INDIAN CULTURE THROUGH
THE AGES
(2 VOLS.)

INDIAN CULTURE THROUGH THE AGES

In Two Volumes

Volume-II

PUBLIC LIFE AND POLITICAL INSTITUTION

S. V. VENKETESWARA

GYAN PUBLISHING HOUSE

New Delhi 110 002

INDIAN CULTURE THROUGH THE AGES

Reprinted, 1996

Published in India by
Gyan Publishing House
5, Ansari Road
New Delhi-110 002

Printed at Goyal Offset Printers, Delhi-110 035

PREFACE

THIS volume deals with Indian Polity through the ages. An attempt is made to sketch, in the light of the original sources, the Public Life in India from the earliest ages down to the beginnings of British rule. The careful reader will find that the chronological aspect has been kept in mind throughout so as to bring out the evolution of institutions. The author's aim has been to differentiate, as far as possible, the actual from the ideal: political philosophy and speculation from Public Life and from those institutions in which the life and the ideal came to crystallize.

The author's thanks are due to the Mysore University for subsidising the publication of this volume, to Principal Rollo for going through the MSS. and to his pupil and Research scholar Mr. T. Srinivasa Murti, M.A., for help in correcting the proofs and preparing the Index.

CONTENTS

CHAPTER I

VEDIC FOUNDATIONS

I

POLITICAL COMMUNITIES

INDIAN peoples lived in communities from the earliest times. The word *kō* or *kōn* in Proto-Dravidian means shepherd or cowherd, and was applied to royalty when it came to be evolved. The Vedic words *gopa* and *gopati* have a similar signification. Communal organisation among the Aryas was pastoral or agricultural like the Dravidian, but came to be pre-eminently agricultural in historical times.[1] It is likely that the Indo-Iranian struggle gave this turn to the economic life of the Aryas in India with a partiality for the cow and the bull, while the Iranians preferred the sheep and the dog. In South India pastoral life retained its importance even in later historical times, as the sheep retained its place along with the buffalo.

The communal organisation of the Veda existed for various political and quasi-political purposes. The members of every community were bound by the tie of kinship, as they were supposed to have a common ancestry.[2] They contributed to the upkeep of the body politic, and their forces were arrayed in communal contingents. They had their common chieftain

[1] Hence such expressions as *gavyamgrāma* applied to the Bharatas.

[2] *Grāmān sajānayo yantu* in *T.S.*, II, 1, 3 and II, 3, 1; *Viśo yudhmāh*; *viśam viśam* in *R.-V.*, IV, 24, 4.

and elders, their officers, herdsmen, guards and policemen,[1] and in some localities, masters of the horse and of the elephants.[2] Some village communities had no chieftain at their head, but were entirely self-governing corporations even in the earliest ages. They had their citadels, military forces and republican officers, whose number is specified as ten in some later Vedic texts.[3] The communal organisation of the Vedic period was not, therefore, so simple and uniform as is usually supposed.

In every community, whether monarchical or republican, we find evidence of an effective and powerful aristocracy wielding influence over the people at large. They were the best of men, 'born with a golden armour', and fit to lead the people.[4] This is easy to understand, as ancient India set as great store by heredity and swore as much by citizen *arety* as ancient Greece. In some hymns we are assured that the aristocrats never bent low before the wishes of the people.[5] They were in power because they were men of intellect and excellence, and the king or chieftain had to treat them with respect and pray for concord.[6]

[1] *Kulapa* in *R.-V.*, X, 84, 4; *balihṛtah* in *R.-V.*, VII, 6, 5 and VI, 39, 5; *purusha* in *R.V.*, IV, 6, 4; *jīvagṛbh* in *R.-V.*, IV, 2, 6 and X, 97, 11.

[2] *Niyutvantah* in *R.-V.*, V, 54, 8 and IV, 46, 2; *ibhya* in *R.-V.*, V, 58, 2 and V, 60, 8.

[3] *Gaṇaśrī* in *R.-V.*, I, 65, 4, V, 58, 2 and V, 60, 8; *daśabhirvīraih* in *T.B.*, II, 6, 3. Cf. *R.-V.*, VII, 104, 15, V, 34, 5 and VIII, 61, 8. The '*puram*' of the texts means 'fortification.' There is no clear evidence of city life in this period.

[4] *Naryāh* in *R.-V.*, IV, 25, 4 and V, 57, 5; *sujātāh* and *janushā rukmavakshasah* in *R.-V.*, X, 91, 2.

[5] *Janam janam janyo nātimanyate* in *R.-V.*, IV, 25, 4.

[6] *Nṛtamā nṛṇām* in *T.S.*, IV, 1, 4; *nama it kṛṇoti* in *R.-V.*, X, 34, 8 and *A.-V.*, XI, 1, 26.

In republican communities the aristocrats had apparently the appellation of *Rājaka*. We find it mentioned in one hymn[1] that Chitra was Rājā but others were only *Rājakas*. This can be understood in the light of the later Licchavi constitution where every aristocrat was styled Rājā. We find many republics[2] known as *vrātas*, *gaṇas*, *śardhas* and *gṛtsas*; some of which were mighty organisations, military or commercial, possessing chariots, horses and fighting men; and others were of the order of craft-guilds—of potters, smiths, hunters, bird-catchers, etc. These republics settled on the land and survived in historical times. They were then classified as military, political or economic bodies.

Even after kingship was evolved in some of these communities, the king was dependent on the elders for military aid, religious worship and economic resources. A chronic condition of warfare in this period, and the important part played by the Aryan horses, coats of mail and elephants, threw him into dependence on the aristocracy. The conquest of enemy villages and the beating off of hostile invasions alike depended on the efficiency of the cavalry. Contributions could sometimes be extracted by force, but more often had to be induced by respect instead of being demanded. A good king looked on himself as the honoured guest of the people.[3] When he took the field, victory had to be prayed for, and the *Purohita* had emerged into importance even in the age of the

[1] *R.-V.*, VIII, 21, 8 and *T.B.*, II, 6, 3.

[2] *R.-V.*, V, 53, 11; *T.S.*, IV, 5, 3; *Ś.B.*, XIII, 5, 2; *niyutvanto grāmajitah* in *R.-V.*, V, 54, 8 and *Ś.B.*, XIII, 5, 4.

[3] *Viśām atithih* in *R.-V.*, II, 2, 8.

earliest hymns.[1] It was the royal care to conciliate the fighting class who had their own meetings and councils of war.[2]

There are instances of integrations of communities, whether republican or monarchical. These are implied in epithets like *pañchajanāh* and *saptajanāh*. Yāska and Sāyaṇa refer these terms to classes of people or castes. But there are epithets[3] which point to their settlement in various tracts of land as different political powers. Sāyaṇa's interpretation involves a social puzzle, as only four castes are known to Vedic sociology. He is constrained to find a fifth caste in the Nishādas, one of the numerous non-Aryan peoples. The five communities formed a coalition against the Bharatas. *Saptajanāh* denoted likewise a confederation of seven peoples who were settled in the basin of the river Indus and its tributaries, whence this appellation. The most prominent evidence of a confederacy of monarchical communities is furnished at the 'Battle of the Ten Kings' described in one of the earliest books of the *Ṛg-Veda*.

II

KINGSHIP

But the foremost feature of the period was the evolution of kingship. The institution of monarchy was sometimes due to military necessity. Frequent warfare with the Asuras made unity of counsel and promptness in action essential among the

[1] *R.-V.*, VII, 18, 13. [2] *Vidatha* in *R.-V.*, III, 38, 5.
[3] *R.-V.*, III, 8; *Ś.B.*, XIII, 5, 4, 23. *Pañchajanāh*, *saptajanāh*, *pañchakṛshṭayah* and *pañchabhūmāh* in *R.-V.*, VII.

Aryan forces. 'Asuras have kings, and are led to battle victoriously. Let us have kings likewise,' thought the Aryas, and they were all agreed.[1] Though this theory of the origin of monarchy is imbedded only in a late text, there are some early texts which could not be explained unless we take them as echoing the idea that 'war begat the king.' 'The man of valour and sense has been chosen king.' 'Oh, kinsmen, recognise this elect as the strongest among you.' 'Congratulate the elected warrior as the mightiest among you.' 'May this king be the sole power among the people.'[2] The king, so appointed, led the people from victory to victory by his valour. He drove away the enemies from the territory occupied by his tribe. The choice of the leader in war evidently rested with the elders of the community, and his tenure depended on their pleasure.[3] Hence his prayer to be dear to them. For even after the war was over, he was continued in power so that the people might be 'free from fear.'[4]

But a peaceful and patriarchal monarchy seems to have preceded this military monarchy. In several early passages the functions of the king are described as those of watching over the welfare of the people and maintaining the prosperity of the state. The king was in charge of their secular welfare, and in this sense their honoured guest, beloved of all subjects. He was elected the head of the community to protect

[1] *A.B.*, I, 14-23: *Devā abruvan | arājatayā vai no jayanti rājānam karavāmaheti tatheti.*

[2] *R.-V.*, X, 103: *Imam sajātā anu vīrayadhvam*; *A.-V.*, VI, 97, 3: *Imam vīram anuharshadhvam ugram*; IV, 22, 1: *Imam viśām ekavṛsham kṛṇu tvam.*

[3] *A.-V.*, III, 5, 7; *T.S.*, I, 6, 2.

[4] *R.-V.*, X, 92, 4.

the people in their laws and observances and see that they did not prey upon each other.[1] For an explanation of this last fragmentary text we have to turn to the *Mahābhārata* where is recorded an ancient tradition to the effect that men were like fishes, the bigger preying on the smaller (*matsyanyāya*).[2] The people at large suffered injustice at the hands of the mighty who deprived them of their wealth and ravished their wives. They therefore finally submitted to the rule of law (*daṇḍanīti*) and elected a king to see that it was administered. There is no evidence in the hymns of any theory of social contract as in the Post-Vedic period.

Other theories are deducible from the Brāhmaṇa texts.[3] Indra was chosen king among the gods because he was the strongest and the most valiant, the most vigorous and perfect, capable of carrying through any work to completion. This coincides with the view that the king represented the supreme will and executive, like the god Varuṇa. Like him, too, he was the lord of *dharma*, and had attained the supreme state because people looked up to him on matters of *dharma*. Another text relates that Indra became king (*adhipati*) among the gods because he was invested by Prajāpati with the solar lustre which was in the form of a gold ornament.[4] 'This symbolises the truth (*satyam*). But *satyam* and *dharma* are the same.' 'The help of *dharma* enables the weaker to rule the stronger.'

[1] *A.-V.*, I, 9, 3; *T.S.*, I, 6, 1; III, 5, 4; *K.S.*, I, 14; V, 6.

[2] Śānti., 58; cf. *R.-V.*, X, 124, 8: *viśo rājānam vṛṇānā.*

[3] *A.B.*, VIII, 4, 12; *Ś.B.*, IV, 1, 4; V, 3, 3, 9.

[4] *T.B.*, II, 2, 10: *haras* and *rukma*; *T.A.*, I, 26; I, 4, 15; *Ś.B.*, V, 4, 4, 5; V, 1, 11.

The king was the upholder of the *dharma*, like the Brāhman well-versed in holy writ. Hence, though one, he ruled over many.

It was necessary that the person of the king, who was the embodiment of *satyam* and *dharma*, should be sacred and inviolable, and that he should be exempt from punishment for his acts, for 'the king can do no wrong, as his actions are for the supreme good of the state.' Therefore the priests gently touched his back with the staff to guide him safely over judicial punishment.[1] At the same time the human character of the king was emphasised. He was 'the son of so and so' and was crowned to administer the *dharma*, with the help of the Brāhmans 'who prosper by righteousness and see that the cosmic order is maintained.' The *Purohita* was one half of the Kshatriya, and Brahma and Kshatra were 'established' on the throne. There was nothing higher than the *dharma*: it was 'the power of the powerful.' 'Therefore is the king weaker than the Brāhman, whose intelligence guides, like Mitra, the royal will to administer the *dharma*.'[2]

This *dharma* is explained in the texts.[3] First there was the *varṇa-dharma*, which was maintained to obviate a confusion of social orders. This was symbolised by the handing over of the sacrificial sword at the *Rājasūya* to Brāhmans, Kshatriyas and others in due order. The Brāhmans are described as spiritual researchers, as practising continence and

[1] *Ś.B.*, V, 4, 4, 7.

[2] *R.-V.*, VI, 75, 10: *ṛtāvṛdhaḥ*; *A.-V.*, V, 17, 1; *Ś.B.*, V, 4, 4, 15; XI, 2, 7, 16; *A.B.*, VII, 26; *B.U.*, I, 4, 15.

[3] *Ś.B.*, V, 4, 4, 19; *R.-V.*, X. 16, 6; *Ch. U.*, II, 23, 1.

as seekers after truth and righteousness. Even the Kshatriya was admitted to the ceremony only on condition of exchanging his own weapons for those of the Brāhman, for Soma had pervaded the latter on account of his continence (*brahmacharya*). There were expiatory rites for allowing non-Aryan ministers (*ratnins*) to co-operate at the sacrifice. There was, secondly, the *dharma* of the *āśramas* or stations in life, elaborated in the latest Vedic period.

The king, elected by the people, could be superseded, if there was general dissatisfaction with his rule. In the early period of the institution of kingship everything seems to have gone on well. But the latest hymns of the *Ṛg-Veda* contain prayers for his security, and some Vedic texts have pointed references to kings who were driven away apparently after their attempts at absolutism.[1] Sometimes there were rival parties in the state and the king was exiled (*aparuddha*) as the result of a revolution. Restoration by royalists might come in due course, and the party in power invited all the people to unite in welcoming the exile back to the country: He was wandering far in other realms till 'the Aśvins came to his rescue and his kinsmen rallied round him.' Then, 'the common people, carpenters, smiths, fisher-folk and others and the friendly kings stood by his side, and the king-makers (*rāja-kṛtah*), especially the *Sūta* and the *Grāmaṇī*, accepted his sovereignty.' All texts[2] agree that the power and stability of kingship depended on the suffrages of the people. Hence the expressions

[1] *R.-V.*, X, 173, 1; *A.-V.*, XII, 1, 17.

[2] *A.-V.*, III, 3-5: *upastīn parṇa mahyam tvam sarvān kṛṇvabhito janān*; *T.B.*, II, 4, 5; III, 12, 9; *V.S.*, 20, 9; *K.S.*, 38, 4.

like *dhruvagopah* and the prayer that the subjects may continue to be loyal to the king.

III

THE CONSECRATION

The selected king had to undergo the ceremony of consecration described in the *Saṁhitā* and commented upon in the *Brāhmaṇa* literature. This was a ceremonial impressive in its character and symbolical in its significance. It meant the purification of the king-elect with water which was at first used to anoint him (*akta*), and later to bathe his head (*mūrdhābhisheka*). The ceremony demanded the co-operation of all classes in the state by representatives, and of the officers, who had to attend on the king in person. It was incomplete if such co-operation could not be enlisted; and an incomplete or imperfect ceremony always lost its religious merit. The tiger-skin, which he was required to tread, symbolised valour in hunting out the wicked; and the lion-skin, his being a lion of justice.[1] The sword with which he was invested had a like significance. He was reminded of his principal duties when the priest acclaimed that he was Mitra in kindness, Varuṇa in virtue and Indra in valour tempered by justice.[2] The king's coronation oath likewise was of political significance and had a religious sanction. He swore to reign in goodness and truth, on pain of incurring the wrath of the gods and bringing ruin on himself and his family if he violated

[1] *A.-V.*, IV, 8, 4: *Vyāghro adhi vaiyāghrye vikramasva diśo mahīh.*

[2] *T.S.*, I, 8, 16; *V.S.*, X, 28; *K.S.*, XV, 8; *Ś.B.*, V, 4, 3: *Suśevah, satyadharmā* and *visvaujas.*

his promises in the letter or the spirit. It was only after this ceremonial was over that he was entitled to the designation Rājā. He showered on his subjects the blessings of plenty like god Savitā, and 'suffused the quarters with glory, splendour and righteousness.'[1]

The coronation ceremony began with an offering to Nirṛiti to avert famine in the country, for Nirṛiti was the earth devoid of vegetation.[2] On the next seven successive days there were prayers to various gods for plenty and prosperity, and for 'forgiveness of sins committed in the village or the forest, in the court-hall or in private life, and in relations with noble and commoner.' The king had then to perform sacrifices at the houses of the twelve ministers (*ratnins*): he had perforce to be on good terms with them. Then the gods were addressed to invest him with power, pre-eminence and lordship of the people,[3] whom he was to lead along the path of righteousness and enlightenment.

After this baptism with water (*abhisheka*) the king was made to tread on a tiger-skin under which was a silver charm to ward off death. Evil influences were expelled with charms of lead and copper. He was then conducted to the throne in a three-horse chariot. Holy waters were now sprinkled on him by representatives of all the castes; the Brāhman used for this purpose a *palāśa* leaf which symbolised purity and lustre (*tvishi*), the Kshatriya, an *audumbara* (fig) which meant strength, the Vaiśya, an *aśvattha* (sacred

[1] *T.S.*, I, 8, 16; *A.B.*, VIII, 19, 1: *Suślokān sumaṅgalān satyarājān.*
[2] *T.B.*, I, 6, 1.
[3] *T.S.*, I, 8, 10: *Kshatra*, *ādhipatya* and *jānarājya*.

fig) which made for increase and prosperity among the people, and a *Janya* (friendly prince), a *nyagrodha* (banyan) in the interests of shelter and protection.[1] The *mantras* used were regarded as symbolical. As the waters flow eternal, unperturbed by external influences, so was the king to be unruffled in temper, and his rule secure and lasting (*sthāvaram*). He was to shower blessings on his subjects, as the showers now fell on him.

The king now wore a turban or a crown. Among some peoples it was not the vogue, for they held that 'the crown hides his real bodily form.'[2] He took the coronation oath made solemn by the sanction of religion: 'May my life, offspring etc., be cut off if I work against your interests.'[3]

He then took his seat on the throne (*āsandi*) of hard *khadhira* wood. As the banyan tree waxes strong by its branches rooting themselves on all sides, so was the king's dignity to be rooted in the affection of his subjects—Brāhman, Kshatriya, Vaiśya and *Phala.*[4] Then came the formal proclamation that he was the king of the state and lord of its people. A text

[1] *T.S.*, I, 8, 11; *Ś.B.*, V, 3, 4; *T.B.*, I, 7, 8. It is likely that *janya* means a person of aristocratic birth, the head of a *jana*, on the analogy of *narya* (cf. *nara*). Compare also *janam janam janyo nālimanyate*, which is in the tenth book of the *R.-V.*, and would make nonsense if, with Jayaswal, we take *janya* as meaning *Śūdra* or 'a man of a hostile tribe' (*Hindu Polity*, Part II, p. 25). Bhāskara on *T.B.*, I, 7, 8 explains *janya : pratirāja ityeke mitrajana ityanye.*

[2] *Ś.B.*, V, 3, 5, 28.

[3] *A.B.*, VIII, 15 : *Āyuh prajām vriñjīthāh yadi te druhyeyam ; Evam Kshatriyam śāpayitvā abhishiñcheta.*

[4] *Phala* denotes the industrial classes as in *Mbh*; Sabhā, 78, 2. *Phalato bhūmito vāpi* (*dhanam*). It has a variant reading *vastrāṇi*. The sense is, obviously, the product of labour, as differentiated from produce of land. Cf. p. 29 *infra*.

shows that the formula was originally applied to the Bharatas, and was later made general. The conception is one of tribal, not yet of territorial, sovereignty, as pointed out by the commentator Kātyāyana, who explains that he was 'king of the people, as the territory was not fixed but fluctuating.' 'Oh tribesmen, here is your king.' 'Oh king, you are the ruler of all and conqueror of the self; be you king for ever, steadfast in aim and true to yourself.' 'We look up to you to cultivate the resources of the state, to preserve what is valuable, and to maintain peace, prosperity and progress.'[1]

But the ideal of the state was not to be entirely material and moral prosperity. The Brāhman class valued also spiritual and moral progress. The consecrating priest, therefore, adds to the formula for all, given above, the formula for the elect in these words: 'Soma is the deathless king of us, dwellers in eternity, and for the time being we swear allegiance to this human king likewise.'[2] The interest of the formula is to impress on the king that the loyalty of the Brāhman class was conditional on good rule, consistent with the ideals of *satyam* and *dharma.*

The king now alighted from the throne and wore the skin of the boar. This was symbolical of extension of territory for the tribesmen, as the boar was, in myth, responsible for lifting the earth from the waters. He then drove to the court-hall in a chariot drawn by four horses, for he had now won the co-operation

[1] *Ś.B.*, V, 2, 1; *Kṛshyai tvā kshemāya tvā rayyai tvā poshāya tvā;* Also *Asyai viśah | esha vo amī rājā.*

[2] *Somosmākam Brāhmaṇānām* which the commentator Bhāṣkara supplements by *adhunā ayam cha.*

of the three estates of the realm and of the other people.

At the court-house they solemnly touched him with the rods of justice (*daṇḍaih*) to beat injustice and partiality out of him, so that he might be fit to punish others, though above such punishment himself. Then they presented him with the sword of justice, which he in turn passed on to his kinsmen and officers, enlisting their co-operation : 'By this sword protect me.' Then they played a symbolical game of dice, the bet being a cow brought by one of the kinsmen (*sajātāh*).

The coronation ceremony was not originally intended to confer kingship in perpetuity. The idea of dynasty was absent, and was incompatible with the sanction implied in the coronation oath. At the same time there was no idea of interfering with the king's position so long as he was good, as he was above *daṇḍa*. But the king could be driven out with his family or even slain, if he were wicked or false. As the sacredness of the office grew and the necessity of avoiding a disputed succession became apparent, we find an implied provision in the ceremonies that royalty was to descend to the crown-prince in due course. At the coronation the priest was to employ the single *vyāhṛti*, *bhūh*; if the king had been the crown-prince, *bhūh* and *bhuvah*; and for the third generation, *bhūh*, *bhuvah* and *suvah*. The ceremony was to be repeated at every succession to the crown, as the oath taken by one king was not necessarily binding on another, and the subjects swore loyalty to the new king by acclamation.

The sanctity that thus hedged the person of the king, helped by the influence of the principle of heredity, is responsible for the evolution of hereditary monarchy. In the latest Ṛg-Vedic age monarchy passed from father to son, and Trasadasyu was succeeded by his son. The *Aitareya Brāhmaṇa* knows Parikshit and his son Pārikshiti, who is the same as Viśvajanina of the *Atharva-Veda*. By this time indeed most monarchies appear to have become hereditary. Lastly, the *Śatapatha Brāhmaṇa* mentions dynasties of kings who ruled successively for ten generations.[1] This is in keeping with the tradition recorded by Megasthenes that in ancient India the succession was generally hereditary after the times of Svayambhu, Budha and Kratu, but that when a failure of heirs occurred in the royal house Indians elected their sovereign on the principle of merit.[2]

If a monarch had been deposed whether for misdeeds or owing to a popular insurrection, there was a special ceremony for his restoration known as *sautrāmaṇi*. 'Soma restores his kingdom to him who, being king, has not come by his own. For Soma enables the sacrifice to be conducted, and thus the gods are induced to shower blessings on the people. Through the intervention of Soma the king is restored by the gods, and becomes a sacrificer to the gods.'[3] Soma was the king of the Brāhmans. The king was restored only if he could satisfy them that he would rule aright.

[1] *R.V.*, X, 33, 4: *Rājānam Trāsadasyavam*; *A.B.*, VIII, 17, 5: *Iyam janā abhi utkrośata samrājam sāmrājyam bhojam bhojapitaram svarājam svārājyam virājam vairājyam, parameshṭhinam pārameshṭhyam rājānam rājapitaram*; *A.B.*, VI, 32, 10: *Pārikshityāh*; *Ś.B.*, XII, 9, 3: *Daśapūrusham rājyam*.

[2] McCrindle, p. 200.

[3] *T.B.*, I, 4, 2.

IV

VEDIC AND WESTERN KINGSHIP

The position of the Vedic king may be compared with that of the king in other ancient societies. Like the Homeric and the Teutonic king he was priest, commander and judge, and held a privileged position in society. But there were vital points of contrast. The main function of the king was to administer the affairs of the state. This he was to do in consultation with his ministers and people. A king who was true to his coronation oath (*Satya Rāja*) never fought shy of popular assemblies where the voice of the people was expressed.[1] It was his anxious care to act in accordance with the wishes and feelings of the Assembly, for 'in the people lay his strength' and the permanence of his tenure.[2] When there were different parties and factions in the state the king was to bring about concord and harmony among them by kind words and sweet persuasion.[3] Even the wishes of the women-folk (*jāyāh*) were to be considered, and he had to carry them with him.[4]

The king was the fountain of justice and the chief judge. He administered equity rather than law, and it was done in company with well-born men in the open court (*sabhā*).[5] He administered justice impartially according to customary law and equity (*dharma*). Every member of the court was an exponent

[1] *R.-V.*, IX, 92, 6: *samitīriyānah*.
[2] *Ś.B.*, V, 4, 4; *T.B.*, II, 6, 8: *dhruvāya te samitih kalpatāmiha*.
[3] *Rājā chid ebhyo nama it kṛṇoti.* [4] *R.-V.*, X, 173, 1.
[5] *R.-V.*, VII, 1, 4; *V.S.*, X, 27.

of the *dharma*. But neither king nor noble was invested with such sanctity as attached to those in Greece, who were supposed to have *themistes* from Zeus.

He was responsible for the defence of the people from enemies, and led them in war.[1] But consultation with the nobles was essential in matters of war and peace, and they met in formal council. His authority was unquestioned and unfettered in the field, and he led those who furnished the tribal contingents in cavalry, elephants, chariots and infantry. He pulled down the cities of his enemies in offensive warfare, and acquired booty which he equitably distributed among his followers.

His was the duty of maintaining peace and order in the state and of seeing that men attended to their own legitimate duties and not to other people's business. The king carefully watched the actions of the people and stimulated work conducive to social happiness. His valour and dignity of demeanour checked evil-doers in their evil courses, and gave shelter to the weak and oppressed, like the many-armed banyan tree. Thus he both protected and punished the people.[2]

The king was the symbol of the state, and its representative in dealing with other states. His personality commanded respect and he was the head of the state (*mūrdhāsi rāṭ*), the most noble of the nobles, the mightiest of the mighty, sitting in durbar with his ministers. His personal magnetism (*tvesha samdṛś*)

[1] *A.-V.*, VI, 88, 3; *A.B.*, VIII, 12, 17.

[2] *T.S.*, I, 8, 16: *Mitrosi suśevah*; *A.B.*, VII, 31: *viśe tvā yantrāya dhartrāya.*

derived heightened glory from the sanctity of the coronation ceremony. And his position of dignity was maintained by gifts and taxes.[1]

But the most characteristic function of the king was as the upholder of the *dharma*. All auspicious circumstances attended a king who was true to himself and to his people, for they rallied round him and made him unassailable. To this end he had a threefold duty. He was to cast off sloth and be ever wakeful and working.[2] Secondly, he was to set an example to his subjects in righteous conduct and orderly life, even like Varuṇa, the *Satyadharmā*.[3] Thirdly, he was to see that the people walked along the path of *dharma* and that sin and vice did not stalk abroad.[4]

There is in some hymns the functional comparison of kingship with the divine Powers. He was 'Varuṇa, ruling over men, Indra slaying the Asuras and Tvashṭa animating all beings.' But in most texts he is connected with Varuṇa and Indra, as the Brāhman is with Bṛhaspati and Mitra, and the people at large (*viś*) with Vishṇu. 'So him, become Indra, his fellows recognise as superior; he becomes the best of his fellows.' 'Brahma is the conceiver and Kshatra the doer, because Mitra is intelligence and Varuṇa is will. Whatever deed Varuṇa did unsped by Mitra, the priesthood, therein forsooth he succeeded not.' In one hymn Trasadasyu describes himself as resembling Indra and as semi-divine (*ardhadeva*). But

[1] *A.-V.*, XII, 1, 17: *Dharmaṇā dhṛtam*; *Ś.B.*, V, 3, 3, 9: *paramatā vai sa yo dharmasya patih.*

[2] *R.-V.*, V, 11, 1: *gopā jāgṛvih.*

[3] *R.-V.*, X: *suvratah*; *T.S.*, I, 8, 16.

[4] *R.-V.*, I, 91, 8; *R.-V.*, X, 92, 14.

all this[1] is in the language of Vedic symbolism. The functions of the king bore comparison with those of the gods, and so indeed did those of the entire Kshatriya class who are described in one of the Brāhmaṇa texts as having a divine origin.[2] Every sacrificer was next-door to divinity, as there was an identification of the subject (sacrificer) and the god who was the object of worship. This identification is increasingly insisted on as the Vedic age passes into that of the Vedānta (Upanishads). 'Being Brahman, one realises that Brahman in oneself and becomes Brahman.' But neither of these considerations would justify our reading anything like a Divine Right Theory into the Vedic texts.[3] At the consecration the king was reminded of his human descent and character, and of the greater King beyond the temporal power, to whom the Brāhman class owed an unwavering loyalty. The law was higher than the king, whose strength lay in justice and righteousness and not in a cloak of divinity. The point of difference was that he could not be subjected to punishment like an ordinary citizen. It was only when the summit of injustice was reached that he was punished by expulsion and loss of his throne.

V

FORMS OF KINGSHIP

There were several grades or classes of kings. Some appear in the earliest books of the *Ṛg-Veda*, and

[1] *R.V.*, IV, 42; *T.S.*, II, 2, 11, 6; *Ś.B.*, 1, 3, 4; II, 5, 3; IV, 1, 4, 1.

[2] *Ś.B.*, V, 1, 5; V, 3, 5; II, 2, 2 which describes Brāhmans as *manushya-deva*.

[3] As is done by Ghosal: *Hindu Political Theories*, p. 172.

some only in the later books.[1] One of the latest hymns even suggests a kingdom of the world, whether as a theoretical political conception or as a reflection of what was found in practice.[2] Some of these terms appear to be used in a metaphorical sense, like *Virāṭ* in the latest books, but such use implies grades of kingship superior to an ordinary king. The Brāhmaṇa texts present other titles.[3]

In the later Vedic collections we have clearer evidence of some sort of gradation: 'The *Adhirāja* shines among kings.'[4] This is certainly clearer than a similar passage in the *Ṛg-Veda* relating to the appointment of an *Adhirāja* and his relationship to other kings. There are a few other passages of the kind: 'The *Virāṭ* comes (in royal procession) after the *Svarāṭ*.' 'The *Virāṭ* became *Adhirāja*.' The *Bhūma* appears with autocratic powers in one of the hymns, and the *Sārvabhauma* with imperial sway in the later Brāhmaṇa texts.

Applications of these epithets to the various gods give some indication of the relative prominence of the title-holders in actual political life.[5] Maruts are *Samrāṭs*, perhaps in the same sense as the eye is *Samrāṭ*, and the newly wedded wife is *Samrājñī*, which

[1] *R.-V.*, III, 46, 1; IV, 21, 1; VIII, 19, 32; VIII, 37, 3: *Svarāṭ* and *Samrāṭ*. *R.-V.*, X, 128, 9: *Ekarāṭ* and *Adhirāṭ*.

[2] *R.-V.*, X, 121, 3: *Eka id rājā jagato babhūva*.

[3] *Sārvabhauma*, *Rājādhirāja* and *Sahyasāhi*.

[4] *A.-V.*, VI, 98, 1; *T.S.*, II, 4, 14: *Adhirājo rājasu rājayāti*; *R.-V.*, X, 128, 9: *ugram chettāram adhirājam akran*; *A.-V.*, VIII, 9, 9: *Virāṭ svarājamabhyeti paśchāt*; *R.-V.*, I, 188, 5; *T.S.*, I, 7, 1.

[5] Agni is *Samrāṭ* and *Svarāṭ*; Varuṇa is *Samrāṭ*, *Virāṭ* and *Samrāṭ-pati*, who could bestow *Sāmrājyam*.

R.-V., VII, 82, 2; *T. S.*, I, 7, 11: *Samrājā ugrā vṛshabhā divaspatī*; *T.B.*, II, 5, 7; *K.S.*, XXXVIII, 4; *V.S.*, XX, 5; *R.V.*, X, 85, 4: *Samrājñī Śvaśure . . . Śvaśruvām*.

suggests the idea of a republican organisation. The same idea appears in one of the earliest hymns of the *Ṛg-Veda*, which speaks of one of the *Samrāṭs* becoming *Virāṭ*, and in two later texts.[1] The position of the *Svarāṭ*, who had apparently given up the glories of conquest and was content with the less renowned victories of peace, appears indicated in the passage describing the worshipped Indra as *Rājā* and *Adhirāja*, while the real Indra in the Beyond was *Svarāṭ*.[2]

The conservative instinct of India asserts itself in retaining these titles even after the terms had lost their original denotation. This accounts apparently for the indiscriminate use of the epithets[3] in some passages, and their association with localities in some others. The king of the East was *Samrāṭ*, in tradition, alike in the Brāhmaṇas and the *Mahābhārata*, where the title descends to Jarāsandha in proto-historic times. Similarly, the Middle Country or the Doab of the Ganges and the Jumna had its rulers designated *Rājā*, alike among the Kuru-Pāñchālas and the Vaśośīnaras. *Bhojas* were kings of the Satvats in the South. The Nīchyas and Apāchyas of the West had *Svarāṭ*, while

[1] *Ṛ.-V.*, VI, 36, 3: *samrādeko virājati*; *K.S.*, V, 6; and *M.S.*, I, 6, 7.

[2] *T.S.*, II, 1, 6: *ayam Indro rājā ayam Indro adhirājā asau Indrah svarāṭ*.

[3] *A.B.*, VIII, 14, 2; VIII, 29, 1; *Ś.B.*, XI, 3, 1; *B.U.*, IV, 1, 1. That the significance attaching to these terms is geographical and not political in the *A. B.* appears from its arranging the terms indiscriminately in different passages. In one we have *sāmrājyam*, *vairājyam*, *bhaujyam*, *svārājyam*, *pāramaiśvaryam*, *mahārājyam* and *ādhipatyam*, whereas later in the same book we have the same list repeated as *sāmrājyam*, *bhaujyam*, *svārājyam*, *vairājyam*, and *pārameshṭhyam* for *pāramaiśvaryam*. Similarly we have *virāṭ* standing for the South in the passage cited above, but identified with the West in *T.B.*, I, 7, 7, showing that in this Brāhmaṇa the significance is political and not geographical.

Vairājyam obtained among the Uttara-Kurus and Madrās of the North.

Elsewhere there is no local significance attaching to these terms. *Virāṭ* is defined as conqueror of the co-rulers, *Samrāṭ*, of enemies, and *Viśvarāṭ*, of all;[1] and the North is described as *Svarāṭ*, the South as *Virāṭ* and the West as *Samrāṭ*. The *Śatapatha Brāhmaṇa* sets the seal on the political significance of these terms by associating each with an important religious ceremony. One became a *Rājā* if he performed the *rājasūya* sacrifice, and *Samrāṭ*, if the *vājapeya*. The title of *Sārvabhauma* was established only after a successful celebration of the *aśvamedha* sacrifice.[2] The transition from the political and religious significance of the appellations to the economic is found only in later historical texts. Dual kingship (*Dvirāṭ*) among some of the communities appears as early as the *Atharva-Veda*.[3]

VI

MINISTERS AND OTHER OFFICERS OF STATE

The most prominent of the royal officers are the *Ratnins*, 'the jewels of state.' The fifth book of the *Ṛg-Veda* mentions the Crowned Queen (*Mahishī*, 'the powerful one'), the sixth book the Treasurer and Charioteer (*Kshatta*) who was originally the 'distributor' of royal goods and favour, and the seventh book the *Purohita* and the *Senāni*. The *Purohita* prayed in the *sabhā* while the king was in the field, and the *Senāni* (later *Senāpati*) was the commander of the forces. The last two books mention *Taksha*, the

[1] *T.S.*, I, 8, 13: *Virāḍasi sapatnahā samrāḍasi bhrātṛvyahā viśvārāḍasi viśvāsām nāshṭrāṇām hantā.*

[2] *Ś.B.*, IX, 3, 4, 8.

[3] *A.-V.*, V, 20, 9.

Architect, whose chief implement was the chisel (*kuliśa*).[1]

Other ministers of the crown appear in later Vedic texts.[2] Prominence must be given here to the *Sūta* and *Grāmaṇī*. The last is described as a priceless gem,[3] but the *Sūta* is considered superior to him, and his person was sacred and inviolable. Both these are connected with the Commander-in-chief, and so also was the *Saṅgrahītā*. Sāyaṇa describes this last officer as Treasurer, and *Sūta* as Master of the Horse. But Bhaṭṭa Bhāskara rightly explains *Saṅgrahītā* as the holder of the reins,[4] and his interpretation is acceptable, especially as there is a prayer to the Aśvins at his house in the *ratnahavis* sacrifice. It may be presumed that in the later Vedic period the *Sūta's* functions as head of the cavalry passed on to the *Saṅgrahītā*.[5] The *Grāmaṇī* commanded the local militia of the township, which was in groups, whence the sacrifice to the Maruts.

The *Yajur-Veda*[6] adds *Bhāgadugh* and *Akshāvāpa*, who are obviously the Collector of revenue and the Accountant, and the *Rājanya* (*Yuvarāja*, heir-apparent) and two more Queens. Some texts place *Taksha* and *Rathakāra*, the Architect and the Engineer,

[1] *R.-V.*, III, 2, 1; V, 2, 2; VI, 13, 2; VII, 18, 13; IX, 112, 1; X, 86, 5.

[2] *A.-V.*, III, 5, 6; *T.S.*, IV, 5, 4.

[3] *A.-V.*, III, 5, 7; *Ś.B.*, V, 3, 1: *amūlyakam ratnam*.
Ahantya in *T.S.*, IV, 5, 2, 1; *Ahanti* in *V.S.*, VI, 18; *ahantva* in *K.S.*, XVII, 2; and *M.S.*, II, 9, 3.

[4] *Raśmigrāhi* or *rajjubhirnihantā*; *vide* commentary on *T.S.*, I, 8, 15.

[5] *T.B.*, I, 7, 9: *Sahasaṅgrahītrā rathe vāhane ratham ādadhāti*. *Rathaestha* is the term for the conqueror in the *Yajur-Veda* (*V.S.*, XXII, 22) and for the Kshatriya class in the *Avesta*.

[6] *M.-S.*, II, 6, 5; IV, 3, 8; *T.S.*, I, 8, 15; *Ś.B.*, V, 3, 1.

between the Collector and the Accountant in the list of ministers at whose houses the king was to offer sacrifices. It may be remembered that the chief architect was so prominent in Egypt that he was also the Prime Minister. In India he was the maker of chariots which played a prominent part in warfare. Other texts introduce a chief huntsman and a courier, whose sister was also a left-hand wife of the king's.

In the latest period[1] we find a briefer list of *Rājanya* or *Yuvarāja*, *Purohita*, *Mahishī*, *Sūta* and *Grāmaṇī*, *Kshatta* and *Saṅgrahītā*. The three main departments now were those of finance, justice and war. The *Purohita* was the chief judge, the *Kshatta* presided over the public, and *Mahishī* over the house hold, finance. The four departments of the army (*chaturaṅgasena*) were under the *Yuvarāja*, *Grāmaṇī* and *Saṅgrahītā*, and the *Sūta* was Minister of Diplomacy. The *Ratnins* appear to have exercised great influence on the administration. They are spoken of as king-makers and as responsible for the appointment or deposition of kings.[2]

Among the other officers of state, importance was attached to the *Ibhya* or *Ibha*, the aristocrat who had the privilege of riding the elephant. He was looked on as *Amā* (*amātya*), was in personal attendance on the king, and sometimes was lord of entire villages.[3] Some *Ibhas* were lords of a hundred villages. The

[1] *P.B.*, XIX, 1, 4.

[2] *Rājakartṛ* in *A.B.*, VIII, 17, 5 : *Rāshṭrasya pradātārah* and *apa ādātārah* in *T.B.*, I, 7, 6. There seems to be no warrant for the interpretation of the term *Ratnin* by the authors of the 'Vedic Index' as 'receivers of gifts.' The *Ś.B.* describes the *Grāmaṇī* as a 'priceless gem' and the other ministers as gems of the state.

[3] *R.-V.*, IV, 4, 1. *M.S.*, has *amāvan*.

Cf. *Ibhyagrāma* in *Ch. U.*, I, 10, 1 ; *Śatapati* in *M.S.*, IV, 14, 12.

Ibhya had as his subordinates the elephant-keepers, as ministers like *Kshatta* had their assistants[1] in the treasury according to Mahīdhara, and in charioteering according to Sāyaṇa. Police officers, *Ugra* and *Jīvagṛbh*[2] appear along with a Mediator (*Madhya-maśī*). Among the local officers of the village mentioned in Vedic texts are the guard, herdsman and *Dāvapa* whose duty was to quench the forest fires.[3] It is possible that all these were regarded as *purushas* or *rājapurushas*.[4]

VII

POLITICAL ASSEMBLIES

Popular gatherings were full of life and were convivial in character: 'Here and there are men moving in free, joyous, vigorous life. Now are they sitting in solemn deliberation, then marching on with flags up-hoisted. They are speaking sweetly in persuasion, or loud in quarrel, intent on pleasing their

[1] *Anukshattṛ* in *V.S.*, XXX, 11 and *T.B.*, III, 4, 9. Sāyaṇa explains *Kshattṛ* as Chamberlain (*antahpurādhyaksha*) in one place (Com. on *Ś.B.*, V, 3, 1, 7) and as Finance Minister (*āyavyayādhyaksha*) in his commentary on *Ś.B.*, XIII, 4, 2, 3. Harisvāmin interprets it as Treasurer (*kośādhyaksha*) in his commentary on *Ś.B.*, XIII, 5, 4, 6. In another place *Anukshattṛ* is explained as Assistant Charioteer (*sāratheranuchara*) by Sāyaṇa, and this would equate *Kshattṛ* and *Sārathi* (Com. on *T.B.*, III, 4, 7, 1). The last sense appears supported by *Ś.B.*, XIII, 5, 2 : *Kshattṛ haye haye kshattah*.

[2] *R.-V.*, VII, 38, 6 ; X, 97, 11.

[3] *Pāyu* in *R.-V.*, IV, 2, 6 ; *Paśupā* in *R.-V.*, IV, 6, 4 ; *Dāvapa* in *V.S.*, XXX, 16 and *T.B.*, III, 4, 11.

[4] *R.-V.*, VI, 39, 5. This explains the 'Porus' of the Greek records which appears to be the name of an office and not that of an individual. We are told of two chiefs named 'Porus' contemporary with Alexander, and one with Augustus. Peshawar (*Purushapura*) was apparently so known as it was the seat of a 'Purusha' in later times. Cp. *Pulisāni* in Aśoka inscriptions.

colleagues or winning them to a sense of duty. Eating and drinking they take counsel together, and finally rise for the worship of Concord.'[1]

The populace of the Vedic period were organised in various bodies.[2] Of these, the *samiti* met for political deliberation, and was a sort of folk-mote. We have actual references to kings having been present at meetings of the *samiti* and guiding the discussions there, like the king of the Pāñchālas or the Videhas.[3] The composition of this body can be judged from the description: 'flowing together from every side, the people came in streams to the *samiti*.'[4] There is evidence of active discussions and prayers for concord: 'May deliberations be one-pointed; discussions to the same intent; and resolutions to the same effect.' 'Oh *Rāja* Soma, sow the seeds of agreement among them.' It was the duty of the King-President to conduct the deliberations to a successful conclusion and to bring about a concensus of opinion. In such agreement lay his strength and security as well as the prosperity of the state.[5] There are charms and spells in the *Atharva-Veda* to secure this result.[6]

The next important public body was the *sabhā*. It was at first a hall alike of council and of sacrifice,

[1] *A.-V.*, III, 30, 5 and 6:

Jāyasvantah chittino mā viyaushṭhā sam rādhayantah sadhurāścharantah | Anyonyasmai valgu vadantah sadrichīnān vah sammanasah kṛṇomi | Samānī prāpā saha vonnabhāgah samāne yoktre saha vo yunajmi.

[2] *A.-V.*, XII, 1, 56; *R.-V.*, V, 59, 2: *saṅgrāma samiti.* Cf. *A.-V.*, XV, 9, 2: *sabhā cha samitiścha senā cha.*

[3] *R.-V.*, IX, 92, 6: *Rājeva satyah samitīriyānah.* *Ch. U.*, V, 3. *B. U.*, VI, 2.

[4] *Sadhṛichīh* and *sarvā diśah.*

[5] *R.-V.*, IX, 191, 3; *A.-V.*, XI, 1, 26: *Soma rājan samjñānam āvapa ebhyah*; *A.-V.*, VI, 88, 3: *Dhruvāya te samitih kalpatām iha.*

[6] *A.-V.*, III, 30, 35.

where the *Purohita* acted while the king was in the field: so Agni is referred to as *Sabhya* in numerous hymns. The *sabhā* was a smaller body than the *samiti*, because only well-born men met here, and women were excluded.[1] Men of learning and character made their mark here, and were therefore known as *Sabheya* and *Sabhāsaha*, and speeches worthy of the body are referred to in one hymn.[2] Sometimes there were sharp repartees and offensive speeches, as thieves and criminals were dragged before it, and the richest and most influential men had to submit to the decisions of their peers assembled here.[3] Among the sins warded off by hymns at the ceremony of sacred unction are those committed in the *sabhā*. The scholiast Mahīdhara explains these sins as consisting of attacking or reviling great men and of partisanship or partiality in deciding disputes.[4] The *sabhā* had, however, high traditions. There are frequent prayers for sons who as youths would be worthy of sitting on this body.[5] The Court-house was used for administering justice, and its members are dedicated to *dharma* in the *Yajur-Veda*.[6] It was also used for gambling and, if later tradition be accepted as

[1] *R.-V.*, VII, 1, 4: *sujātāh*. Cf. *A.-V.*, III, 29: *Sabhāsada rājānah*. *M.S.* IV, 7, 4.

[2] *R.-V.*, II, 24, 13; VI, 28, 6; X, 71, 10; I, 167, 3. Grassmann interprets *sahah* (*R.-V.*, I, 56, 2) as *sahasā* and Bloomfield considers the meaning obscure (*J.A.O.S.*, 1928, p. 216). But the form persisted in later times. Cp. *ghaṭikāsāhasa* in vol. i, p. 244 of my book, a term which can be contrasted with *ghaṭikā sāmānya* in the Niḍamarru plates of Jayasimha.

[3] *A.-V.*, VII, 12, 3; *R.-V.*, VII, 104, 10: *Ripuh stenah steyakṛt dabhrametu*.

[4] *T.S.*, I, 8, 3; *V.S.*, III, 45; XX, 17. Cf. *R.-V.*, X, 34, 6.

[5] *R.-V.*, I, 91, 120.

[6] *V.S.*, XXX, 6; *T.B.*, III, 4.

a guide, for popular amusements like dancing and music.[1]

The next assembly of importance is the *vidatha*, which was apparently a sacrificial gathering which met in a special hall erected for the purpose. The *Rathakāra* is in one passage described as pleasing the *vidatha*,—a reference probably to his building the hall. In another hymn there is clear mention of the fire which was kindled there being a sacred fire carefully kept. The speeches made here were in a low tone,[2] as contrasted with those in the *sabhā*. In one early passage[3] the *Samrāṭ* is described as *Vidathya* and some of the councillors as distinguishing themselves. Women were sometimes present at the *vidatha* unlike the *sabhā*.[4] That this body had also a military character may be inferred from its being placed under the protection of Indra, who is invoked on the eve of war, for gathering resources in men, horses and elephants.[5]

VIII

QUASI-POLITICAL GATHERINGS

The most important of the non-political gatherings of the people was for social and educational purposes.

[1] Whence the conception of *dabhrasabhā* of Naṭarāja Sabhāpati in historical times.

[2] *R.-V.*, X, 91, 8: *Mēdhākāram vidathasya prasādhanam.* Cf. *T.B.*, III, 5: *Medhāyai rathakāram* and *R.-V.*, IV, 6, 2: *Agnir mandro vidatheshu prachetāh. Ibid*, V, 89, 2; VII, 1, 4: *Vidathasya dhībhir kshatram rājānah pradivo dadhāthe. A.-V.*, I, 13, 4: *Sā no mṛḍa vidathe gṛṇānā.*

[3] *R.-V.*, IV, 27, 2; II, 27, 12: *vidatheshu praśastah.*

[4] *A.-V.*, VII, 38, 4; *Ibid*, V, 10, 12: *Indrāya gupto vidathā ni-chikyat.*

[5] *T.S.*, IV, 7, 15: *Yah pushṭāni saṁsṛjati trayāṇi.*

It was called *samana*,[1] which appears to be another term for *parishad*, a form of popular festivity where poets went to win laurels. Fires were kindled as at the *vidatha*, and the gathering lasted through the night. Its social character is evident from the fact that women attended,—elderly women and courtesans in early times, and even young women in the later Vedic period.[2] Bowmen exhibited feats of skill, and horse races added merriment to the occasion. When the assembly had a more literary character, it was styled a *parishad*, was presided over by *Īśāna*,[3] and held discussions regarding matters of learning (*vidyās*).

A purely religious assembly was the *sadas*[4] and its president was styled *Sadasaspati*. Membership of this body was apparently confined to the *Purohitas* who were friendly with one another and were technically known as *Sādanya* or *Sadasya*. The function of the *sadas* was to offer sacrifices.

Of other gatherings we get only faint glimpses. Some were of the nature of Roman 'contios' and were convoked only to listen to the golden deeds of heroes, to fire the audience with enthusiasm.[5] There were sub-gatherings of the *gaṇas*, *vrātas*, etc.

Side by side with the gatherings of the folk there existed the local or communal gatherings of the groups. The *saṅgrāma* or *sena* had contingents from the localities where the fighting men assembled in

[1] *R.-V.*, X, 143, 4: *samane parshato narā*; II, 16, 7; X, 69, 11.

[2] *R.-V.*, IV, 58, 8; VI, 75, 4; VII, 2, 5; *A.-V.*, II, 36, 1.

[3] *Pārasakara Gṛhyasūtra*, III, 13, 4.

[4] *T.S.*, VI, 5, 1; *R.-V.*, I, 91, 20; *T.B.*, III, 12, 9; *Ś.B.*, II, 10: *Sadasya devayajanam me dehi; Sādanyam vidathyam sabheyam.*

[5] *R.-V.*, X, 39, 5: *Purāṇā vām vīryā prabravā jane.*

groups known as *śardha.*[1] There were *śardhas* of cavalry, of valiant heroes and of chariots : and in local or communal contingents they swelled to form the host.

Local communities were Aryan or non-Aryan. The Aryan *gaṇas* included all kinsmen, and often belonged to the family of some eponymous ancestor. One such of the Kaṇwas is specifically mentioned in the *Ṛg-Veda.*[2] Hymns of the *Yajur-Veda*[3] explain that not only men of all ages and grades, but even women had a voice in local polity and had to be conciliated. The presiding deity of the Aryan *gaṇa* was Brahmaṇaspati, and under his blessings they fought the non-Aryan *gaṇa* (*phala*) and their leaders like Vala.[4]

Some non-Aryan communities (*viś*) worshipped the Maruts and were in seven divisions like the Maruts. We are told in one passage that the *aśvattha* tree was sacred to them, and they apparently met underneath it. This picture in the later Vedic texts[5] accords with what we find still existing among communities like the Kuvi-Khonds : 'The village assembly of the Kuvis meets under a tree in the centre of the village. All round the trunk are flat stone-seats arranged for the elders to sit on, and the headman sits at the centre

[1] *R.-V.*, I, 71, 8 : *śardham anavadyam yuvānam ; R.-V.*, I, 53, 11 : *śardham śardham.* Zimmer thought that the reference is to the host arrayed in clan, village and family, but various texts show that the term applies to the several component parts of the military system : *R.-V.*, V, 33, 5 ; 53, 10 ; 54, 10 ; 85, 4.

[2] *R.-V.*, I, 42, 10.

[3] *T.S.*, IV, 5, 4 : *mahadbhyaḥ kshullakebhyaḥ* ; II, 3, 9.

[4] *Rukvatā gaṇena valam ruroja phaligam.* Cf. p. 11 *supra.*

[5] *T.S.*, II, 3, 1 : *Marutām ojah aśvatthah | viśam avagacchati | sapta bhavanti.* The gods sit there : *vide A-V.*, V, 4, 3 ; *Ch. U.*, VIII, 5, 3.

near the trunk of the tree. Meetings of the village council are held after due notice, and decide matters of family and matrimonial affairs and cases arising out of these.'

Gṛtsas and *Vrātas* were apparently religious orders which had some sort of political organisation. The chieftain at their head appears in the latest book of the *Ṛg-Veda* attended on by the heads of localities. In the latest period we find some of them devoted to religion (*arhants*) and others to fighting (*yaudhas*). The former set included the singers and saints whose organs had atrophied by continuous practice of continence. Necessities of proselytism resulted in the admission, to these orders, of men of the lower grades in society and even of men of dubious character. They had recruits even from the Brāhman community, for we are told of special chants employed to enable some of these to regain admission to the orthodox fold. It is of interest that these bodies of vagrants did not live by industry or by commerce. There was military discipline among them, and their chief was armed with a goad. [1]

The *Gṛtsas* were in the orthodox fold. Already in one of the earliest books of the *Ṛg-Veda* [2] we find Agni and Varuṇa described as *gṛtsas*, and some mortals also sharing the appellation. Bands of sages designated as *gṛtsamadas* are frequently mentioned in another of the earliest books, and their attachment to their society is implied in the epithet *gṛtsamadāh*. There is apparent

[1] *R.-V.*, X, 34, 12; 177, 2; *A.-V*, VII, 72, 2; Book XV; *P. B.* XVII.

[2] *R.-V.*, VII, 86, 7: *martyam gṛtsam*; II, 4, 9; 39, 8: *gṛtsamadāsaḥ*.

etymological connection between them and the *gṛdhras* of the later books of the *Ṛg-Veda*, who are styled *kavi* and are led by a *Śyena*.[1] The semi-mythical associations of *gṛdhra* and *śyena*[2] settle down to *terra firma*, as the famous family of the Gotamas are described as *gṛdhras* in the latest book of the *Ṛg-Veda* and the *gāyatrī* hymn is referred to as revealed by a *Śyena*, in the Brāhmaṇa texts. An early passage of the *Yajur-Veda*[3] mentions *gṛtsas* and their chieftains along with *gaṇas* and *vrātas*. The *gṛtsas* became famous in later literature (Epic and Purāṇic) as originating the social divisions of the people into the four castes.

Among the professional or craft guilds of the Vedic age we have notices of potters, blacksmiths, carpenters, engineers, and makers of bows and arrows. There were also social groups among the masses, like those of hunters, bird-catchers, elephant-catchers, dog-breeders, and gamesters.

It is specially interesting to note evidences of organisation among the ladies of the time. A *strī-samsādam* or assembly of ladies is mentioned in the *Taittirīya Saṁhitā*[4] as having discussed the privileges and disabilities due to sex. The *Ugaṇas* of the *Rudra* hymn are apparently military bodies for both offensive and defensive purposes.[5] Among

[1] *R.-V.*, IX, 97, 57 ; IX, 96, 6.

[2] *Ibid.*, I, 88, 4. The *Aitareya Upanishad* describes the spiritual march of the disembodied soul as 'swift like the hawk' (*śyeno javasā*). Perhaps we have similar symbolism in the *Rāmāyaṇa* where Jaṭāyu who took up the cause of Sītā against Rāvaṇa is described as a *gṛdhra* or chieftain of *gṛdhras*, an order famous for their wanderings in forest tracts.

[3] *T.S.*, IV, 5, 4.

[4] *Ibid.*, II, 3.

[5] *Ibid.*, IV, 5, 5 : *āvyādhinī vividhyantī*.

non-Aryan people women were also engaged in the manufacture of arms.[1]

IX

INTER-STATE RELATIONS

The growth of a doctrine of *dharma* influenced the relations of the Aryan states to one another on the one hand, and to the non-Aryan on the other. The tendency was to humanise the relations both in war and in peace. In war the relations of an Aryan to a non-Aryan state were to some extent conditioned by a reciprocity of dealing. Fair fighting was hardly possible with peoples like the Nāgas who excelled in the arts of magic and mesmerism, and had military and material resources in no way inferior to the Aryan; the Rākshasas whose warfare was full of surprises, such as fighting from ambush, and who practised deception; and the Piśāchas who used unfair contrivances like thorns and hurdles hidden underground.[2] Nor was it easy to maintain principles of chivalry when Dāsa hosts like Namuchi's let loose an army of amazons to seduce Aryan soldiery in the ranks or even their trusted leaders. At first the tendency[3] was to beat them by their own methods. There is a hymn in praise of an iron-pointed arrow which was tipped with poison.[4] But there gradually grew a tendency to trust more and more to organised hosts and to humane methods of fighting.[5] The might of the cavalry and

[1] *R.-V.*, V, 30, 9: *Striyo hi dāsīh āyudhāni chakre.*

[2] *T.B.*, II, 4; *G.B.*, I, 10.

[3] Reflected in *R.-V.*, V, 30, 9; *A.-V.*, VII, 38, 2; *T.S.*, VII, 4, 19, 3.

[4] *R.-V.*, VI, 75, 15.

[5] *R.-V.*, II, 104, 16 records the resentment of Vasishṭha when Viśvāmitra accused him of being a sorcerer (*yātudhāna*).

chariots in warfare is described in the earliest books, as also the hand-to-hand fighting[1] among the infantry. Elephants appear only in the latest books.[2] The evolution of such organised fighting in place of ruthless slaughter is an early stage in the humanisation of warfare.

The next stage was reached when the Aryas fell to fighting among themselves. The *Yajur-Veda* and the Brāhmaṇas are redolent of the warfare of Aryan and Asura states. The worshippers of the *Devas* relied on their superior mental and moral power to vanquish the united arms of the *Asuras*, rather than on force or fraud. Very often too, there were treaties made and compacts observed. We have the evolution of military strategy and tactics as early as the Battle of the Ten Kings,[3] when the enemies of Sudās tried to cut off his forces by diverting the course of the river Rāvi.

The greatest achievement of the age was in the establishment of diplomatic relations between one state and another. The office of *Sūta* does not find mention in the *Ṛg-Veda*, but he figures as a *Ratnin* in the *Yajur-Veda*, and his importance gradually grows until the *Śatapatha Brāhmaṇa* considers him and the *Grāmaṇī* as king-makers (*rājakṛt*). The person of the *Sūta* is described as inviolable, and his influence went on increasing in the administration. The *Taittirīya Saṁhitā* introduces *Dūta* and *Prahita*. The one was a diplomatic envoy accredited to a foreign state, and the other an officer on a secret mission. Such diplomatic relations were carried on with non-Aryan

[1] *R.-V.*, V, 84, 4 : *mushṭika*. [2] *R.-V.*, I, 84, 17.
[3] *R.-V.*, VII.

3

states also. We read in one passage: 'the messengers of the Rākshasas are come.'[1]

X

THE IDEAL STATE

The ideal state of Aryan political philosophy is reflected in the texts of the latest Vedic age. King Aśvapati of Kekaya says[2] that there was in his dominion 'no thief, no villain, no drunkard; none who neglected religious rites, none uncultured, no man incontinent and gay as a libertine, no woman who was unchaste.' This was a body politic painted in roseate hues, but the ideal is clear. The principle ot polity was, not *laissez faire*, but that of saving men and women from an inclination to do wrong, and providing for the education of the adult and the adolescent. A righteous king had the right of punishing rebels (*śaṭrūyataḥ*) as well as the duty of beating off foreign invasions.[3] The head of the state was also to see that plenty and prosperity reigned in the state, and that there was not only active production of wealth but equitable distribution.[4] His rule was to be benign and kindly, and he was to undertake works of religious merit and to adjust the relations among his subjects.[5]

[1] *T.A.*, IV, 33, 3. [2] *Ch. Up.*, V, 11, 7.

[3] *A.-V.*, VI, 88, 3.

[4] *Athā mano vasudēyāya kṛṇushva tato na ugro vibhajā vasūni* (*A.-V.*, IV, 4, 4.)

[5] *Indrendra manushyāh parehi saṁ hi ajñāsthāh valgaih saṁvidānah* | *Sa tvāyam āhuta sve sadhasthe sa devān yajñāt sa u kalpayāt viśah*|| (*A.-V.*, III, 4, 6.)

CHAPTER II

POST-VEDIC LIFE AND IDEALS

I

POLITICAL THOUGHT

IN the Post-Vedic age we have abundant evidence of political speculation. Though polity was not yet recognised as a branch of the Veda or as one of the *vidyas*, schools of political thought grew up side by side with Vedic studies. There is evidence in the *Mahābhārata* of the schools associated with Bâhudantiputra and Viśālāksha, who are identifiable with Indra and Maheśvara. Schools of grammar associated with these names were well known in Pāṇini's day. The connection of polity with military science is indicated in Kauṇapadanta who has been identified with Bhīshma, and with music in Piśuna identified with Nārada. If Vātavyādhi, referred to by Kauṭilya, be identified with Uddhava, we get a similar association of political and ethical studies.

The identification of Bhīshma is based on a later text which may, however, embody an early tradition. The emphasis on the army as an element of sovereignty seems also to support the identity, conditions of war justifying his political principles. Similarly Piśuna's championship of a sound finance as the paramount consideration implies a diplomacy which would keep the enemies divided (*mitrabheda*), for war would deplete the treasury. The school of Piśuna may be associated with Avanti, as the minister of Agnimitra is styled Āchārya Piśuna in Kāḷidāsa's drama; and Agnimitra's policy, like that of the classical Nārada, cleft Vidarbha in twain. 'Vātavyādhi' denotes an unhealthy constitution where the members defied control. It could be strengthened and energised only by external alliances (*mitralābha*) of the kind for which Uddhava was responsible in the Epic story.

We have similar association of political and other studies in Ghoṭamukha, who appears in Kauṭilya's *Arthaśāstra* and in Vātsyāyana's *Kāmasūtras*; in Kātyāyana or Vararuchi, the author of a grammar as well as founder of a political school; in Vāmadeva figuring as a political teacher;[1] and among later writers, in Maya the founder of schools in architecture and polity, and in Satyāchārya whose political and astrological views are discussed respectively in Kāmandaka's *Nītisāra* and Varāhamihira's *Bṛhatsaṁhitā*. Whether every one of these identifications be tenable or not, it will be evident that principles of polity were in the process of formation long before the historical period, and that they were associated with the founders of other schools of study branching off from the Vedic. Buddhist *Brahmajālasutta* denounces the Brāhmans who were engaged in king-craft and in the arts of war and peace.

Some of the schools of polity are traceable in history. Bharadvāja, styled also Kaṇika by Kauṭilya,[2] is the hero of the *Kaṇikopākhyāna* in the *Mahābhārata*, and of Droṇāchārya's school. His views on the aims of an unscrupulous minister agree with those attributed

[1] *Mbh*:. Śānti, 61, 94.

[2] Kauṭilya, V, 5.

to that teacher by Karṇa. Both in the Epic and in the *Kauṭilīya* he is said to have advocated deliberation with only one minister.[1] Chārāyaṇa *alias* Dīrghachārāyaṇa appears in Buddhist literature as the king-maker who deposed Pasenadi (Prasenajit) of Kosala in favour of the crown-prince. Tradition regards Kauṭilya as the King-maker and the real founder of the fortunes of the Maurya dynasty. It is interesting that political thought in all these cases, and even in later ages, is associated with ministers rather than with kings. Perhaps the only royal name which could possibly be traced in the long list of political writers is that of Puloma. It suggests Puḷumāvi, the Sātavāhana king, whose name appears in the Purāṇas in many places as Puloma. His doctrines, apparently unknown to Kauṭilya, are mentioned in Kāmandaka's *Nītisāra*.

It is interesting that different schools of thought are associated with different parts of India. Bharadvāja wrote for a Sauvīra king of the West, and is represented in the Epics and the Purāṇas[2] as living on the upper Ganges, at Haridvār or at Prayāg. Śukra or Uśanas was the minister of a mythical king, Pṛthu Vainya, and his ancient work was known as *Daṇḍanīti*. A king of Girivraja is known as *Daṇḍadhara*,[3] and the school may have originated in Magadha. Chārāyaṇa belonged to Oudh, and was contemporary with Pasenadi and the Buddha. The Ambhīyas mentioned by Kauṭilya can similarly be connected with Taxila, whose king Ambhi was a contemporary of Alexander the Great. Maya and

[1] *Mbh.*: Ādi, 153, 91. [2] *Ibid*: Śānti, 58, 120.
[3] *Ibid*: Karṇa, 18, 696.

Puloma are probably of the Dekhan, and Kauṭilya belonged to Magadha. Bṛhaspati [1] refers his work especially to the land of the Bharatas, i.e., the Doab of the Ganges and the Jumna.

The science of polity was known by different names. The earliest is *Rājadharma* or *Rājaśāstra* 'the body of rules governing the conduct of kings,' as it is styled in the *Mahābhārata*.[2] The chapters in the Epic dealing with the subject show that the designation is not without significance, for the rules of polity formulated there have an ethical bearing. In the same work there is reference to the *Rājanīti* of Bṛhaspati. Aśvaghosha refers to the *Rājaśāstras* of Bhṛgu and Aṅgiras, which were probably the original texts of Bṛhaspati and Śukra. But the more popular designation of the latter work is *daṇḍaśāstram* or *daṇḍanīti*, a treatise on which subject is also attributed to Prajāpati.[3] We find here a shifting of the emphasis from righteousness (*dharma*) to expediency (*nīti* or *naya*). Kauṭilya adopts the same term (*daṇḍanīti*) and analyses it into rules of expediency or diplomacy (*naya*) and of the strength of states (*bala*). The term *artha-śāstra* has probably a wider connotation and includes economics (*vārtā*) [4] as well as politics (*daṇḍanīti*). It is used both by Kauṭilya and Bṛhaspati, but, even in Kauṭilya's day, Economics parted company from Politics, and the essence of the latter science was

[1] Bṛhaspati, III, 74.

[2] According to this tradition (Śānti, 58, 82f.) Śaṅkara or Viśālāksha came first after Brahma, and was followed by Bāhudantaka, Bṛhaspati, Śukra, Bharadvāja, Gauraśiras and Vyāsa in order of time. Elsewhere, it introduces Vasu Uparichara of Chedi and Svāyambhuva Manu before Bṛhaspati, and makes Śukra the minister of King Vainya.

[3] *Mbh.:* Śānti, 31 and 58.

[4] Kauṭilya, I, 4: *Tasyāmāyattā lokayātrā.*

Diplomacy (*nīti* or *naya*). Thus we have the *Nītisāra* of Sukra [1] and Kāmandaka and the *Nayaśāstra*, told in the form of stories and fables in the *Pañchatantra*. We can place in chronological order the *Rājadharma*, the *Rājaśāstra* of Bhṛgu and Aṅgiras, the *Arthaśāstra* of Kauṭilya and Bṛhaspati, and the *Artha* or *Naya śāstras* of the *Pañchatantra* and other story-books. In Kāmandaka's view *nīti* was the real soul of state-craft. But the diplomacy here implied was applied to practical politics, and thus was *Rājatantra* evolved. Maya is spoken of by Kāmandaka as *tantrakuśala*.[2] This view continued, down to mediaeval times, as will be obvious from the *Nītiratnākara* of Chaṇḍikeśvara and the *Nītivākyāmṛta* of Somadeva.

In the course of this development the science of polity lost more and more of its sacred character and became essentially secular and practical. Ancient doctrine was that usage was the test of *dharma*, but the school of Śaṅkha did not agree with this view. Bhīma observed that kings should gather wisdom from various sources, and not from the Vedas alone. Bṛhaspati held that the texts could be understood, not solely by discussion or dialectics, but by experience. Uśanas would never accept anything which could not stand the test of reason.[3] The body of political doctrine was gradually parting company with ethics and equity, and was taking its stand in the cold light of logic and rationalism, and in the exigencies of practical politics.

[1] Śukra styles *nīti* as *lokasthitikṛt*—securing the maintenance of states and as *dharmārthakāmamūlam*, i.e., the basis of all the other activities of man. The sense is obvious, that government and order are the necessary conditions of all other activity.

[2] Kāmandaka, I, 7 ; VIII, 20

[3] *Mbh.* : Śānti, 132, 141 and 142.

II

THEORIES AS TO THE ORIGIN OF MONARCHY

The period was fruitful in theories as to the origin of kingship. First is the theory of a social compact following anarchy, detailed in the Śānti Parva of the *Mahābhārata.*[1] There was general lack of security, and men were like fish eating the smaller ones of their kind. This reign of lust and domination was followed by a rule of law *(daṇḍanīti)*, and a king was chosen to administer it. He had no powers of initiative, but was merely the instrument of the popular will.[2]

A second theory was that of Social Contract. In return for taxation the king was bound to hold himself responsible for the safety and security of his subjects and for meting out proper punishment to wrong-doers. His portion was a tenth, an eighth, or a sixth of the agricultural produce, 2 per cent of the stock of gold and cattle, 5 per cent on merchandise, and a sixth of fruits, roots and forest produce. He was entitled also to one day's labour every month from artisans.[3] The king was thus only the highest paid officer and servant of the state.[4]

A third theory was that the king was the best, the most excellent man in the state. In the *Jātakas* we are told that the tribal republics chose men who were

[1] Śānti, 67; *Rāmāyaṇa*: Ayod. Kāṇḍ., 67, 31: *Matsyā iva narā nityam bhakshayanti parasparam.* Cf. *Mbh.*: Śānti, 14, 38: *Jale matsyānivābhakshyān durbalam balavattarāh.*

[2] *Mbh.*: Śānti, 58, 111. Cf. Sumerian conditions before Utu-Khegal.

[3] Gautama, X, 24 and 27; X, 46; Baudhāyana, VII, 5, 10; Vishṇu, III, 66. One off-shoot of this Contract theory was the king's liability to restore stolen property.

[4] *Rām.*: Ayod. Kāṇḍa, 75, 24. Cf. Āryadeva, V, 77: *Gaṇadāsasya te darp ah shaḍbhāgena bhṛtasya kah.*

'handsome, auspicious, commanding, perfect.'[1] In the Buddha's day they chose 'the finest looking, the largest, the handsomest, the strongest man' as king. The king was 'the chosen and approved of all.' He was 'the lord of protectors.' He was *Rājā*, 'one who pleased all by his virtue.'[2] Here we have the idea of peaceful and patriarchal monarchy. The king was set over the people to lead society in *satyam* and *dharma*, to enable every individual and class to lead the highest and best life possible for each. He was to take paternal care of his people.[3]

III

IDEAL OF KINGSHIP

Kingship in the Post-Vedic age was a civil monarchy, not sacerdotal or military. We find no military title among those of the king,[4] and militarism was expressly forbidden: 'Bṛhaspati has laid down that a wise king should always avoid war for the acquisition of territory.'[5] Nor was there any idea of Divine Right. 'The king who is virtuous is a part of the gods. He who is otherwise is a part of the demons.' A king who was unable to protect his subjects was to be slain by them, according to Vāmadeva.[6] Instances of kings deposed for wickedness like Khananetra, disinherited for disease like Devāpi, or for wickedness like Asamañja[7], abound in the Epic texts. The Jātakas likewise make it clear that the king's mastery

[1] *Jātaka*, II, 249. The king was *mahāsammata* or *mahājanasammata*.
[2] *Mbh.* : Śānti, 28, 138 ; 31, 32 ; 56, 11.
[3] *Rām.* : Ayod. Kāṇḍ., 75, 23 : *bhūtāni putravat*.
[4] *Narapati*, *Bhūpati*, *Bhaṭṭāraka*, *Mahārāja*, etc.
[5] *Mbh.*: Śānti. 69, 23. [6] Cp. *Mbh.* : Śānti, 92, 9.
[7] *Mbh.* : Aśvamedha, 4, 8 and 9 ; Udyoga, 148, 27 ; Śānti, 57, 9.

was only over evil-doers, not over all, and they have instances of people who had killed their kings.[1]

At the coronation ceremony all sorts and classes of subjects took part—Brāhmans, territorial chieftains, merchants and Śūdras;[2] even women, unmarried girls, traders and soldiers are specifically mentioned. Before them and the neighbouring kings and princes the king took his Coronation Oath (*pratijñā*): 'I will carry out the *dharma* as laid down in the *nīti* and will never be guided by selfish interests.'[3]

The Queen did not ascend the throne with the king in Vedic times; but now she did, and every wife of the king, even a Śūdra wife, took part in the ceremony.[4] Already in the later Vedic period the queen was seen to wear her crown (*ushṇīśa*), and instances of female rulers were known, e.g., Uśinarāṇi, and Subhadrikā of Kampila.[5]

In the *Rāmāyaṇa* not only were the subjects consulted at the coronation of the crown-prince but the *parishad* of princes from the various states.[6] The qualification of the heir-apparent was not merely birth and fealty to the king but popularity in the state. Sometimes it was not the eldest son who succeeded, but the one who was chosen for his virtues. A good instance in point is Puru who was crowned, though he

[1] *Jātakas*, Nos. 73 and 432. [2] *Rām.*: Yud. Kāṇḍ., 128, 62.

[3] *Mbh.*: Śānti, 59, 106 and 107: *Yaśchātra dharmo nītyukto daṇḍanītivyapāśrayah | tamaśaṅkah karishyāmi svavaśo na kadāchana.||*

[4] *Mbh.*: Śānti, 39, 44: *Upaveśya mahātmānam Kṛishṇām cha* . . . Cf. *Rām.*: Bāla Kāṇḍ., 14, 35; Yud. Kāṇḍ., 128, 59.

[5] *R.-V.*, X, 59, 10; *V. S.*, XXIII, 18.

[6] *Rām.*: Ayod. Kāṇḍ., 1, 45: *Nānā nagaravāstavyān pṛthak jānapadānapi rājān*, etc. Also Ayod. Kāṇḍ., 3, 40.

was the youngest son, by Yayāti, backed by the consent of his people.[1]

The king was looked upon as the ideal of the state in *satyam* and *dharma*. He was to salute the people as well as be saluted by them; to show himself to the people every day in the forenoon; and to consult his ministers on all matters of state, both individually and collectively. He had the duty of holding *sabhas*, *utsavas* and *samājas*, i.e., popular festivals and processions. He was to show the people what was right, and to lead them away from the path of unrighteousness: to be like a father unto his people.[2] His was to be a life of unremitting toil, a life of selfless service like that of the expectant mother, living for her child and suppressing her selfish inclinations.[3] The country was his God, and he was the symbol of the state. That king was the best whose subjects had no fear of him and no need to conceal their resources from him, whose subjects never planned plots or conspiracies, but were guided in daily life by righteousness and self-restraint, and lived in harmony and peace with one another.[4] In fact, the duty of the king was to break up such unions of the people as political conspiracies or economic combinations.[5] He had also the

[1] *Mbh.*: Śānti, 28, 98.

[2] *Rām.*: Ayod. Kāṇḍ., 67, 34; Araṇ. Kāṇḍ., 50, 9; Ayod. Kāṇḍ., 100, 52: *kachchiddarśayase nityam manushyāṇām vibhūshitam | uddhāyoddhāya pūrvānhe rājaputra mahāpathe* || Ayod. Kāṇḍ., 67, 31: *vibhajan sādhvasādhūni*.

[3] *Mbh.*: Śānti, 56, 45: *Garbhiṇīdharmah—svayam priyam parityajya lokasya hitamedhate*.

[4] *Mbh.*: Śānti, 56, 35 and 36: *Agūḍhavibhavāh*; *asaṅghāte ratāh* and *na cha saṅgharshaśīlinah*.

[5] *Mbh.*: Śānti, 57, 10: *Paurasaṅghātabhedanam*; *vide* also *Rām.*: Ayod. Kāṇḍ., 67.

sacred duty of looking after ruined temples and edifices.[1]

We are told that the king combined the functions of Agni, Indra, Soma, Varuṇa and Yama, or the Sun, Agni, Mrtyu, Kubera and Yama.[2] He nipped evil deeds in the bud by his department of spies, cleansed those impure in heart and turned them to the right path, awarded punishments and rewards according to desert, and gave or took away wealth according to circumstances. The incessant watchfulness of the king and the need for constant vigilance are emphasised. He used his spies for checkmating the designs of evil-doers, and his spies were everywhere—in the bazaars and fields of sport, meeting places and streets, parks and pleasure-gardens, halls of learned discussion, court-halls and high-ways, inns and brothels.[3] But there is no evidence of allegiance being due to the king in all circumstances. *Bhakti* has sometimes been taken in this sense, but the Grammarians make it clear that the idea implied in it is territorial and not political.[4]

IV

THE MINISTRY

The king was helped by ministers and by a Council of ministers (*parishad*). The general term for the minister in the *Rāmāyaṇa* is *Amātya*, i.e., one near the

[1] *Mbh.*: Śānti, 57, 7: *Ketanānām cha jīrṇānām avekshā chaiva sīdatām.*

[2] *Rām.*: Ayod. Kāṇḍ., 40; Śānti, 67; Manu, VII, 8.

[3] *Mbh.*: Śānti, 68, 11 and 12.

[4] Kātyāyana on Pāṇini, IV, 3, 100: One of Madrabhakti is Mādraka and of Vriji is Vrijika.

person of the king, and *Amātyas* are classified as *Mantrins* and *Sachivas.*[1] In the *Kauṭilīya,*[2] *Amātyas* are differentiated from *Mantrins.* In the *Jātaka* texts the ministers are called *Rājakartaro.* This may mean 'king-makers', as the election of a new king partially depended on them.[3] Their number is given as six.

In the Buddhist texts we have the king's household officers described as the potter, basket-maker, gardener, barber, cook and appraiser. Elsewhere we have mention of the charioteer, the keeper of the king's purse, the store-keeper, the *Dauvārika,* who was the guardian of the city-gates, or of the frontiers, the *Nāgaraguttika* who arrested robbers and ruled the night, and the *Choraghātaka* or executioner. There is also mention of musicians, dancers and singers, elephant-tamers and archers. But none of these is included among the king's ministers.[4]

The *Amātyas* (*amacchas*) were the great officers of state (*Mahāmātras*). They formed a class like the Brāhmaṇa and the Vaiśya, and were probably hereditary, as *Amātyakula* is mentioned like *Rājanyakula.*[5] One of the prominent *Amātyas* was the *Arthadharmānuśāsaka*; another the *Senāpati,* who was sometimes the most important, and a third was the Judge (*Viniśchayāmātya*) whom the king consulted as regards

[1] *Rām.*: Yud. Kāṇḍ., 130, 17-20. In the *Manusmriti, sachiva* is a generic term, and *amātya* is the keeper of counsel (*daṇḍadhara*).

[2] Kauṭilya, I, Chap. 8.

[3] *Mahāgovinda Suttānta* in *Dīgha Nikāya,* II, 233. The same term *Rājakartārah* occurs in the *Rāmāyaṇa* (Bāla Kāṇḍ., 79, 1), but in the sense of ministers rather than king-makers.

[4] *Jāt.,* Vol. I, p. 121, 124, 126 and 137; II, p. 377 and 379; III, p. 41, 59 and 193; IV, p. 43, 382; V, p. 123, 290-292.

[5] *Chullavagga,* VII, 3, 5; *Jāt.,* I, 260; III, 376; II, 98 and 125.

punishments to be inflicted, and who could protest against unjust judgments in order to save the innocent.[1] Another *Amātya* was the *Rajjugrāhaka*, who measured lands and granted remissions,[2] and whose sense of justice and fair-play is emphasised. Still another was the *Purohita*. He was the king's adviser, friend and inseparable companion. He sometimes acted as a judge, and as such could reverse the orders of the *Senāpati*. He guarded the king's treasures and had a part in settling the succession to the crown.[3] The Superintendent of weights and measures (*Droṇamāpaka*) was also a *Mahāmātra*, as well as the *Grāmabhojaka*, or head of the township. It is clear that these *Amātyas* or ministers of the crown were differentiated from the royal household officers even before the historical period. They eventually became heads of departments. Their number became standardised at 18, and they were designated *Tīrthas*.

The ministerial Council consisted of these and some others. The classical list in the *Mahābhārata* includes 54 members selected on a caste basis—4 Brāhmaṇas, 18 Kshatriyas, 21 Vaiśyas, 3 Śūdras and 8 ministers.[4] It is clear that there was a very large representation of Kshatriyas and Vaiśyas and a small sprinkling of Brāhmaṇas and Sūdras, so that the former classes bore the brunt of the responsibility. The purpose of summoning the *parishad* was, of course, to enlist the co-operation of the representatives

[1] *Jāt.*, III, 104.
[2] *Ibid*, IV, 169.
[3] *Ibid*, III, 417 ; V, 1 ; II, 187 ; I, 439 ; III, 238.
[4] *Mbh.* : Śānti, 85, 12 : *Chaturo Brāhmaṇān | Kshatriyān daśa chāshṭau cha | Vaiśyān ekaviṁśati | trīṁścha Śūdrān | Ashṭānām mantriṇām madhye mantram rājopadhārayet |*

of the people in the special needs of the administration in times of stress. One prominent object was to enable the king to maintain the harmonious working of the administration.

The qualifications of ministers are indicated in several passages in the *Rāmāyaṇa*, the *Mahābhārata* and the Buddhist texts. The ministers were to be high-born, war-like, learned, shrewd, and of high character. One clever minister was better than a thousand.[1] Those who were to be the executive were tested by being subjected to temptations, and men who led a pure and godly life, and had an ancestral experience of affairs, were to be preferred. Alertness and dexterity were additional qualifications in the Executive Councillors.[2] As regards the ministers forming the advisory Council (*mantrins*), they were to be consulted in private as well as in Council.[3] The *Upādhyāya* was to be well-versed in polity. The *Dūta* was to be intelligent, a native of the country and one who would faithfully carry out his mission. The *Senāpati* was to be one attached to the person of the king, steadfast and faithful.[4]

There was an inner Council of 8 ministers, who formed the Executive. The eight *amātyas* of Daśaratha are described,[5] consistently with these criteria, as lions of justice meting out punishments and distributing rewards without favour or partiality; as experts in finance who replenished

[1] *Rām.*: Ayod. Kāṇḍ., 100, 23.

[2] *Ibid*: 100, 27: *Amātyān upadhātītān pitṛpaitāmahān śuchīn.*

[3] *Ibid*: 100, 72: *Mantribhistvam yathoddishṭaih chaturbhih tribhireva vā | kachchit samastairvyastaiścha mantram mantrayase midhah* ||

[4] *Rām.*: Ayod. Kāṇḍ., 100, 15 and 36.

[5] *Rām.*: Bāla Kāṇḍ., 7, 3 and 8–17.

the treasury without injuring the people, by arranging that public burdens fell on men according to their ability to contribute to the state fisc; as men of personality who could be entrusted with affairs of war and peace and foreign relations; as masters of diplomacy who could keep secret counsel and devise clever expedients; as well-versed in the science of polity, and clever in the art of sweet persuasion. The functions detailed here agree with those described by Bharadvāja, who says that 'the ministers were concerned with general deliberation on policy (*mantra*) and its execution, matters of public finance, military affairs and relations on the frontiers, provision for the protection of princes, and provisions against national calamities.'[1]

The ministers of Yudhishṭhira are thus described.[2] Bhīma was *Yuvarāja*, and Vidura the master of political deliberation and the six-fold art of diplomacy. Nakula was the chief army-officer charged with the organisation, payment and disposition of the troops. Sañjaya was the minister of finance, in charge of receipts and disbursement of the resources of the state. Arjuna was the Commander-in-Chief, in defensive warfare and in suppressing internal rebellions. Dhaumya was the *Purohita*, the general adviser in administration, and in special charge of the department of religion. Sahadeva was the Aide-de-Camp and Private Secretary to the Emperor. The only point of

[1] *Mantro mantraphalāvāptih karmānushṭhānam āyavyayakarma daṇḍapraṇayanam amitrāṭavīpratishedhah rājyarakshaṇam vyasanapratīkārah kumārarakshaṇam abhishekam cha kumārāṇām āyattam amātyeshu*, cited by Kauṭilya in Book VIII, Chap. I.

[2] *Mbh.*, Śānti, Ch. IV.

interest here, as compared with the other passages, is the mention of two heads of departments in the army—the Commander-in-Chief and the Paymaster of the Forces.

Amātyas are frequently referred to and described in the Buddhist texts. In one place a king, sick of worldly life, hands over the kingdom to his ministers. Sometimes they were in temporary custody of the kingdom. They formed a class and were probably hereditary.[1] Some of them were Brāhmans,—the *Purohita*, who is also styled *Āchārya* and *Guru*, and the *Arthadharmānuśāsaka* were always Brāhmans. The *Senāpati*, who had also judicial functions, and the *Uparāja* were always Kshatriyas, and generally related to the king. The *Senāpati* sometimes acted as Viceroy.[2]

The *Rajjugrāhakāmātya* was the Survey and Settlement officer. The *Dauvārikāmātya* kept out-castes and vagabonds away from the royal precincts. When the king was in the city, he blew his horn three times a day and closed the city-gates after night-fall.[3] He issued directions in regard to the foreigners resident in the city. All these *amātyas* were also known as *Rājabhogyas* (*Rājabhoggas*), i.e., royal officers. It is interesting to notice that a man of the Chaṇḍāḷa caste was the Executioner and went by the side of the king at processions. He had a hatchet and a thorny rope in his hand, was dressed in yellow and adorned with red flowers.[4] Thus the various castes were represented in the ministry.

[1] *Jāt.*, II, 2; I, 260; II, 98 and 125 (*amātyakula*); V, 125.
[2] *Ibid*: V, 459.
[3] *Ibid*: II, 279; IV, 382
[4] *Ibid*: III, 41 and 179.

V

THE ASSEMBLIES

The people of the capital city and the country at large (*paurajānapadāh*) are frequently mentioned in the Epic texts as assembling on important political occasions. It is clear from the context that they had some voice in the administration. There is, however, no evidence that they had a regular constitution, or that they were summoned, or had specific rules of working, or definite functions or powers. It is mostly in connection with the election of the king that we have the populace assembling of its own accord and exercising its voice, both in the Epics and in the Jātaka texts. In the populace were differentiated leaders of the guilds (*naigamas*), and other corporations (*gaṇas*), besides the leaders of the people at large.[1] A general concensus of opinion among the people on any matter was known as *samaya* or *samvit*.

It is clear, however, that while there was no assembly of the people at large, there were assemblies of groups or sections, in normal and effective working. Such assemblies of cities are mentioned in the Jātakas. The *cchandaka* of Sakalanagara was the resolution of the city-corporation or *paura* as contrasted with that of the *negama*. The *grāma* was a Brāhman corporation,[2] and other caste groups had their own institutions (*jāti-samūha*). Merchants were organised in *saṅghas*, and their guilds (*śreṇi*) had political influence. The *Rāmāyaṇa* refers to *grāmaghoshamahattarāh* or

[1] *Rām.*: Ayod. Kāṇḍ., 4, 14; 3, 24: *Paurajānapadaśreshṭhāh naigamāścha gaṇaissaha.*

[2] Kullūka on Manu, VIII, 219.

leaders of *grāmas* and *ghoshas*, and Patañjali explains *ghosha* as a township with corporate arms and its own seal. *Śreṇis* and *śreṇibaddhas* are mentioned among Kshatriya corporations in the *Mahābhārata*.[1] According to Manu, these groups entered into relations with one another, and their contracts and agreements (*samvit*) were binding on the state. Some kings were merely presidents of *śreṇis* and had to carry out their behests.[2] Gautama lays down that each had its own laws and local usages and that the usages of the *kula* (family), *jāti* (caste), and *deśa* (locality) were valid.[3] The *deśasaṅghas* or local groups may be analysed in the light of Gautama's text as those of agriculturists, merchants, cowherds, bankers and artisans. Each was known as a *varga*, which probably means a subdivision of the people. The *Mahāvagga*[4] speaks of *saṅghas* of 4, 5, 10, 20, and 21 *vargas*. Jātaka texts mention groups and further subdivisions of the same, each having its own *śreṇi*. Pāṇini uses the term *saṅgha* in the generic sense, and *pūga* to denote economic organisations. The generic sense of *saṅgha* is also clear from the *Rāmāyaṇa*.[5] *Goshṭhi* and *samāja* were gatherings of the people for social purposes.[6]

Gaṇa is explained as a fraternity of Brāhmans by the commentators on Manu and Nārada-*Smṛiti*.[7] But

[1] *Mbh.* : Aśva., 4 ; *Rām.* : Ayod. Kāṇḍ., 79, 4.

[2] *Rājānaḥ śreṇibaddhāścha* in *Mbh.* : Śānti, 14, 4.

[3] Gautama, XI, 21.

[4] IX, 4, 1.

[5] Ayod. Kāṇḍ., 6, 20 ; 81, 12 ; Bāla Kāṇḍ., 5, 12 and 13 : *Vadhūnāṭakasaṅghaiścha* ; *sāmantarājasaṅghaiścha*.

[6] *Vinaya*, IV, 226. The Buddhist texts mention *saṅgha*, *gaṇa*, *pūga* and *śreṇi* as organisations without the sanction of one of which no woman could take orders as a Buddhist nun.

[7] Manu, IV, 209 ; Nārada, I, 7.

in most passages it means only some corporation or a confederation of corporations. In the *Rāmāyaṇa* we are told of *gaṇas* into which the *naigamas* were divided.[1] In later ages the *naigama-sabhā* denoted a larger assembly than the *śreṇi*.[2] The *naigama-sabhā* was therefore something like a merchant guild of the town. But it should not be identified with a political or municipal corporation (*paura*). In one Jātaka text[3] the election of a king is described as sanctioned by the will of the whole *nagara*, as contrasted with the *negama*. This latter assembly of the *nagara* was the *paura*. *Naigama* and *paura* are also differentiated in the *Rāmāyaṇa*.[4] The *paura* had written resolutions recorded. These are called *chiraka* by Vasishṭha. Gautama makes it clear[5] that there was special social dignity attaching to membership of the city corporation. He says a Brāhmán must rise from his seat and do honour to a Śūdra who has been a member of a *paura*. Members of the *paura* were to be treated as equals in spite of differences in age up to 10 years. Their influence on the government of the kingdom as a whole is clear from such regulations as the following: The king shall conduct the affairs of state in consultation not only with the *mantrins* but also with the *nagaras*.[6]

VI

REPUBLICAN ORGANISATIONS

We have information as regards the working of group organisations in various localities. Some of

[1] *Rām.*: Ayod. Kāṇḍ., 4, 14 and 40. [2] *Ep. Ind.*, Vol. VIII, p. 32.

[3] *Cchandaka* of Sakalauagara, in Vol. I, p. 399.

[4] Yud. Kāṇḍ., 127. 16. [5] Gautama, VI, 9 to 11.

[6] *Mantribhissaha nāgaraiścha kāryāṇi kuryāt* in Vasishṭha, XVI, 19.

these were based on birth (*kula*), and were apparently bound by the tie of kinship. Others consisted of several families who were of the same caste or profession (*jāti*). A mere professional guild, consisting of various classes of members, was known as a *pūga*. The presidents of these were known as *Grāmaṇī* or *Grāmaṇika*, e.g., *grāma-grāmaṇika* and *pūga-grāmaṇika*. In the *gaṇa* there was an equal status for every *kula* and *jāti*.[1] Larger than these organisations, and probably composed of several *gaṇas*, was the *saṅgha*. A good instance of the latter is the Andhaka-Vrishṇi-Kukura-Bhoja-saṅgha which consisted of eighteen *kulas*.[2] An executive council of elders is mentioned in connection with this federation. It is clear that there were integrations of tribal republics, and federations of these integrations. We know from the Buddhist records that the great federations of the Licchavis and the Mallas were formed in this period. These were different from temporary confederacies. The *Jaina-sūtras* mention that Mahāvīra was met by the eighteen confederate kings of Kāśi and Kosala, the nine Mallakis and nine Licchavis, who instituted an illumination in his honour.[3] The only dangers of these federations arose from want of secrecy in deliberation, the discussions sometimes getting heated and resulting in rupture, jealousy and rancour among the factions.[4]

Buddhist and Jaina records give details of these self-governing republics. The Mallas had their own

[1] *Mbh.*: Śānti, 107; cf. *Ang. Nik.*, III, 76: *kuleshu pratyekā-adhipatyam*.

[2] *Mbh.*: Sabhā, 14.

[3] *S.B.E.*, XXII, 286.

[4] *Mbh.*: Śānti, 107, 8: *Bhedamulo vināśo hi gaṇānām upalakshaye | mantrasamvaraṇam duhkham bahūnām iti me matih.* ||

officers.[1] The *Rājā* of the Śākyas of Kapilavāstu was elected by the people, presided over their meetings, and conducted the business of the State. Every village had its people meeting in the village grove, and each township appointed its own rulers. There was no supreme government at Kapilavāstu; but there was a congregation of priests and ten families of laymen.[2] There was considerable attention to 'town-planning' in the case of these cities and villages. In Kundagrāma the northern and southern quarters were distinguished,[3] and in Vaṇiyagrāma the families of high, low and middle classes had different quarters.[4]

Pāṇini mentions several republics.[5] It is important to note that they contained members of various castes: a member of the Mālava *gaṇa* was styled a Mālava or Mālavya, according to his caste. Some of these *saṅghas* were military corporations and others economic, but all alike were politically sovereign. He refers to the seal and crest of a *gaṇa* (*aṅka* and *lakshaṇa*). There was a separation of powers, the judiciary from the military and civil, among the Licchavis for instance. The prosperity and permanence of these republican bodies depended on qualities of leadership, combining intelligence and secretiveness, in their officers, and faithfulness and loyalty in the men.[6] He mentions as military republics (*āyudhajīvins*) the Vṛka, Dāmani,

[1] *Ang. Nik.*, 42, 4. [2] Beal., II, 14.

[3] Uttara Khattiya and dāhiṇa māhāṇa.

[4] *Uvāsagadasao*, pp. 5 and 6.

[5] *Avadāna Śataka*, Vol. II, p. 103: *Kechit deśāh gaṇādhīnāh kechit rājādhīnāh*; Pāṇini, III, 3, 86; V, 3, 114.

[6] *Mbh.*: Śānti. 107.

Trigartashashṭha,[1] Yaudheyas, Pārśvas, Asuras and Rākshasas. He also names six other communities: Madrās, Vrijji, Rājan, Andhaka-Vṛshṇi, Mahārāja, and Bharga. In Buddhist literature we find mention of the Śākyas, Koḷiyas (of Rāmagrāma), Licchavis, Videhas, Mallas, Moriyas (of Pippalavana), Būḷis (of Allakappa) and Bhargas (near the Vatsas).

VII

GOVERNMENT OF THE LICCHAVIS OF VEŚĀLI

Foremost of these republics was that of the Licchavis of Veśāli, who dominated the Vajra country. The *Rāmāyaṇa* and *Vishṇu Purāṇa* have traditions that here was an ancient state founded by Viśāla, a son of Ikshvāku, and that the Licchavi kings were renowned for their valour, virtue and longevity.[2] Buddhist tradition has it that the city of Veśāli was four or five *li* in circuit, the older city sixty or seventy *li*, and the country 5,000 *li*. These are called respectively *ābhyantara* and *bāhira Vaiśālakāh*.[3] These three concentric portions were peopled respectively by seven, fourteen and twenty-one thousand families. There were three concentric walls in the Buddha's day, and each wall was a *gāvuta* distant from the other.[4] There were 7,707 Rājas or aristocrats in the State, and each had 'a storeyed building, pinnacle, pleasure-grounds and lotus-ponds.'[5] The prosperity

[1] Named in tradition recorded in *Kāśikā* as Kauṇḍopartha, Daṇḍaki, Kaushṭaki, Jalamaṇi, Brahmagupta and Gaṇaki.

[2] *Rām.*: Bāla Kāṇḍ., 47.

[3] *Jaina-sūtras* in *S.B.E.*, Vol. 45, p. 321.

[4] Watters: *Yuan Chwang*, II, 63; *Jāt.*, I, 504; Rockhill: *Life of the Buddha*, p. 62.

[5] *Vinaya*, II, 171; *Jāt.*, III, 1.

of the city is also mentioned in the *Mahāvattu*, which describes the people as diligent and valorous. They knew no luxury or ease, but were full of warlike, boisterous life.[1] Theft was unknown among them, or even falsehood or faithlessness. There were public feasts and festivals on the 8th, 14th, and 15th day of each fortnight when animals were slaughtered for food. The greatest festival was the *sabbarāttivaro* or *sabbarātticharo*[2] which I would identify with *Śivarātri* (*śarvarātri*) which is on the fourteenth day of the fortnight; and I am supported in this identification by the legend of 'Āmrātakeśvara' on the figure of a linga with *triśūla* on both sides, excavated from Basarh. There was no prejudice against foreigners in this city: A minister of king Virūdhaka fled to Veśāli from the jealousy of other ministers, and was shortly afterwards elected a *Nāyaka* or city officer there.

The Licchavis had a *Rājā*, an *Uparāja*, a Commander, and a Treasurer chosen from among the 7,707 Rājas, who probably represented the Foundation families. The total population was 168,000. We are told that each of these Rājas had a viceroy, a general, and a treasurer. But even the ordinary citizens of Veśāli considered themselves independent, and none of them suffered from an 'inferiority complex.'[3] Gautama Buddha was struck with the greatness of the Licchavis and attributed it to their union, respect for ancient traditions and institutions, reverence for elders

[1] *Apramattāh* and *ātapinah* ; *Sutta Nipāta*, II, 268 ; *Aṅg. Nik.* III. 76.

[2] *Sam. Nik.* I, 201. *Arch. Sur. Rep.*, 1903-4.

[3] *Lalita Vistara*, Ch. III : *Ekaika eva manyate aham rājā aham rājā iti.*

and for religion, protection of holy men, and the holding of full and frequent assemblies.[1]

They met in their mote-hall (*santāgāra*) frequently where they listened to their elders and discussed all matters. They were seated in order of precedence by a special officer known as *Āsanaprajñāpaka.* The proposer was *Jñaptṛ*, and the proposal was put thrice. Silence was taken to imply consent.[2] Voting tickets were collected by the special officer appointed by the assembly.[3] A sick man, though absent, had his vote.[4] There was a quorum.[5] Record-keepers registered the decisions of the assembly.

The liberty of the citizen was jealously guarded. There was a register of crimes and punishments. A suspect or accused was subjected to a preliminary enquiry at the court of the *Viniśchaya mahāmātras*, and, if found guilty, passed on to the court of the *Vyavahārikas*, who were learned in law and custom. The appellate court was presided over by the *Sūtradharas.* The final appeal lay to the *Ashṭakulaka*, apparently a court of eight, composed of representatives of the eight *kulas.* Their decision had to be confirmed by the *Senāpati* and the *Uparāja.* The *Atthakathā*[6] says that at every step the criminal could be released if found innocent, and that he was passed on to the next stage only if considered guilty. No sentences were passed unless all these officers had found the accused guilty. In the latter event the matter went up to the *Rājā* who consulted the *Puveṇi*

[1] *Dīg. Nik.* (*S.B.E.*, Vol. XI, pp. 3-6).
[2] *Suttas* (*S.B.E.*, IX, p. 3) ; *Vinaya* (*S.B.E.*, XX, 408 ; I, 170).
[3] *Vinaya*, III, 25 : *Śalākāgrāhāpaka*.
[4] *S.B.E.*, XIII, 277.
[5] *Ibid.*, p. 307.
[6] *J.A.S.B.*, for 1838, p. 993.

pustaka (Book of Precedents and Usages): 'There it is written, to him who commits such a crime such a punishment is awarded.'

The *saṅgha* or *gaṇa* of the Licchavis was thus a self-governing body having a corporate existence, and sovereign power. It had its own treasury, laws and discipline, and conduct of foreign policy and wars. It was in fact a republican government as described in the *Avadāna* and the *Mahābhārata*.[1] No transaction was valid unless there was a quorum, to see to which was the duty of the *Gaṇa-pūraka*; and the decision of the majority was binding.

VIII

GOVERNMENT OF THE BUDDHIST CHURCH

The organisation of the Buddhist Church followed that of the lay administration of Veśāli, as is clear from the accounts of the Veśāli Council. Ajita was the *Āsanaprajñāpaka*. The motion was *jñapti* and the resolution, if passed, *pratijñā*. Only opposers of a motion spoke. The quorum was 20, and was made up by the *Gaṇa-pūraka*.[2] 'At a *ñatti-dutiya* the votes (*chhanda*) of absentees must be collected and conveyed.' Otherwise the resolution was invalid. But it was optional to the members present to use the opinions so conveyed.[3] Decision was by the majority (*bhūyasī-yakam*). The voting-tickets (of wood) were taken by the *Śalākāgrāhaka* who was to be free from partiality, malice, folly or fear, and endowed with discrimination.

[1] *Jāt.*, I, 422: *gaṇabandhana*; *Mbh*, Śānti, 107.

[2] *Chullavagga*, XII, 2, 7; *Vinaya* (*S.B.E.*, XX, 408); *Mahāvagga*, IX, 4, 1; *S.B.E.*, XIII, p. 307.

[3] *S.B.E.*, XVII, p. 266.

The tickets were taken in secret ballot (*gulhakam*) when colours of two kinds were used for them, or in 'whisper' (*karṇajalpakam*) or openly (*vivṛtam*). If the speeches at the *saṅgha* became irrelevant or noisy, the matter was referred to a committee for decision if possible, and, when the committee could not agree, to the *saṅgha* again. Settlement by committee was known as *sammukha-vinaya*.[1] Once settled, the question was not to be re-opened. There were four record-keepers.

Dissent in the *saṅgha* had already appeared in regard to the expulsion of a Bhikku in the Buddha's time, and he felt helpless to heal the strife. It was the unlawful practices of the Vrijjian monks that led to the Council of Veśāli. Yaśas, who was excommunicated, appealed to the laymen of Veśāli, and when this appeal proved fruitless, he summoned monks from Avanti and Kauśāmbi to the council. The committee of eight appointed by the council agreed with him, and he won the case.[2]

One great defect in the organisation of the Buddhist Church was the lack of a co-ordinating agency. The personality of the Buddha had served the purpose during his life-time. Even after his death the *saṅgha* had no power to make new laws, except by a legal fiction, in the way of explaining or expounding his laws: 'The truths and the rules of the order which I have set forth and laid down for you all, let them, after I am gone, be the Teacher unto you.'[3] The local community of Bhikkus was a democracy; but a resolution, if on a grave matter, could be referred to another

[1] *Chuḷḷavagga*, XII, 2, 7 and 8; 4, 14 and 21.
[2] *Mahāvagga* X, I, 5; *Chuḷḷavagga*, XII, 2, 7. [3] *S.B.E.*, XI, p. 112.

local community in which there was a large number of Bhikkus.[1] The matter was referred to a committee only in case the discussion in the general body took an irrelevant turn. If the committee differed, the *saṅgha* reconsidered the matter and decided by a majority. But the taking of votes in the general body was irregular if the vote-taker knew that the opinion of the majority would be against the law. In this case 'he was to reject the vote as wrongly taken.'[2]

The voting was considered invalid also when the matter in dispute was not clearly stated, or was trivial, or had not been previously subjected to arbitration. It was ignored when the voters were insincere or under extraneous influences, or when there was fear of a schism in the *saṅgha*. In these safeguards we discern an anxiety for the maintenance of the *status quo*. The enormous power of the polling officer reminds us of that of the Spartan Ephors whenever the people had made a 'crooked decree.' But the provision for a previous arbitration, which was compulsory, shows the Indian genius for compromise and conciliation before matters were pushed to a breaking-point in accordance with the decision of the majority. In important matters absolute unanimity was declared essential. At the *uposatha* all were to be present,[3] and the ceremony was not to be held unless the absentees, if any, had sent in their permission. Even if a member were in custody, they were to get him temporarily released. In the case of invalids, they had to be brought to the house of meeting, or the *saṅgha* had to move to their houses and hold the *uposatha* there.

[1] *Chullavagga*, IV, 14, 17f.
[2] *Ibid*: IV, 14, 26.
[3] *Mahāvagga*, II, 23.

IX

LOCAL GOVERNMENT

The *Jātakas* give us a picture of village life in the pre-Mauryan age. The *Gāmabhojaka* or headman of the village was paid by the king,[1] but was probably a chief elected by the villagers. When he fell out with the villagers, the matter was taken up by the king, and we have an instance where he was dismissed.[2] Ordinary quarrels among the villagers went to him for settlement, and he could fine the guilty. He was to see that the villagers led a regular life and were free from trouble. He guarded the village against robbers. He prohibited indiscriminate slaughter of animals and the sale of liquor. He supplied food and seeds in famine times as against the security of the next crops. But he was not in a position to lord it over the villagers. In one case we are told of a villager who beat a *Gāmabhojaka* who had been guilty of misconduct and drove him out of the village.[3]

The name *Gāmabhojaka* seems to show that he was in enjoyment of certain rights in the village, in contrast for instance, with *Rājabhogga* and *Nagaraguttika*, who certainly were royal officers. But we find him described as an *Amaccha*, and in one place it is stated clearly that he was in receipt of some pay from the king. He can therefore be compared with the *Rājabhogas* who are described as paid officers (*bhaṭṭa vetanaharo*) and with *Nagaraguttikas* or keepers of the peace in towns. In another place we read that Bimbisāra, king of Magadha, had 80,000 *Gāmikas*

[1] *Jāt.*, I, 354: *Rājabalim labhitvā*; *Vinaya*, III, 222.

[2] *Ibid.*, I, 198.

[3] *Ibid*, I, 483; IV, 115; II, 135.

under him, whom he assembled and instructed in politics and ethics.[1] The *Gāmikas* here must be the same as the *Gāmabhojakas* of other passages. We are told by Manu[2] that there were officers who were lords of villages ranging from 1 to 1000. It may therefore be presumed that the *Gāmabhojaka* was a prominent magistrate of the village, who also received some remuneration from the state.

When we come to city-life in the period, what strikes us most is the attention to town-planning. The city of Ayodhya[3] was 12 *yojanas* by three in extent, and had its roads and highways clearly laid out, and its bazaars and markets well arranged. The fortress was well provided with means of defence. The buildings were tall and majestic. It was the resort of merchants from various foreign countries, of foreign princes and artisans, dramatists and dancers. The city was in the form of an octagon, built on a level plain, and provided with rest-houses, baths and feeding houses. The cities of the non-Aryans, like Rāvaṇa's Laṅkā, were no less remarkable for splendour, and even surpassed the Aryan in strength and impregnability. The chief duty of the City Prefect was to see that watch was kept of aliens entering the city, that its gates were guarded and closed at night, and incendiarism guarded against. The last was a necessary duty in an age when people apparently lived in wooden houses. A fire incident or an accident might assume the dimensions of a general conflagration as at Laṅkā, or at Lāvāṇakam in the Vatsa country in the Buddha's day.

[1] *Mahāvagga*, V, 1: *dittha dhammike atthe anusasitvā.*

[2] Manu, VII, 115. [3] *Rām.*: Bāla Kāṇḍ., 5; Sund. Kāṇḍ.

It is clear that there was a tendency for villages to develop into townships, and new towns and cities frequently sprang up. The city of Śrāvasti grew up and replaced Ayodhya in importance. Several causes contributed to the formation of cities. Taxila and Benares attracted men, as centres of learning; and Ujjain as a centre of the fine arts. Religion was responsible for the growth of Gaya, where the Vishṇupāda temple had a sanctity already before the time of Yāska. But the most important cities were those created by the administration. The best illustration is Pāṭalīputra.

The ancient capital of Magadha was the mountain fastness of Girivraja. The stately capital Rājagṛha was built by Bimbisāra. Wars of imperial expansion on the north-west brought the frontier village of Pāṭalī into prominence. It was the centre of operations against the Licchavi country in the reign of Ajātaśatru, whose ministers Sunīta and Vamśakara laid the foundation of a fortress or citadel on the spot. The place attracted a population on account of political and economic relations with Veśāli, and became the nucleus of a city. The Magadha emperor Udaya made it his capital, and it became the most famous city in all India.[1]

X

TAXATION

Among the canons of taxation evolved in this period we can trace those of Equity and Economy. One sound principle was that a tax was not to fall on

[1] S. V. Venkateswara; *Ancient History of Magadha* (*Ind. Ant.* for 1915 and 1916).

capital (*mūlam*) or on the means of production.[1] It was to be progressive in the case of new industries so that people might be encouraged to engage in them.[2] In any case, a tax was to fall only on the surplus left over after the reasonable and legitimate wants of the producers were met. The similes in regard to the milking of the cow after the calf had had its fill (*vatsaupamyena*), or the gathering of the honey by the bees without detriment to the flowers (*madhudoham*), are interesting in this connection.[3] Taxes on industrial classes and commodities were to be carefully considered with reference to the amounts and sources of profits, the difficulties involved, and the expenses incidental to production.[4]

There was some regard for the convenience of the tax-payer, and we find an insistence on the fixity or the consistency of assessment, more or less on the lines of the modern canons of Convenience and Certainty. The taxes were to be collected in accordance with the precedents of previous years, the amounts not exceeding what was ordered in consonance with the general principles, and to be collected at the times convenient to the tax-payer. There was to be no harshness in the collection of revenue.[5]

The sources of revenue were land-tax, customs, excise, and fines from the Law Courts.[6] The first varied at different times and places, from a sixth to a

[1] *Mbh.:* Śānti, 87, 18. [2] *Ibid*, 88, 7: *alpam* and *vardhamānam*.

[3] *Ibid*, 87, 19; 88, 4.

[4] *Ibid*, 37: *utpattim dānavṛttim cha śilpam samprekshya śāsakṛt*. Cf. Manu, VII, 127: *yogakshemam cha samprekshya vaṇijām kārayet karān* and VII, 129: *yathā phalena yujyeta*.

[5] *Mbh.:* Śānti, 38: *ānupūrvyeṇa sāntvena yathākālam yathāvidhi*.

[6] *Ibid*, 71: *balishashṭhena śulkena daṇḍenādhāparādhinām*.

tenth, and it amounted to even a fourth in cases where the taxes could not be readily assessed and collected, as in the woods.[1] In levying the taxes on commodities, importance was attached to the effects of the consumption on the people at large. They were to be so graded that commodities of noxious consumption were surcharged, while the necessaries of life and auxiliaries of production, which were imported from abroad and were of lasting benefit to the country, were not only untaxed but encouraged by bounties.

The general principle was that the State should not fleece or oppress the people by taxation.[2] There are traces of the doctrine that the king was to live on his own (*svayam*) and should supplement his resources only where the incomes were easily and naturally forthcoming.[3] To this end he was to attract men from various quarters to bring their merchandise to the country. The opening up of trade[4] and the general material prosperity thus caused would replenish his treasury in the natural course. There was to be no interference with the normal course of industry and trade. He had a customary right to a land-tax of one-sixth the yield, and to two per cent of property, a seventh of the sales, and a sixteenth of the live stock. Labourers were not to be encouraged to form combinations which interfered with the smooth working of industry, and the State was to break up such unions.[5]

[1] *Rām.*: Ayod. Kāṇḍ., 1, 19; 6, 11. [2] *Ibid*, Bāla Kāṇḍ., 11.
[3] *Mbh.*: Śānti, 41, 42: *sañjātam upajīvan*.
[4] *Rām.*: Bāla Kāṇḍ., 14.
[5] *Mbh.*: Śānti, 57, 10, *op. cit.*

XI

JUSTICE

The importance of the judiciary and the need for its separation were emphasised. The ethical standard of the State could not be maintained unless the good were protected and the wicked punished.[1] Fear of punishment was to operate so as to prevent injury even to men off their guard or asleep. Punishment was for those who were unable to restrain themselves.[2] The judge who meted out condign punishment was unaffected by the consequences of his act and incurred no sin.[3] At the same time it was not to be callously exercised: the judge or the king who ordered a death sentence was to fast in penance for a night, and the *Purohita* who advised it for three nights. The Court of Law was almighty and could call on any person to attend it, and failure to answer summons was a high crime visited with the first degree of amercement.[4] The sanction of religion was used to reinforce the authority of the temporal power. It was an old adage reproduced both in the *Manusmṛti* and in the *Rāmāyaṇa* that one who underwent trial and punishment was *ipso facto* freed from the sin of the act, and was purged and purified by the process. If the State deliberately let a proved criminal escape, the sin of the act fell on the judge or the State officer ordering the release. Whether punished or let off, therefore, submission to legal procedure and

[1] *Mbh.*: Śānti, 14, 57.
[2] *Ibid*, 14, 36; Gautama, XI, 28.
[3] *Mbh.*: Śānti, 31, 15.
[4] *Ibid*, 14, 110.

the resulting penalties absolved the criminal once for all.[1]

The king himself was now considered as subject to law and his punishment was a thousand times that of an ordinary citizen.[2] If a learned man offended, punishment was increased, e.g., property stolen by a Śūdra thief had to be restored eight-fold, and there was double this fine for the other classes. In the story of Anāthapiṇḍika's purchase of the king's gardens at Śrāvasti, the judge held that the king was bound to keep the contract.[3]

The sources of Law were the code of sacred laws (*dharmaśāstras*), Case Law (*vyavahāra*), custom and tradition (*charitra*) and the king's orders (*śāsana*). There were, besides, the regulations of the caste-guilds, and the traditional observances of families, which were binding on the respective groups.[4] 'Justice is to be administered according to Vedas, Aṅgas, Dharmaśāstras and Purāṇa. The laws of countries, castes and families also have binding authority, if not opposed to these.' 'Cultivators, traders, herdsmen, money-lenders and artisans can lay down rules for their respective classes.'[5]

The Law Court was *sabhā* or *parishad*.[6] It had an odd number of judges who were to be bold men of years and experience. In civil cases ten Brāhmans

[1] *Rām.*: Bāla Kāṇḍ., I, 18, 32f : *Rājabhirdhṛtadaṇḍāstu kṛtvā pāpāni mānavāh| nirmalāssvargamāyānti santah sukṛtino yathā|| śāsanādvā vimokshādvā stenah stenādvimuchyate|rājā tvaśāsan pāpasya tadavāpnoti kilbisham||*.

[2] Manu, VIII, 336. [3] Gautama, XII, 17 ; *Chullavagga*, VI, 4, 9. The position *per contra* has been considered in *Ante* vol. I, p. 40.

[4] *Mbh.* : Śānti, 35, 19.

[5] Gautama, XI, 19-21. Cp. Hammurabi's Code in Sumer, which was an integration of local codes.

[6] Nārada, III, 18 : *vṛddhāh* and *dharmam vadantah*.

formed a court, but there was to be at least one Brāhman well-versed in sacred lore and belonging to a family which led the Vedic life. For such men were 'incapable of favouring or injuring created beings.'[1] They were 'embodiments of political wisdom and moral rectitude.' The *Jātakas* refer to rules of procedure inscribed on golden tablets, and to recorded decisions.[2] A decrease in litigation was the test of the proper administration of justice.[3]

XII

INTER-STATE RELATIONS

The relations in peace and war assumed a more civilized and humane character. It was part of the ethics of warfare in the *Rāmāyaṇa* that non-combatants were not to be hit in battle, or those unarmed or otherwise engaged; those who had accepted defeat and were fleeing from the field, or those who ran away under the guise of non-combatants.[4]

The *Mahābhārata* gives a longer category of those who were thus immune: soldiers who were sleeping, thirsty or insane; who had their armour off; who were starting on a journey or moving on elsewhere. Nor were they to be molested when eating or drinking; when they had been crushed or wounded, disabled or maimed; when they were in fright or just getting into array, or just cast off their ranks in rout. Servants of

[1] Gautama, 28, 51.

[2] *Jāt.*, V, 125; II, 2.

[3] Āpastamba, II, 11.

[4] *Ye cha bāṇairviyudhyanti viviktam aparāparam | śabdavedyam cha vitatam laghuhastāh viśāradāh||*. The commentator explains the epithets as meaning respectively *asahāyam*, *vamśasya ekatantum*, *pracchannam* and *palāyitam*. Those who were the sole stay of their families were not to be killed.

fighters, camp-followers, menials and other non-combatants always enjoyed immunity. Gautama adds ambassadors or envoys to the list.[1] Beating the crushed enemy was condemned on all hands: 'Aryas forbid the slaying of one who has laid down his arms, one who cries for quarter, and one who prays abjectly for terms of truce,' says Āpastamba.[2]

War was to be waged only as the last resort when peaceful methods had been exhausted. For it was full of horrors and its results were uncertain. Once war was declared, it was the duty of the Kshatriya to fight to the end, bitter though it be. But he was to do so in an organised way and according to standards of ethics and codes of honour. There were various kinds of array mentioned in the *Rāmāyaṇa* and the *Jātakas*. The Aryas would not employ the stratagems which found favour with their enemies.[3] They would not meet the enemy when he was unprepared ; they would rouse him by giving him formal notice or indications like cattle-lifting. All was not fair in war, though it involved incidents like cutting off the enemy's supplies, and demolishing forts and embankments.[4] Barbed or poisoned weapons were not to be used even in the thick of the fight or attempts made at a wholesale or indiscriminate slaughter.[5] Women taken in war were to be treated gallantly and sent home under safe escort, if they would not stay with the conqueror.[6] In the conquered country local customs were to be

[1] *Mbh.*: Śānti, 100, 27ff. Cf. Manu, VII, 91 and 93 ; Gautama, X, 18.

[2] II, 5, 10.

[3] *Rām.* : Yud. Kāṇḍ., 100 ; Manu, VII, 104.

[4] Manu, VII, 196 ; *Mbh.* : Śānti, 68 ; 103, 13.

[5] Manu, VII ; 90 ; *Mbh.* : Śānti, 103, 13 ; *Rām* : Ayod. Kāṇḍ., 65, 6.

[6] *Mbh.* : Śānti, 96, 5.

retained.[1] Pensions were to be given to widows of fallen soldiers.[2]

We discern some principles of civilized diplomacy. The person of the *Dūta*, or envoy, was already sacrosanct, even when he was considered as exceeding his instructions and not acting merely as the mouth-piece of his master. But an erring envoy could be subjected to other penalties, to anything short of deprivation of life.[3] He could be disfigured, mutilated, shorn of his hair, etc. The slayer of an envoy and his ministers were destined for the depths of hell.[4] It was recognised, however, that the envoy who proved false to his master and did not communicate his instructions, deserved death.[5]

The presence of numerous States in India—many of them with high ideals of government—led to the evolution of a system of inter-state diplomacy and the development of relations along the lines of matrimonial and political alliances.

The times of the Buddha witnessed some of these. Bimbisāra of Magadha was helped in his conquest of the Aṅga country by a political alliance with the Nāga king of Kampilya. The same king of Magadha had matrimonial alliances with Kosala and Veśāli. Ajātaśatru, after his wars with Kosala, concluded a treaty which was sealed by his marriage with a Kosala

[1] *Rām.*: Ayod. Kāṇḍ., 9, 30: *deśadharmastu pūjyatām.*

[2] *Mbh.*: Sabhā, 5, 57.

[3] *Rām.*: Sund. Kāṇḍ., 52, 2; Yud. Kāṇḍ., 25,21; *Rām.*: Sund. Kāṇḍ., 52, 15: *Vairupyam aṅgeshu kaśābhighāto mauṇḍyam tathā lakshaṇasannipātah| etān hi dūte pravadanti daṇḍān vadhastu dūtasya na nah śrutopi||*

[4] *Mbh.*: Śānti, 85, 26: *Dūtasya hantā nirayam āviśet sachivaissaha|*

[5] *Rām.*: Yud. Kāṇḍa, 20, 18: *yastu hitvā matam bhartuh svamatam samprabhāshate| anuktavādī dūtah san sa dūto vadhamarhati||*

princess. His contemporary, Udayana of Kauśâmbi, was an enemy of the Kosala king who incited the revolt of the Vatsas under Aruṇi, according to tradition embodied in Harsha's *Ratnāvaḷī*. The same king is represented as marrying a Ceylonese princess, which probably signalised the development of foreign commerce by sea. Udayana's marriage with an Aṅga princess and his war with Kalinga are mentioned in the *Priyadarśikā*, and his alliance with Magadha following his marriage with princess Padmâvatī, is the main plot of the *Svapnavāsavadatta*. It enabled him to suppress the revolt of the Vatsas and to reign in peace.

By far the most interesting point in these transactions is the diplomacy of Yaugandharāyaṇa, the minister of Udayana. He was able to outwit Sālankâyana, the minister of Avanti, according to the tradition embodied in Bhâsa's *Pratijñā Yaugandharāyaṇa*. His master had been imprisoned at Ujjain. But the minister was able to relieve him by adopting guises, using a cypher-writing and a code language. He created trouble in Avanti, to cover the retreat of his master and his bride Vāsavadattā. When he found the political difficulties of Kauśâmbi insurmountable without extraneous aid, he prevailed upon the queen to sanction the diplomatic marriage of his sovereign with the Magadha princess.[1]

[1] S. V. Venkateswara: *Ancient History of Magadha* (*Ind. Ant.* for 1915 and 1916).

CHAPTER III

INSTITUTIONS OF THE MAURYA AGE

I

THE MONARCHY

THE Court was maintained in splendour and ostentation. The king was attended by a female guard of armed slaves. He got up about 3 a.m. and went to bed about 9 p.m. He interviewed his priests and kitchen-officials, formed his plans and heard reports from officers. He took rest only in the middle of the day for an hour and a half. He received his ambassadors in the forenoon, and reviewed his military forces in the afternoon. There was a particular kind of work posted for each eighth part of the day and of the night. Kauṭilya gives us details of this daily routine.[1]

Megasthenes speaks of the king's physical exercises, of the massaging of his limbs, and of his delight in the chase and in witnessing gladiatorial contests and combats of animals. He appeared in public in the audience hall and in the law courts. When he left the capital, his person was well guarded. There was a constant fear of plots against his person, and he had to change his bed-chamber every night. Kauṭilya has detailed the precautions against attempts on the person of the king. There were secret underground passages in the palace leading from one chamber to

[1] Bk. I, ch. 19.

another. When the king marched out of the city to witness festive shows, fairs, processions or sacrifices, he was protected by a strong force and the police lined the roads and pathways.

It is clear from these accounts[1] that the Maurya emperor was not a 'do-nothing' monarch, but led an active and strenuous life. Confirmation on this point appears in the inscriptions of Aśoka. The Minor Rock Inscription I contains his most important precept: 'Let small and great exert themselves.' In the Kalinga Edict he gives his ideal of good government: 'the king is to his subjects even as a father; he loves them even as he loves himself; the subjects are to the king even as his children.' Agreeably to this ideal, he tells us[2] that he had made arrangements for the prompt despatch of business at all times and in all places. Whether he was eating his food or resting in his private chambers, whether he was at his physical or religious exercises, at his study or at worship, in parks or pleasure-gardens, his men had been instructed to acquaint him with urgent matters so that he could see to the prompt and personal despatch of State business.[3]

[1] *Megasthenes*, Extract 27; Kauṭilya, Bk. I, Ch. 20. [2] *R.E.* VI.

[3] *Savēkāle bhuñjamānasa me orodhanamhi gabhāgāramhi vachamhi va vinītamhi cha uyānesu cha savata paṭivēdakā stitā* (Lines 3 and 4). These expressions have been variously rendered. I would render *gabhāgāramhi* as 'at worship.' *Garbhagṛha* is the *sanctum sanctorum* in temples. *Vachamhi* is 'study,' and *vachabhūmi*, in *R.E.* XII, is a place of study or school. My interpretations are based on expressions in the Jātaka texts (*pāṭham vachesi*, *śilpam vachesi*), and in Vātsyāyana's list of *Kalas* (No. 31. *pustaka vāchanam*). *Vacha* has been interpreted as *Vraja* (cow-pen), but Michelson pointed out the phonetic difficulty long ago (*J.A.O.S*, No. 46, p. 259), and that of explaining the change of *ja* to *cha* in Girnar. In *R.E.* VI, we have *Vachasi* and *Vachamhi*. *Vinītamhi* would mean athletic exercise or physical discipline, and appears as the last but two in the list of the *Kalas*. (*Ibid*, No. 62. *Vainayikīnām vidyānām jñānam*.)

Justin has a statement that the rule of Chandragupta Maurya was oppressive.[1] But there is nothing to corroborate this statement, in the Indian sources. Kauṭilya recommends that the king should check his subordinates by division of functions and frequent change of officers.[2] Even in regard to the republican governments of the time, Kauṭilya's prescription is that they should be overthrown not by force but by diplomacy. Whatever may have been the nature of the administration under Chandragupta, in Aśoka's time there was no despotic government but a regular constitution. His Council gave orders to his *Yuktas* both in general financial policy and in details.[3] His principal provincial officers were empowered to grant remissions of revenue and to award punishment.[4] He had officers in charge of the various departments, frontiers and cities. His ministerial Council had power to revise even the imperial orders, as well as to take action in emergent situations.[5] It is clear that the government was a paternal and benevolent monarchy working on constitutional principles.

[1] Bk. XV, 4.
[2] XXII, 27.
[3] *R.E.* III, line 6.
[4] *P.E.* IV.
[5] *ya cha kimchi mukhato āñapayāmi svayam dāpakam vā srāvāpakam vā ya vā puna mahāmātresu āchāyike aropitam bhavati tāya athāya vivādo nijhatī vā santo parisāyam ānantaram pativedatavāyam me sarvatra savē kale* (*R. E.* VI, lines 5-8). Mr. Jayaswal has it that *mukhato* signifies the *oral* orders of Aśoka. I would translate it as 'first or tentative order—subject to confirmation,' in the light of the contrast of *mukhato* and *antato* in literature, e.g., *T.U.*, III. 10. The contingency arises out of the king's anxiety to save delay in issuing orders. Cf. Kauṭilya, p. 39, Ch. 19, para. 1; *Rājānamuttishṭhamānamanūttishṭhante bhṛtyāh........tasmādutthānamātmanah kurvīta*: 'If a king is energetic, his officers will be equally energetic...........Hence the king shall ever be wakeful.' For the sense of *ātyāyika* (*āchāyike*), see Kauṭilya, Bk. I, Ch. 19.

II

THE MINISTRY

There were discussions among political thinkers and publicists as to the strength, the composition and the working of the ministry, and we find some of them referred to in Kauṭilya's work.

Bharadvāja had held that classmates of the king were to be preferred for the office, Viśālāksha that they should be men whose secrets were known to the king, and Parāśara that nothing succeeded like success, and men of proved fidelity were the best choice. Piśuna preferred men of proficiency in matters of finance, Kauṇapadanta would ensure an all-round ability by selecting men whose ancestors had been ministers, Vātavyādhi considered new men as likely to be safer for the king, and Bāhudantiputra regarded experience of practical politics as the highest criterion. It is clear that each thinker had in mind some department of ministerial work, and that his opinion was in accord with the conditions and needs of his time.

As regards the strength of the ministerial Council (*mantriparishad*), the Mānavas had suggested 12, the school of Bṛhaspati 16, and that of Uśanas 20. There was apparently the need for widening the ranks, as matters of administration grew more and more complicated with the growth of time. Kauṭilya therefore advised his king to have as many men as he thought necessary (*yathāsāmarthyam*), but to have consultation only with three or four members on any subject, so that different points of view might be presented and secrecy maintained at the same time.

In every State there was the need for differentiating the deliberative and consultative ministry (*Mantrins*) from the officers charged with the executive and administrative work (*Amātyas*). Kauṭilya would, therefore, choose the latter class of ministers in accordance with their experience and their capacity for particular kinds of work.[1] But he would have only men of tested fidelity with whom to take counsel. The test was to be carried out with the help of the institutes of espionage (*samsthāh*) and the parties of wandering spies (*samchārāh*).[2]

But in issues of far-reaching importance he was to consult not only these three or four[3] but the whole ministerial Council (*mantriparishad*), and be guided by the majority in regard to both the end to be achieved and the means to be adopted. The council was to deliberate on all measures of administration. The deliberations were to be strictly confidential and the proceedings maintained without possibility of disclosure. The councillors were to be watched carefully till the matter resolved upon had been taken in hand. With these safeguards, the ministers were to be consulted both individually and in council, and they were to give their opinions with reasons. The ministers who were away from the station were also to be consulted by correspondence.[4]

[1] Ch. 8. *Amātya* would thus correspond to the *Rājakarta* or *Ibha* of Vedic times, and *Ibhya* in the Aśoka inscriptions, which has puzzled scholars. The key is in *T.S.*, I, 1, 14: *yāhi rājeva amavān ibhena.*

[2] Chs. 11 and 12.

[3] Which is also in accord with the practice mentioned in the *Rāmāyaṇa*.

[4] *Patrasampr ēshaṇa* (Ch. XV).

The passage already cited from Aśoka's inscriptions shows how the *mantriparishad* (*parishā*) worked under him. It gave instructions to the *Yuktas*, especially on matters of finance, and had control of accounts. It instructed his *dharma* officers.[1] It recorded and modified, where necessary, the orders passed by the emperor, and he was content if it informed him of its decisions and disposals. If traditions be believed, the *parishā* supported the Yuvarāja (Samprati, the grandson of Aśoka) in setting at naught Aśoka's over-liberal grants to Buddhist monasteries, when the emperor was in his dotage. 'Great was the emperor Aśoka Maurya, and very liberal in making gifts, but he had no power to give even a gooseberry fruit (*āmalaka*).'[2] About the middle of the reign there had been a decentralisation of power, and the *Rajjukas* were authorised to grant such reliefs or remissions and such punishments as were consistent with good government and with the needs of the subjects. The *Rajjukas*, who were provincial officers, were also of ministerial rank (*Mahāmātras*).[3]

III

THE DEPARTMENTS

The Departments of the Central Government were 18 in number and their heads were known as *tīrthas*.[4]

[1] *P.E.* VII. [2] *Divyāvadāna*, No. 29. [3] *P.E.* IV.

[4] *Ashṭādaśa tīrthāh* (Bk. i, ch. 12). Dr. Shama Sastri rightly refers to Mallinātha's citation of the list, at the beginning of this chapter; but Dr. Sastri's translation would give us 20. His mistake consists in taking the *paura* and *vyavahārika* as separate officers and the *mantriparishad* as an officer separate from the *adhyaksha*. We know from Aśoka that *pauravyavahārikas* were the city officers (e.g., Minor *R.E.* 1). The 'Assembly of Ministers' obviously cannot be regarded as an officer, but the President (*adhyaksha*) of the Assembly (*mantriparishad*) was one of

Megasthenes speaks of 'the class of councillors' as nominating the heads of departments—the governors, deputy governors, district officers, treasury officers, generals, admirals and directors of agriculture. But the list of the *tīrthas* given by Kauṭilya does not include any military officers other than the *Senāpati*, nor any of the market officers, though Megasthenes clearly states that the chief officers of State were those of the army, the city and the markets. The enumeration of *tīrthas* here mentioned is, however, followed in later books with a few variations. We may presume therefore that the central government had got its final cast by this time, and that all other elements, the military, the sacerdotal and the economic, were subordinated to the civil.

The other heads of departments mentioned by Kauṭilya[1] were military or economic officers. To the former class belong the superintendents of ships, horses, elephants, chariots and infantry; to the latter, those of commerce, weights and measures, tolls, weaving, agriculture, labour, artisans, and merchants.

IV

PROVINCIAL GOVERNMENT

Kauṭilya notes that the empire was divided into four provinces, and that the provincial capital, or

the 18. Thus we get the correct number of *tīthas* as 18, as understood by commentator Mallinātha (on *Raghuvaṁśa*, xvii, 68).

For attempts to get exactly the 18 officers from the list see Nag (*Les Theories Diplomatique*, p. 28), who takes *nāyaka paura* as one officer; and Mr. Jayaswal, who follows Dr. Shama Sastri in taking *paura* and *vyavahāraka* as different officers but leaves out *Āṭavika*, the forest officer. ('*Hindu Polity*' part ii, p. 134).

[1] Bks. ii and iv.

sthānīya, was the seat of a viceroy (*uparāja*), who had a miniature court. The provinces in Aśoka's reign were Taxila, Tosali, Ujjain and Suvarṇagiri. The Kauśāmbi edict is addressed to the *Mahāmātras* there, from which Dr. Hultzsch infers that Kauśāmbi was probably the headquarters of a fifth province. But the term *Mahāmātras* does not necessarily denote that they must be officers in a provincial capital, as even *Nāgarakas* (city officers) are styled *Mahāmātras* in the Kalinga Edict. Aśoka's governor at Ujjain was a royal prince (*kumāra*), and Aśoka was himself viceroy of Ujjain under his father. Taxila (Takshaśila) was the seat of Kuṇāla according to Buddhist traditions. Suvarṇagiri was the headquarters of the southern viceroy, who was a prince (*āryaputra*) and had jurisdiction over the district of Isila (Chitaldrug) and probably also over Maski (in the Nizam's dominions) and Yerragudi (Kurnool district) where Aśoka's inscriptions have recently been found. The eastern capital Tosali was under a *kumāra*, who had jurisdiction likewise over Jaugaḍa in the Samāpa country. It is clear that the provinces of the empire were entrusted to royal princes (*kumāra* or *āryaputra*).

Aśoka's governor of Girnar was Tushāspa, a *Yavana*.[1] He could have been little more than a district officer. Such districts were known as *āhāla* (*āhāra*). Each provincial governor was assisted by *Mahāmātras* or, as they are called in one place, *Prādeśikas*, corresponding apparently to the district officers mentioned by Megasthenes. Thus we have in the inscriptions specific mention of the *Mahāmātras*

[1] *Ep. Ind.*, vol. viii, p. 47.

in charge of Isila, Kauśāmbi, Tosaḷi and Samāpa. In two places [1] there are references to a Council (*parishad*) of the *Mahāmātras*, which was responsible only to the king and received its orders direct from him. A similar instance is found in the *Divyāvadāna* tradition which narrates that the *Mahāmātras* of Taxila received orders direct from the emperor in regard to the blinding of Kuṇāla.

The connecting links between the provincial government and the localities consisted of the *Rajjukas*, the *Pradeśikas*, the *Yuktas* and the *Purushas*. The *Rajjukas* or *Rajjugrāhakas* appear already in the Jātaka literature, and were officers of revenue survey and settlement in the early period. But Aśoka invested them with authority to award remissions of revenue as well as to mete out punishments.[2] We are told that they were to instruct the *Yuktas*.[3] Kauṭilya says that the *Chorarajjukas* had to make good the losses from theft.[4] It would appear therefore that the *Rajjukas* in this period had both revenue and judicial functions. This would agree with the account of Megasthenes that they 'superintended the rivers, measured the land, as is done in Egypt, and inspected the sluices by which water is let out from the main canals into their branches, so that every one may have an equitable supply of it. The same persons have charge also of the huntsmen, and are entrusted with the power of rewarding or punishing them according to their deserts. They collect the taxes, and superintend the occupations connected with land, as those of

[1] *R. E.*, iii and vi.

[2] *Abhihāre cha daṇḍe cha.*

[3] *P. E.* vii.

[4] Kauṭ., iv, 13.

woodcutters, carpenters, blacksmiths and miners.' The *Yuktas* were secretaries of some sort who had to codify the royal orders [1] and to go about the country on tour. The *Purushas* were of three ranks, were acquainted with the king's wishes, controlled the *Rajjukas*, and were 'placed in charge of many people.' [2]

There were safeguards against the provincial governor asserting independence or growing too powerful like a Warden of the Marches. In the first place, the emperor's periodical tours (*anusamyāna*) and his personal contact with his subjects ensured their loyalty to him and checkmated the designs of an ambitious viceroy. Secondly, there were the *Yuktas* touring about and the *Prādeśikas* receiving instructions direct from the central government and carrying them out in the districts and rural tracts. Thirdly, the imperial orders were sometimes addressed to the *Mahāmātras* associated with the viceroy direct from the capital and without the knowledge of that officer. Such a situation is implied in the story of the blinding of Viceroy Kuṇāla under a forged order of Aśoka, issued by his Queen Tishyarakshitā. Fourthly, we have seen that the *Rajjukas* were given power by the emperor, obviously without reference to the provincial government, to reward and punish the people in their charge. These safeguards appear to be no matters of accident, especially when we bear in mind that the viceroys were princes and that a whole section of the *Arthaśāstra* is devoted to the circumventing of the designs of princes on the throne.

[1] *R. E.* iii.

[2] *P. E.* iv and vii.

V

LOCAL GOVERNMENT

Megasthenes gives us details about the municipal administration of Patna. The Municipal Council consisted of 30 members in six boards of five each, each board being probably a development of the non-official panchāyat system which obtained in India from time immemorial. In their collective capacity the commissioners controlled all matters affecting the general interest, such as the keeping of public buildings in proper repair, the regulation of prices and the care of markets, harbours and temples. The work of the boards is thus described: 'The members of the first look after everything relating to the industrial arts, carefully protecting the artisans, but enforcing the use of good materials and the performance of a fair day's work for fair wages. Those of the second attend to the entertainment of foreigners. To these they assign lodgings, and they keep watch over their modes of life by means of those persons whom they give them as assistants. They escort them on the way when they leave the country: or in the event of their dying, forward their property to their relatives. They take care of them when they are sick and, if they die, bury them. The third body consists of those who inquire when and how births and deaths occur, with the view of levying a tax, and in order that births and deaths among both high and low may not escape the cognizance of the government. The fourth superintends trade and commerce. Its members have charge of weights and measures, and see that products in their season are sold by public notice.

No one is allowed to deal in more than one kind of commodity unless he pays a double tax. The fifth class supervises manufactured articles, which are sold by public notice. What is new is separated from what s old, and there is a fine for mixing the two together.[1] The sixth and last class consists of those who collect the tenths of the prices of the articles sold. Fraud in the payment of this tax is punished with death.'[2]

There were numerous other towns, the government of which may have been on more or less similar lines. 2,000 towns are mentioned in the dominions of Porus and 30 in the Āndhra country. The former were probably little more than petty townships. Some of these were district centres for two hundred to four hundred villages. Those at the mouths of the rivers were known as *droṇamukha* and those on level plains as *khārvāṭaka*. The great city was *nagara*, and the sea-port *paṭṭaṇa*. The provincial capital was *sthānīya* and the imperial capital *Rājadhānī*. Some towns were fortified with ditches, ramparts and walls, and had guard-houses for troops (*gulma*). The town was rectangular in plan, and had four wards, each under a special official who enforced absence of traffic in the middle part of the night, except on special nights (*chārarātri*). There were precautions against incendiarism, and punishment for it was severe. Music at unseasonable hours was regarded as a nuisance. Kauṭilya describes towns as under individual magistrates. But it is not true to say that town panchāyats

[1] Kauṭilya explains it thus: Tolls on commodities shall generally be determined by taking into consideration whether the commodities are old or fresh, and how they have been manufactured. (Bk. II, ch. 22; Bk. IV, ch. 2).

[2] McCrindle: *Indike*, p. 87.

are not reflected in the Indian records. One is mentioned in the *Mahābhārata*.[1] In the inscriptions of Aśoka the city-officers are always mentioned in the plural, which suggests the panchāyat. Town-government as described by Kauṭilya is, however, that of a Mayor (*Nāgaraka*) under whom were the local petty officers (*sthānikas* and *gopas*) who kept registers of persons and property. All public places were watched by spies.

The close connection of the government with the villages will be clear not only from the circuits of officers like the *Prādeśika* but from the fact that several of them supplied troops and free labour. Villages were classed under these heads: those that were exempt from taxation (*parihāraka*), those that supplied military contingents (*āyudhīya*), those that gave free labour (*vishṭi*), those that supplied produce in lieu of taxes, and those that paid taxes in corn or in coin at their option. The towns and villages alike had common halls used for social gatherings and public dinners, and for entertainments by dancers, singers and actors. There are complaints that these were distractions from the life of the home and the field.

Villages were autonomous. Each was under its headman (*Grāmaṇī*), who consulted the panchāyat on questions of customary rights and duties. Every family was responsible for the payment of revenue on its lands, and there are traces of a collective responsibility of the families for the payment of revenue. A cluster of five or ten villages was served by a market-town (*saṁgrahaṇa*) and was in charge of a *Gopa*. It

[1] Hopkins, p. 85, note.

was the special care of the state to encourage settlements in new or abandoned tracts. Megasthenes says that husbandmen were 'regarded as a class that is sacred and inviolable ; the tillers of the soil, even when battle is raging in their neighbourhood, are undisturbed by any sense of danger, for the combatants on either side in waging the conflict make carnage of each other, but allow those engaged in husbandry to remain quite unmolested. Besides, they neither ravage an enemy's land with fire nor cut down its trees.'

The most interesting feature of rural life in this period is the absence of the modern tendency of the country population to migrate to towns. 'They entirely avoid going into towns.'[1] The importance of a town was estimated by the number of villages with which it was in intimate contact. The number varied from 5 to 400. Sometimes villages suffered from floods or famine, when the people left the locality and migrated elsewhere. But there is no reference to agricultural population, even in those circumstances, flocking to towns.[2]

The industrial regulations in towns are also interesting. There were numerous crafts and guilds (*śreṇi*), of which the aldermen (*Mukhya*) had official recognition. There were inter-caste clubs (*pūga*), and temporary combinations of workmen. Collective obstruction was known and penalised, as also combinations to raise prices. Towns were connected by high roads (*Rājapatha*) or trade-paths (*vaṇikpatha*), which contained signboards at intervals. The trading corporations of towns were advanced enough to own money and carry on banking operations.

[1] McCrindle, p. 42. [2] Kauṭ., Bk. VII, ch. 4 and Bk. VIII, ch. 4.

There was something of the nature of a 'Domesday Survey' conducted by the village officer (*Gopa*). He fixed the boundaries, classified lands, looked after roads and rest-houses and registered gifts, sales, charities and remissions of taxes. He kept an account of the number of inhabitants, their professions, their live stock, and the amounts that were due from each family to the state. 'He shall also keep an account of the number of young and old men that reside in each house, their history (*charitra*), occupation (*ājīva*), income (*āya*) and expenditure (*vyaya*).' Unfortunately, such family-budgets have not survived.

Among the regulations in regard to cities, it is interesting to notice that foreigners and bands of mendicants (*pāshaṇḍa*) were carefully watched. They were concentrated in some special quarter or distributed among the villages. A civic survey was made, a *Gopa* being in charge of every ten, twenty or forty households; and family-budgets had to be maintained. Besides regulations safeguarding against incendiarism, we find sanitary laws forbidding the throwing of dirt in the street or in reservoirs of water, or in temples or public buildings. There were special regulations in regard to the disposal of dead bodies and to other matters of civic and social hygiene.

VI

REPUBLICS

The contemporaries of Alexander the Great have left records of the republican government they witnessed in India. According to Megasthenes this form of government was widely prevalent. He speaks of localities where people had kings, and others 'where they are self-governed.' Among the 'self-governed' were some peoples governed on aristocratic lines, some military republics, and some true democracies.

There were aristocratic republics on the Beas where 'each of the 5,000 councillors furnishes the state with an elephant.' Among these were the Yaudheyas, 'whose name filled the Greeks with terror,' and whose council *(gaṇa)* exercised their authority with justice and moderation. Another aristocratic republic was that of the Patalēnē, whose constitution was Spartan in character, with two hereditary kings chosen from different houses to lead in war, and a Council of Elders whose authority was paramount. The President of the Council was *Moeres*. The people would not submit to Alexander and had emigrated from their territories. We recognise a Spartan character also in the Musicani whose realm was 'the most opulent in India,' and whose citizens took their meals in common as in Sparta. But they would not recognise slavery, and they regarded 'the excessive pursuit of any art,—the art of war, for instance,—as wickedness.' Near them were the other republics of the Sudras, the Xathroi and the Ossadioi.

Among the military republics are mentioned the Kathaioi, who chose the handsomest man as king, whose women practised *sati*, and whose courage and skill in war were evinced in their defeat of Porus and of the king of the Abhisāras. They dwelt east of the Rāvi. In the territory of Saubhūti, too, there was an admirable system of administration, and men were held in esteem for their personal beauty. In both these states weak, ugly or deformed children were exposed, as in Sparta on Mount Taygetus. The Agalassoi had 3,000 horse and 40,000 foot. They resisted the Greeks bravely, and fired their houses when they could no longer defend them, anticipating the Rajput *jauhar*. The Kshudrakas fought the Greeks all alone.[1] They were proud of their liberty, which, for many ages, they had preserved inviolate. Alexander treated them kindly, in contrast to his usual vindictiveness.

The government of the Ambhashṭhas was likewise republican. They had a Council of Elders and their army of 6,000 horse and 500 chariots was led by three generals. One republic of the Brāhmans is mentioned, styled Brachmanoi by the Greeks, and *Brāhmaṇakā nāma janapadāh* by Patañjali.[2] These philosophers, says Plutarch, encouraged free states to revolt against Alexander, who therefore hanged many of them. Other republics of learning can be traced in the Sālaṅkāyanas who, according to Patañjali, were in three sections, the *Vāmarathas*, the *Kaṭhas* and the *Kapisthalas*, all alike noted for culture and learning.

During Alexander's retreat he met the Malloi, who had formed a league and the Siboi, among whom there was no king.[3] According to Curtius, it was the prospect of meeting the army of the Malloi—a hundred thousand strong—that struck terror into the hearts of Alexander's men, and led to their insisting on a precipitate retreat.[4]

[1] *Ekākibhih kshudrakaih jitam* : Patañjali on Pāṇini, V, 3, 32.

[2] II, p. 298.

[3] *Diodorus*, XVII, 96.

[4] Cp. Indians 'stayed Alexander from any further advance' (*Apollonius of Tyana*, Bk. II, 43).

Kauṭilya classifies the republics as *Rājaśabdopajīvin* and *Vārtāśastropajīvin*. Among the former class of political corporations he places the Licchavis, Vrijjikas, Mallakas, Madrakas, Kukurus, Kurus and Pāñchālas. Among the latter, which were industrial corporations, he includes the guilds of the Kambhojas and the Surāshṭras. But, as we have seen, there were republics of other classes also in Western Hindustan.

VII

JUSTICE

Megasthenes notes that the administration of criminal law was efficient but severe, many offences being punished with death or mutilation. But he adds that the people were honest in trade and had few law suits : 'Indians neither put out money at usury nor know how to borrow. It is contrary to established usage for an Indian either to do or suffer a wrong, and therefore they neither make contracts nor require securities.'[1] In one place he refers to written contracts, though he states elsewhere that the art of writing was unknown. 'Among the Indians one who is unable to recover a loan or a deposit has no remedy at law. All that the creditor can do is to blame himself for trusting a rogue.'[2]

Crimes were rare. 'An Indian has never been convicted of lying . . . . Indians are not litigious.'[3] 'They were accustomed to bring charges for merely wounding and murder.' There were few thefts, and little was locked up in the houses. Megasthenes had seen no convictions for theft amounting to 200

[1] Fr. 27 b. [2] Fr. 27 c. [3] Fr. 13.

drachmas.[1] Punishment was based on the principle of 'an eye for an eye, a tooth for a tooth.' Cropping of the hair was regarded as infamous in the last degree, and was the punishment for heinous offences: such was the importance attached to the conventional observances of caste. Mutilation was punished with mutilation, but that of artisans was punished with death.

The *Arthaśāstra* has elaborate descriptions of the law courts, of the sources of law, of legal procedure, and of the gradation of offences. There were two classes of courts besides the Royal Court, which was the highest court of appeal. The *dharmasthānīya* court tried civil cases, including those of robbery and violence, and matrimonial cases. The *kaṇṭhaka-śodhana* court tried criminal cases, including those of misconduct of officials. Each had three judges. The civil law of the time contained elaborate rules about contract, procedure, etc. There were boards of arbitrators (*panchāyats*) appointed by officials. Religious cases were tried by *parishads*. Cases were heard in the morning. 'There were such courts in every city which was the centre of villages (*saṁgrahaṇa*), in every town on sea or river, at the meeting points of districts, as well as in the capital cities.'[2] It is interesting that perjury was punished severely. As test of truth, sacred law (*dharma*) was preferred to evidence of witnesses as well as to custom (*vyavahāra* and *charitra*). But the king's ordinance (*Rāja-śāsana*) based on reason was held authoritative 'for, in respect of that matter, the original text on which the sacred law was based is not available.'

[1] I. 8., Fr. 35.   [2] Kauṭ., Bk. III, ch. 1.

VIII

MILITARY SYSTEM

Megasthenes describes the enormous standing army, efficiently maintained and equipped by the government. Chandragupta's infantry was three times that of the Nandas, and his cavalry one and a half times; and amounted to 600,000 and 30,000 respectively. Though Aśoka gave up wars after his conquest of Kaliṅga, we do not hear of any retrenchment in military strength or expenditure.

The War Office was in six departments. The older four were efficiently organized. Elephants were used in war to pull chariots.[1] They were 'so teachable that they could learn to throw stones at a mark and to use arms.' The war elephant carried three fighting men, besides the driver—two who shot from the sides and one from behind. Two fighting men sat up in the chariot beside the charioteer. The infantry consisted of hereditary troops, and mercenary guild troops, who were a sort of defence-force used for short expeditions and were less quickly assembled than the forest tribes. But Kauṭilya says that it was on the elephants that the destruction of the enemy's army depended.[2] To these four limbs of the army Megasthenes adds two new departments: the Admiralty, and Supply and service. The last included drummers, mechanics, grooms and grass-cutters. Kauṭilya mentions that fixed and mobile engines such as the *śataghnī* were in use, and that the arts of mining, countermining and flooding mines were known and employed. The army must therefore

[1] Fr. 16.   [2] Bk. VII, ch. 11.

have contained a number of mechanics, artisans and camp-followers. An army medical corps was provided, including doctors and nurses. There were sappers and miners and, possibly, a corps of airmen.[1]

As regards the Admiralty department, Kauṭilya says that it let ships out on hire for the transport of passengers and of merchandise. There were mechanical contrivances *(srotoyantra)*. Ships were of various classes—ocean-going ones which touched at harbours *(samyātyah)*, merchantmen *(pravahaṇa)*, yachts used in pearl-fisheries *(grahiṇyah)*, vessels used in navigable rivers *(mahānāvāh)*, tiny craft *(kshudrakāh)* and pirate boats *(himsrikāh)*. It was the business of the Lord Admiral to see that the last were pursued and destroyed and that the use of the others was regulated. He was helped by a Superintendent of Ocean Mines.[2]

IX

PUBLIC WORKS

The Public Works Department is prominently in evidence. We are told that irrigation works were under the Superintendent of the Admiralty. The department measured lands and gave every one his fair share of water. A rain gauge is mentioned.[3] There was a regular system of navigable canals and rivers (*kulyā*). Coastal traffic (*kulapatha*) and ocean routes on the high seas are mentioned. Roads were maintained in order, with pillars set up to serve as sign-posts and with mile-stones. Grand trunk roads

[1] *Khanaka ākāśa divārātri yodhinām purushāṇām* : Bks. IX and X.
[2] Bk. II, ch. 30.
[3] *Varsha māna* (Bk. II, Ch. V).

connected the various parts of the empire with the capital.

Evidence of the attention paid to irrigation, even in the remotest provinces of the empire, comes to us from a strange source. The Junāgaḍh inscription of Rudradāman records how Chandragupta's brother-in-law formed the Sudarśana lake by damming up a small stream and how the supplementary canals and water-courses were constructed by Aśoka.

The duties of the Public Works Department included the planting of trees. These were in avenues for shade and shelter along roads, or in gardens of fruits like the mango (*āmravāṭika*), as such were laid out under the directions of one of Aśoka's queens. Aśoka had also herb-gardens attached to hospitals, where there were medicinal arrangements for animals as well as for men. Such work extended not only to the frontiers of the empire but to the neighbouring kingdoms as well.[1] The department was also in charge of the forests.[2]

X

QUASI-POLITICAL ORGANISATIONS

The state considered it its duty to found and encourage public institutions, which were, in some cases, of political significance. Of this class are the institutions known as *samāja*, *vimāna*, and *darśana* mentioned in the Aśoka inscriptions, and referred to here and there in Sanskrit and Pāḷi texts.

The *samāja* (*samajjo*) is described in the *Sigālovāda Sutta*. It was a social gathering usually attended with dancing, music, recitations, conjuring

[1] *R. E.* II. [2] *Kauṭ*, Bk. II, Ch. II.

tricks and acrobatic shows. From the *Vinaya* texts we learn of a *samajjo* and that, at it, not only amusements but also food was provided; that high officials were invited and had special seats; and that it took place at the top of a hill. Rhys Davids considers[1] this last detail of high places, i.e., sacred places, as pointing to a religious motive actuating the whole proceeding. But we have a reference in the *Rāmāyaṇa* to a *samāja* held in connection with the triumphal entry of the king.[2] It appears therefore that the *samāja* was a convivial gathering, and had the nature of a political triumph or demonstration. It is used in this sense in the Jātaka texts.[3] Meat and wine were in use, and this accounts for Aśoka's forbidding such festivals.[4]

Vimāna is described in the *Vimānavattu*. It was a public gathering at which sacred symbols or divine images installed in aerial chariots were shown to the people, and instructions were given on the relation of a virtuous or vicious life to the life after death. These occasions were of socio-religious significance, and therefore Aśoka encouraged them. Such observances continued later both among the Buddhists and the Jainas.[5]

Kauṭilya mentions *utsavas* and *pravahaṇas* as popular institutions, which it was the business of the state to encourage and to regulate: 'The king shall go to witness festive trades, fairs, processions and sacrificial performances when they are regulated by

[1] *Dialogues of the Buddha*, p. 8.

[2] *Samājaścha mayā dṛshṭo gītavāditranisvanah* in Sund. Kāṇḍ., V, 34.

[3] III, 541.

[4] *R. E.* I.

[5] *Jaina Jātakas* (Lahore, 1925), p. 69; Fa-Hien: Legge's trans., p. 79.

bands of police.'[1] In one place he asks the king to take advantage of the *pravahaṇa* to test the fidelity of his ministers.[2] *Utsavas* were to be encouraged, and were marks of a city under prosperous rule.[3]

The *darśanas* mentioned by Aśoka refer to *divya-rūpas*, i.e., the exhibition of divine beings, like the Buddha as elephant (*hasti*). Sometimes there were fireworks (*agniskandha*). Sometimes there were also theatrical performances, and action-songs illustrated by paintings and pictures. Patañjali refers to these as the work of *Śaubhikas* and *Chitrapaṭikas*. The *Śaubhikas* showed, for instance, the slaying of Kamsa by Krishṇa on the stage: and the *Chitrapaṭikas* represented the same scene to illustrate the recitations of the *Grandhikas*. These exhibitions continued much later, as is shown by the reference to the *Yamapaṭika* or the narrative of the story of Yama, in Bāṇa's *Harshacharita*.[4]

Already before the Maurya age there were different social groups. Kauṭilya mentions *deśasaṅgha*, *jātisaṅgha* and *kulasaṅgha*, which shows that each group had its own corporate life. The discussions among these bodies are reflected in the *Arthaśāstra*, which enjoins spies in pairs to resort to discussions in the *tīrtha*, *sabhā*, *śālā*, *pūga*, and *jana*.[5] *Tīrtha* is a sacred bath, *śālā* an educational or feeding house, and *jana* a nondescript gathering. *Pūga* was an economic organisation consisting of men of several castes. We are reminded of the *Mahābhārata*, where there is

[1] *Yatra samājotsavapravahaṇāni cha daśavargikādhiṣṭhitam gacchet.*

[2] Ch. X, Bk. I.

[3] *Samājotsavaśālini* in *Rām.*: Ayod. Kāṇḍ., XXIII.

[4] Trans., p. 119.

[5] *Samavāyeshu vivādam kuryuh* in Kauṭ., I, 13, 9.

similar mention of bringing about a split in the corporations so as to overcome them.[1] It shows that there were parties, some of whom were loyalists (*upāśritāh*), others conciliated (*samśritāh*); and an outer circle of the hostile, who were to be subdued by sowing the seeds of dissension among them. Kauṭilya would agree with this policy, as the *saṅghas* were invincible by any other means.

XI

POLITICAL THOUGHT

Greek references to a school of political philosophers known as Brachmanoi show that political thought was not only existent but effective in this period. The doctrines of the earlier schools were very much in the air, and Kauṭilya often refers to them, whether in support of his own view or, more often, as holding views which it was easy to controvert. Three of them are associated with Manu, Śukra and Bṛhaspati, whose doctrines were codified in a later period. And there are a few thinkers, Ghoṭamukha, Chārāyaṇa, Kiñjalka and Piśuna's son, to whom there is reference only in a single passage. But on controversial issues of importance Kauṭilya mentions in regular order seven other writers, whose views may now be put together.

Bharadvāja invariably emphasises the importance of ministers, and he probably lived in an age of do-nothing kings and self-sacrificing ministers. He would have the king rely on a single minister, who was to be selected from among his class-mates and

[1] *Paurajānapadān sarvān samśritopāśritāmstathā | bāhyam janam bhedayitvā bhoktavyo maddhyamas sukham ||* in Śānti, 87, 24.

was to be his confidant and *alter ego*. Even the crown prince was a necessary evil, and was to be immured for the king's safety. A weak king was to surrender before his stronger rival. When the kingship came to be in jeopardy, the minister was to take the throne. Love and anger had their uses for the king, among the various political expedients. It is no wonder that the inaugurator of these views should be regarded in later ages as 'a crooked politician.' His doctrines would apply, granted such ministers as Yaugandharāyaṇa of Kauśāmbi, whose safety might be regarded as even more important to the State than that of the king, as they could deliver both the king and the State from any scrapes or compromising political situations.

Viśālāksha was against autocracy, and championed the cause of the people. He regarded the State as quite secure if the king did not act against popular interests or irritate public opinion by indiscreet utterances. Ministers were never to be in a position to act against the king's will, though they were to give him the benefit of their intelligent advice and opinion. He would have the princes carefully protected. Parāśara was an advocate of fortresses. He would lock up disaffected princes in citadels, and use these as places of refuge for loyal subjects in times of distress. Piśuna was an economist, and would replenish the treasury at any cost. He would have the minister of finance as the premier, and would even allow the king to gamble, if it would yield revenue. Kauṇapadanta[1] would base the rule on force, and would sacrifice all other considerations

[1] Means 'son of Kuṇapadanta'—'the tooth of a bad king.'

to the efficiency of a citizen-army which would support the administration of hereditary ministers. Vātavyādhi considered the acquisition of allies as the greatest asset, in war and peace. He would even under-estimate the evil effects of drink on the king on account of its social advantages.

It is clear that the speculations of these schools were responsible for the evolution of the doctrine of the seven elements of sovereignty or seven props of political power—monarch, ministry, forts, finance, population, army and allies. Every school was partial to one of these factors as contributing to the stability of states. Kauṭilya's own contribution to the discussion is significant. His view is that the relative importance of the various factors was to be gauged from the circumstances. Taking the *conjuncture* of the forces, a statesman was to decide how much of a factor he could afford to sacrifice for the time being, having regard to the political aim then in view, and to the mutual influences of the factors themselves. It is obvious that Kauṭilya relaxes the rigidity of the political canons, in accordance with the pliability of circumstances and the mutability of political conditions.

The end of the State is clearly defined. It was merely an agency for the protection of the people in their pursuit of what was the highest and the noblest in life, in such a fashion that it did not interfere with the rights of others in pursuit of similar aims. The king was therefore to enable each order of society *(varṇa)* and men in each station and grade of life *(āśrama)* to fulfil their functions safely and efficiently. He was to act in accordance with the social and ethical canons of *dharma* laid down in the *śāstras.*[1]

The State was never to neglect the native instincts of local groups and communities, so far as they were consistent with this principle.[2] Local laws, customs and traditions *(saṅgraha)* were maintained in the administration of justice, and foreign traders had the right to be adjudged by their own laws.[3] The king was to preserve the customary laws in conquered territories. Local contracts, and agreements entered into by the members of an association among themselves, were legally valid and enforced by the State.

The king was to regard himself only as an agent of the people in accordance with the original theory of social contract.[4] He was to identify his interests with those of the people,[5] irrespective of his individual views and inclinations. Kings who lost their head and fell into a temper were deposed or exiled by the righteous indignation of their subjects.[6] It was impossible to base one's right to rule on might alone, for force was futile in repressing sedition among the leaders of the people.[7] It was not enough to consider what was for the good of the subjects. In politics or the art of government what mattered was how the people took it, how they felt in regard to a measure, however beneficial it might ultimately prove

[1] *Chalitaśāstrastu śāstrādanyadhābhinivishṭabuddhiḥ anyāyēna rājyam ātmānam cha abhihanti*, Kauṭ., Bk. VIII, ch. 2.

[2] *Dāśasya jātyaḥ saṅghasya dharma grāmasya vāpi yaḥ | uchitas tasya tēnaiva dāya dharmam prakalpayēt* || Bk. III, ch. 7 ; Gautama, XI, 21.

[3] Kauṭ., Bk. VII, ch. 15; Bk. XIII, ch. 4.

[4] Bk. I, ch. 13.

[5] *Na ātmapriyam hitam rājñaḥ prajānām cha priyam hitam.*

[6] Bk. VIII, ch. 2—*prakṛti kōpaiḥ.*

[7] *Daṇḍō hi mahājane kshaptum aśakyaḥ* : Bk. IX, ch. 6.

to be. It follows that the king had the duty of educating the people as to what was best for them. It was thought that this result would be best achieved if both the government and the governed followed what was laid down for the good of the State by sages of intellect, and men free from selfish considerations.[1]

The class of men who laid down the law as to the ultimate good might abuse their trust and degenerate into a close and narrow sacerdotalism. But this result was obviated in India. In the first place, the philosophers lived far away in forest retreats, and were detached from the burning politics of the day. Secondly, there was the body of *dharma* doctrine handed down through the ages, and their actions had to be in conformity with this, as its principles were held to be of potency, independent of time and place. Thirdly, this class of people had no organization, no acknowledged leaders, no machinery for concerted action. They were not concentrated in cities, but distributed far and wide in India. Lastly, while the Brāhman had the power of thought only, the Kshatriya had worldly power, and the Vaiśya the sinews of power in industry and commerce.

It is important to emphasise the fact that the State was not regarded as the ultimate good, but only as a means of attaining the highest good. If there was no facility in a kingdom for leading the highest life, the only course open was to leave it and to migrate to more congenial tracts.[2] Even in normal times, the king

[1] *Paurajānapadaviśvāsam dharmāt gatāh :* Śānti, 83 vv. 45, 46.

[2] *Rājānam anugraham yāchāmahe niranugrahāh paratra gacchāmah iti :* Kauṭ., XIII, 1, 171.

was dependent on the ministry in internal as well as external affairs.[1] There was thus no danger of an unbridled despotism.

XII

INTER-STATE RELATIONS

The system of diplomacy, helped by an elaborate use of espionage, was responsible for the Maurya revolution in Magadha. It was due to the philosophy of Kauṭilya, who exalts the importance of diplomacy (*mantraśakti*) over direct action or resources. Indian diplomacy was characterised by the use of a code-language and systems of cipher-writing. Two such systems have now come down to us—those of Kauṭilya and Mūladeva. It was by diplomacy that the strength of the republics (*kulasaṅgha*) was undermined by an ambitious emperor. The Maurya emperors received ambassadors from foreign princes and sent ambassadors to other lands. The *dūtaka* was often a prince with delegated powers.[2] At the close of the Maurya period, the fortunes of the declining empire were bolstered up by the diplomacy of Mūladeva, who plotted the overthrow of the Śuṅgas. In the succeeding century began the diplomatic relations between China and the foreign dynasties in India. Indian ambassadors were insulted and imprisoned in China, but the person of the foreign envoy was held sacred and inviolable in India. Even in the remote west coast, Nambūdiri Brāhmans were used as envoys.

[1] *Paratantraḥ sadā rājā . . . . . kuto rājñaḥ svatantratā :* Śānti, vv. 139, 140.

[2] *Ep. Ind.*, vol. XI, p. 177.

CHAPTER IV

HINDU VIEW OF CIVIC LIFE

EARLY HINDU POLITY

IN the early centuries A.D. we find an elaboration of political theory in the *Śukranītisāra*, and Bṛhaspati's *Arthaśāstra*, as well as in the *Pañchatantra*, Bhartṛhari's *Nītiśataka*, and the dramatic works of Aśvaghosha, Bhāsa, Kāḷidāsa, Bhāravi and Bhavabhūti. Inscriptions reflect the conditions of practical politics and administration, and these are supplemented by the observations of Fa-Hien, Yuan Chwang and I'-tsing. Among local variations, those due to the establishment of foreign dynasties in India are revealed in the inscriptions of the Kushāṇas and the Kshaharātas ; and South Indian conditions in the *Śaṅgam* texts. Mutual interactions of systems of polity are noticeable in the inscriptions of the Kshatrapas, the Sātavāhanas and the Pallavas.

I

KINGSHIP

Our accounts vary as to the age at which a prince attained his majority. Kauṭilya had fixed it at sixteen. But the coronation of Khāravela, king of Kalinga, was at twenty-five. During the minority of the Sātavāhana king Gautamīputra, the Queen-mother acted as regent.

The kings worked hard. Fa-Hien saw the king of Nagar giving audience on government business after worship every morning. Of Harsha it has been said that the day was too short for him: he had hardly time for sleep and food.[1] Kingship was usually hereditary, but when there was a vacancy, the ministers appointed the successor. Harsha, like the Chōḷa emperor Rājarāja I and the Chāḷukyan Vikramāditya VI in later times, was called by the ministers to accept the crown. Nandivarman Pallavamalla was elected not only by the ministers and leaders of the people, but by the Professors of the College at Kāñchīpuram.[2] The coronation oath was *pratijñā*. Bṛhadratha Maurya was deposed because he would not keep it. Rudradāman prides himself as being *satya-pratijñā*. At Thāneswar the people were dissatisfied with the king and refused to obey his commands.[3]

Fa-Hien records that the people were free and happy. Only those who cultivated royal lands had to pay land-tax. Offences were punished with fines, and there was no decapitation or corporal punishment except for sedition and for rebellion against the king. State servants were paid salaries, and not by grants of land. The king of Kāñchī held a quinquennial assembly.[4]

Among the peculiar features in politics described by Yuan Chwang is that of the Suvarṇagotra country in the Snow Mountains. It was ruled by a succession of women. 'The husband of the queen was king, but did not govern.'[5] Harsha gave audience to neighbouring princes and statesmen, and was on friendly

[1] Watters, Vol. I, p. 344.
[2] *Ghaṭikayār* in *S. I. I.*, Vol. IV, p. 10 (explained in Vol. I, p. 243 *ante*).
[3] Watters, Vol. I, p. 314.
[4] *Pañchaparishad*, in chap. V.
[5] Watters, *Ibid*, p. 330.

terms with them. He divided his day into three periods, one of which was devoted to affairs of government and one to public works. Families were not registered, or individuals subjected to forced labour or contributions. Of the royal land, one part was for the expenses of government and state worship, one for the public servants, one for rewarding intellectual eminence, and one for gifts to various sects. Taxation being light, every one kept to his hereditary occupation and attended to his patrimony. The king's tenants paid a sixth of the produce as rent. Light duties were paid by tradesmen at ferries and barrier-stations. Officers were maintained by portions of land or assignments of cities.[1]

The people of India are described as of hasty and irresolute temperaments, but of pure moral principles. 'They will not take anything wrongfully, and they yield more than firmness requires. They fear the retribution for sins in other lives, and make light of what conduct produces in this life. They do not practise deceit and they keep their sworn obligations.'[2]

The duties of the king are thus described by Bhāsa: He was to consider beforehand whether a proposed political measure was consistent with equity (*dharma*). The opinions of ministers were then to be invited and discussed. He was to decide whether any occasion that arose was one for sternness or for leniency. He was to be in touch with public opinion, and have a knowledge of local conditions and usages. He was to watch his neighbours and rivals by the agency of spies. His person was to be protected at

[1] Watters, pp. 176-177.
[2] *Ibid.* p. 171.

all costs, but in war even this consideration was to be given up.[1] A king beloved of his people was worthy of being trusted by his neighbours.[2] State affairs were not to be neglected even for a moment,[3] for the ruler was merely the bearer of the burden of the doings of his subjects.[4] Sovereignty was to be won; and was not obtained by begging.[5] The envoy was to play his part, but never to exceed his instructions.[6] The state's portion was usually a sixth of the produce.[7] Kings were not to heap up fortunes, but leave their heirs only their arms and emblems.[8] Popular opinion exonerated the king in times of distress, and held the ministers responsible for having misguided him. Ministers were to be business-like, and not swayed by private considerations in the discharge of public duties. In the country of Sauvīra, ministers looked after the government efficiently in the absence of the king, and saw that no one obtained admission to the palace.[9] Popular festivals and processions were encouraged. Among the *utsavas* mentioned in the dramas are that of Indra,[10] the *Dhanurmaha* festival at Mathura[11] and that of Agastya on Mount Malaya.[12]

[1] *Avimāraka*, Act I. v. 12 :—*Dharmah prāgeva chintyah sachivamatigatih prekshitavyah svabuddhyā | pracchādyau rāgaroshau mrduparushaguṇau kālayogena kāryau || jñeyam lokānuvṛttam parachara nayanaih maṇḍalam prekshitavyam | rakshyo yatnāt ihātmā raṇaśirasi punah sopi nāvekshitavyah||*. Quoted also as Bhāsa's in *Sāraṅgadhara Paddhati*, V.

[2] *Visrambhayatyenam asya paurānurāgah* in *Pratijñā.*, II, 12.

[3] *Pratimā.*, Act IV.

[4] *Bhāravāhī* in *Pratimā.*, Act VII.

[5] *Rājyam nāma nṛpātmajaih sahṛdayairjitvā ripūn bhujyate||talloke na tu yāchyate na tu punardīnāya vā dīyate|| Dūtavākya*, 24.

[6] *Bahumāyoyam dūtah dūtasamudāchārān atikrāntah keshavah : Ibid*, 14.

[7] *Avim.*, IV, 11.

[8] *Pañcharātra*, I, 22.

[9] Act I.

[10] *Bālacharita*, Act I.

[11] *Ibid*, IV, 12.

[12] *Avim.*, Act IV.

There were spies, and a regular department of public intelligence.[1] One duty of the crown prince was to keep a record of the public proceedings.[2]

II

MINISTRY

The ministers were known as *Rājāmātyas*, and Śukra has eight of them, the usual number. The *Purohita* was in charge of religion and justice, and the *Sūta* of diplomacy. The latter officer is styled *Sāndhivigrahika* in Gupta inscriptions. Bṛhaspati lays down that ministers should be chosen for their intelligence.[3] Śukra recommends that they should be transferred from one post to another every three, five or ten years, for 'authority should not be kept in one man's hand for a long time.' There is also an insistence on business being done in writing: 'A king or officer who does state business without a written document (*lekhya*) is practising a fraud on the state.' These written orders were to pass successively through the departments of Home, Justice, Law and Diplomacy, Agriculture and Finance; and then through the *Pradhāna*, *Pratinidhi*, *Yuvarāja* and *Purohita* to the Rāja. Yuan Chwang tells us that Harsha went frequently on tours and that official records were kept by the administration. But these have not survived.

There is evidence of the hold the ministers had on the king and the people. We understand from Rudradāman's inscription that, when he ordered the repairs to the embankment at Girnar without reference

[1] *Pravṛtti purushah* in *Pañcharātra*, Act II. [2] *Ibid*, II, 41.
[3] *Arthaśāstra*, I, 4, 5. (Thomas' edition).

to his ministers, they refused to sanction the expenditure, and he had to charge it to his privy purse. Already at the close of the Maurya period we have traditions of ministers, under the guidance of Yuvarāja Samprati, refusing to carry out Aśoka's orders. But the case of Rudradāman is the more interesting as it shows an assertion of the rights of the ministry on principle, for the grant was required for a public and legitimate affair of the state. In the Gupta period we have a similar instance mentioned of Vasubandhu. Vikramāditya of Śrāvasti, probably Puragupta, gave away ten lakhs of gold coins to the destitute and desolate in spite of the protest of ministers, who complained that they would incur public odium by reason of the new taxes which these gifts rendered necessary. The position of the minister was thus the difficult one of reconciling the will of the king to the wishes of the people. As the *Pañchatantra* puts it, 'the minister who does what is good for the people incurs the king's displeasure, and he who acts in accordance with the king's wishes is hated by the people. It is rarely, therefore, that men are found who are fit for the responsible position of serving the king and the people alike.'

III

DEPARTMENTS

The departments of the administration remained under the control of the *tīrthas*, whose number continued as eighteen, including the prominent ministers who were four or eight.[1] The Sātavāhana

[1] *Pañchatantra*, III; *Śukra.*, p. 115.

inscriptions of Nasik introduce a Superintendent of merchant guilds, and a custodian of their property.[1] In the Gupta period the chief minister was *Kumārāmātya*, who is also styled Yuvarāja and *Bhaṭṭāraka* in inscriptions. Another prince was in charge of the army, and under him was a Paymaster of the Forces. Among other officers were the Superintendent of the Police, the Chamberlain and the Minister for War. Ministership became hereditary.[2] Instances of hereditary ministers are found in Vīrasena, who was in charge of foreign affairs under Chandragupta II, and Prithvīsena who was Commander-in-Chief under Kumāragupta. The father of this Prithvīsena, Śikharasvāmin, had been an officer under Chandragupta II. There were also junior ministers in each department, whose titles[3] give indication of their rank and status.

IV

PROVINCIAL GOVERNMENT

The empire was divided into small provinces in the Gupta period : *rāshṭra* or *maṇḍala*, which included several districts known as *vishaya*.[4] Intermediate between *rāshṭra* and *vishaya* was *bhoga*,[5] and the *vishaya* comprised several *deśas*. In Sātavāhana

[1] The ministers mentioned are: *Mahāsenāpati*, *Pratīhāra*, *Lekhya* and *Bhāṇḍāgārika*.

[2] *Anvayaprāpta-sāchivya* (*Gupta Inscr.* No. 6).

[3] The names of these were : *Daṇḍanāyaka* as contrasted with *Mahādaṇḍanāyaka* and *Kumārāmātya Daṇḍanāyaka* ; *Sāndhivigrahika* with *Mahāpradhāna Mahāsāndhivigrahika* ; *Balādhikṛta* with *Mahābalādhikṛta* and *Raṇabhaṇḍāgāra* with *Mahāraṇabhaṇḍāgāra*.

[4] *Gupta Inscr.* No. 16 mentions a district officer (*vishayapati*) of Skandagupta's time.

[5] *Ind. Ant.*, V, p. 114.

inscriptions the district was known as *hāra* or *āhāra* and was under an *amātya*. A lesser division was a *pathaka*.[1] Inscriptions of Kaṇha mention ministers, treasurers, and secretaries. *Mahārathins* and *mahābhogas* were apparently viceroys of Sātavāhanas, and asserted their independence later on. The Pallavas of Kāñchī had a political organization modelled on that of Hindustan.[2] We have references in their inscriptions to lords of *rāshṭras*, *vishayas*, *koshṭas*, *deśas*, *grāmas* and *vapitthas*; and to *tīrthikas*, *gūmikas* and *nekas*. But the most interesting addition to the list is the officer known as *Rahasyādhikṛta*, who was apparently a confidant and Private Secretary. Below the provincial governors were officers known as *āyuktakas* and *viniyuktakas*.[3]

[1] E. g., *Pratishṭhānapathaka* in Sopāraka-hāra.

[2] *Cf.* The Hiradahaḷḷi Plates of Śivaskandavarman, 1, 3-7:

1-3. *visayesa vattharāja kumāra senāpati*

4. *ratthika madabinu desadhikataḍike gāmā-gāmabhojake*

5. *vallave govallave amchche anandhi ate gumike tuthike*

6. *neyike anne vi cha amhapesanappayulte samcharaitaka*

7. *bhadamanusana* (*kadh . . . o*) *pariharam vitarama. . . . .*

Bühler considers *vattha* to be possibly a mistake for *vanitha* or *bandha*, explained in Hemachandra's *Deśikōśa* by *bhṛtya* (servant). But *vattha* is a Dravidian word meaning a division (lit. a circle), and even now a small sub-division is known as *vaṭṭam* in the West Coast. The word is repeated in *Apitthivattavana* ' . . . *brahmananam* ' in 1.8 of the inscription, and the sense is clearly a political sub-division.

Madabinu is corrected by Bühler into *mundabika* and taken in the sense of a customs officer, and *bhojaka* in the sense of Ināmdar or free-holder. Fleet's conjecture that *Neyika* is *niyukta* may be borne out by inscriptions: *Rāshṭrapati vishayapati grāmakūṭakāyuktaka niyuktakādhikārika* in *Ep. Car.*, XI, Dg. I, l. 56. But it is more natural to take *neka* as *nāyaka* (military or police officer). The king's epithet or *gohalasatasahassappadavino* ('giver of a lakh of ploughs and oxen and of crores of gold') shows that encouragement of agriculture was one of the main objects of the government.

[3] *Gupta Inscr.*, No. 38.—The governors of Skandagupta were Sarvanāga of Antarvedi and Bhīmavarman at Kośāmbi. Other officers mentioned are:—Dhruva, the collector of the royal share in the revenue; Mahattara, Chatbhala and Daṇḍapasakara. No. 46 mentions

The former were apparently permanent officers; the latter a sort of commissioners on special duty.[1] Thus, there was an elaboration of the machinery of administration in districts, divisions and localities.

V

LOCAL GOVERNMENT

Sātavāhana inscriptions tell us something of the administration of towns. There were merchant guilds (*nigamasabhā*) at Karhād and Nasik, the latter of which had expanded into an assembly of all the citizens (*paura*). Its president was Śreshṭhin, and its Registrar of Gifts caused a written contract (*chirakam*) to be drawn up. Among the guilds (*śreṇi*) mentioned in towns are those of oilmongers, boatmen, potters, day labourers, bankers and bamboo-workers. These were probably under the *nigamasabhā*. The guilds received deposits and paid annual or monthly interest on them. In the Pallava country customs duties were collected in *maṇḍapas* by officers known as *maṇḍapis*.

Hāla mentions the *Grāmaṇī*[2], and inscriptions, the *Padraka*, as the village officer. The village community was strong and well organised. There is evidence of the panchāyat in the Gupta inscriptions.[3] To it were added two members appointed from time to time by the town. In Nepalese inscriptions also the panchāyat

Grāmagoshṭīyakula, Talavāṭaka, Dūta, and Sīmakarmakāra, besides Rājaputra, Rājāmātya, Mahākshatika, Mahādaṇḍanāyaka, Mahāpratīhāra, Kumārāmātya, Rājasthānīya, Uparika, Chauroddharaṇika, Daṇḍika and Daṇḍapāsika. No. 55 has Sarvādhyaksha, Adhiyoga, Niyukta, Ājñāsanchārī, Kulaputra, Adhikṛta, Bhaṭa and Cchātra.

[1] As in No. 39, line 76.

[2] *Saptāśati*, vv. 628 and 631.

[3] *Pañchamaṇḍali* named *Pañchakula* in Siyadoni village. See *Ep. Ind.*, I, 167.

appears under the name of *panchāli*. Ushavadāta of Nasik introduced quadrangular rest-houses on highways, water-houses and free ferries; and endowments of the kind were placed with the village communities. The village assembly borrowed from the temple treasury in hard times.[1] There was a strong public opinion in some villages which demanded that accountants, carpenters and other workmen should serve in the village and not outside it.[2] Men who helped in restoring, constructing or maintaining tanks were rewarded with grants of land permanently free from rates.[3] But South Indian inscriptions refer also to 'social porcupines' and public enemies[4] who ruffled the smooth course of village life.

Gupta inscriptions[5] mention the local taxes—*udraṅga* and *uparikara*. *Draṅga* means a city or township[6] and *udraṅga* corresponds to city rates. *Uparikara* was probably an officer's cess, as the term *upari* occurs among the subordinate officers. There is reference also to a *choradaṇḍa* which corresponds probably to the *chorarajju* of the earlier period.

VI

JUSTICE

In the *Mṛcchakaṭika* and the dramas attributed to Bhāsa we have a good picture of the administration of justice. Śūdraka opens with the statement that the officers of the Court cared nothing for family or

[1] No. 397 of 1914. [2] No. 205 of 1919.

[3] *Ep. Ind.*, III, 51 (*kōḍige*). Cf. *sarvamānya* and *iṛai- ili*.

[4] *Grāmakaṇṭaka* and *grāmadrōhi* in *A.S.A.R.* for 1904-5, p. 144. *Mad. Ep. Rep.* for 1900-11, p. 75.

[5] Nos. 21 and 27. [6] *Ind. Ant.*, Vol. IV, p. 175.

descent, but went solely by the character of the parties and the merits of the case.[1] There was an *Adhikaraṇa Bhojaka* (judge), a *Śreshṭhin* (appraiser) and a *Kāyastha*[2] who took down depositions: The last had no reputation for impartiality. They noted the demeanour and carriage of the parties. Torture was permissible in the case of those who were known to withhold the truth.[3] The courts were to administer both law and equity.[4] Evidence of witnesses, when clear and unimpeached, was decisive. The judge gave the verdict, and the punishment was to be fixed by the king.[5] But if the accused was willing to undergo the ordeal by poison, water, weighment or fire, it was to be allowed by the king. In older times Brāhmans were exempt from capital punishment. A guilty Brāhman was to be exiled, and to leave the state bag and baggage. This rule was departed from in the case of Chārudatta, who was sentenced to execution by the king, and two men of the untouchable caste were to carry out the sentence. But the criminal was let off in various contingencies. Sometimes ransom was offered for his release. There was a general release of all prisoners, following the birth of a prince. Another contingency was anarchy or civil war.[6]

In the *Mattavilāsa* we have a skit on the impartiality of the judges, whose palm could be oiled by the great, but whom the innocent need not fear.[7] The evidence of witnesses was binding, but it was not let in

[1] *Kim kulenopadishṭena śīlamevātra kāraṇam* in Act IX, v. 7.
[2] *Kāyastha sarpāspadam nītikshuṇṇapadam* (v. 14).
[3] *Krakacham dātavyam* (v. 43).
[4] *Nyāya* and *dharma*.
[5] *Nirṇaye vayam tu pramāṇam śeshe tu rājā*, 1, 525.
[6] Act X, ll. 304-8.
[7] *Nyāyavṛtterbhayam nāsti.*

when the facts were obvious (*pratyaksha*). There is evidence of arbitration and settlement of disputes without resort to the law courts.[1]

VII

SOUTH INDIAN POLITY

The earliest account of South Indian polity is that found in the *Śaṅgam* texts. These disclose Sanskritic and North Indian influences. But it is possible to detect in them elements which appear to be distinctively Dravidian.

Central Government

There are numerous terms for 'king': *Kōn* or *Kō* apparently denotes a shepherd, like *gopa* in Sanskrit. *Ēndan* or *ēndal* seems to denote the premier person in the state. *Mannan* denotes the hero; and *kuriśil* that he was living on an eminence, in a hill fortress. *Iṛaivan* means capturer or conqueror, and *āṭchi* rule over the people. The king's crown was *muḍi* (tuft of hair), showing that the earliest form of the crown exaggerated rather than concealed the natural mode of wearing the hair.[2] The foreheads of the chieftains were bound with gold, as we find them in the burial urns of Adichchanallūr. The crown was conical in shape and studded with gems.

The king appeared in durbar every morning and held secret council with his ministers at night, as is described in the case of the Pāṇḍyan Neḍun-Chēḻiyan. The king's council at Uṛaiyūr is described as the abode of equity,[3] and the Chōḻas regarded themselves

[1] *Dharmādhikāra* in *Pañcharātra*, I, 39.
[2] See *supra*, p. 11.
[3] *Puṟanāṉūṟu*, 39.

as lions of justice. When the king sat in council, drums were beaten, and they sounded the purpose of the council—whether it was the administration of justice, the giving of alms or the entering on a campaign.

The entourage of the king was of three classes. Five persons were household officers, five were the ministers of state, and eight were the heads of departments. To the first class belonged the head of the nobility (*vaḷḷal*), the astrologer (*vaḷḷuvar*), the chamberlain (*agavar*), the bard (*pāṇar*) and the steward (*aḍiyar-ūḷiyar*). The five ministers were the *Amātya* (*amaichchar*), the *Purohita*, the *Senāpati*, the *Dūta*, and the *Chāra*. The first four figure in the polity of Hindustan; the last was a secret spy and had a ministerial rank in the South Indian state.

The eight heads of departments were: the Accountant-General (*kaṇakkiyar vinaiñar*), the Master of the Ceremonies (*karma-vidhi*), the Treasurer (*kanakachchuṟṟam*), the Palace Guard (*kaḍaikāppār*), the First Citizen (*nagaramāndar*), the Commander (*paḍaitalaivar*), the Master of Elephants (*yānai vīrar*) and the Master of Horse (*īvuḷi maṟavar*). The departments compare with those of North Indian polity. The last three were military officers, and the fourth the head of the police. The fifth reminds one of *Grāmaṇī* in Aryan polity, the first and the third of *Kshatta* and *Saṅgrahīta*, and the second of *Amātya*.

In at least one place[1] there is an analysis of the qualifications of councillors. They were to be men of high birth and sound learning—men of irreproachable character, truthful and pure, free from envy and covetousness, generous and even-minded. It is

[1] *Vāhaippaḍalam*, VIII, 19.

interesting that much more regard was paid to character than capacity. Consistently with this principle, we have frequent references to the influence of poets and men of learning on the administration. One poet appeased the wrath of a Chōḷa king against his rebellious sons. Another exhorted the Chēra king to protect his subjects like children. Poets like Kapilar acted as arbitrators among contending kings. They interceded on behalf of innocent men who had been falsely accused, and were able to save them.[1]

The composition of the council varied with time and locality. In the *Śilappadikāram* for instance, we have the five ministers described as *Mājanam*, *Pārpār*, *Maruttar*, *Nimittar* and *Amaichchar*—the First Citizen, the Brāhman, the Physician, the Augur, and the *Amātya*. This list contrasts with that given above. But the variations are significant, as showing a ministry governing in peace, instead of a war ministry. The Commander, the Messenger and the Spy are replaced by the First Citizen, the Physician and the Augur. Elsewhere we have another list: Priest, Accountant, Judge, Tax-Collector and *Mantrin*.[2] This list is similar to the former one, except that it calls attention to the ministers being heads of the departments of Finance and Justice.

There is no evidence of a further elaboration of the central organisation when the Tamil kingdoms expanded into empires. While Chōḷa inscriptions of historical times are full of significant details as to the working of the local institutions, they are surprisingly sparse in their accounts of the provincial and imperial governments. The policy was one of developing

[1] *Puṟam*, 46f.

[2] *Āśān*, *peruṅkaṇi*, *aṟakkaḷattandaṇar*.

local self-governing institutions so efficiently that they should call for little interference from the central power. The main function of the central government consisted in adjusting local differences when such arose, and in protecting the local authorities, in the just exercise of their rights, against their officers who had misappropriated public funds, and against powerful miscreants in high places who had defied local control. The king and his ministers had also to provide for matters of common policy in the state, like Defence, Irrigation and Public Works. There was thus no need for a very elaborate organisation at the centre.

The central government of the Chōḷas, for instance, consisted of the Emperor, his secretary who put his orders in writing, his chief secretary (*ōlai nāyagan*) and another high dignitary. The Minister of Despatches (*viḍaiyadhikāri*) conveyed the orders to the parties. These orders, approved of by the viceroy and the assemblies, were sent to the Record Office. It is clear that the king's orders were tentative,[1] and became final only after the matter under reference had been fully investigated by the local authorities. The revenue was obtained from taxes on land and on commodities, professions, trades and raw products. Officers were rewarded by gifts of land or by assignments of revenue, and the balance reached the royal treasury. The Chōḷa army consisted of infantry, cavalry, elephant troops and archers. The infantry was manned by artisans. The fleets varied in efficiency. Public works formed another head of expenditure—temples, cities and irrigation works. Labour was never impressed, even when the state was

[1] Cp. p. 74 *supra*.

in financial difficulties. We are told that even Karikāla paid his workmen, though in depreciated coins.

Departments

The king's revenue came from cesses (*vari*), tolls (*śuṅkam*), tribute (*kappam*), land-tax (*irai*), presents (*pariśu*), mines and fisheries (*ulka* and *tirai*).[1] *Vari* indicates that the idea in taxation was that every man must pay his own mite or quota towards the expenses of administration. *Śunka* is toll. *Ulaka* seems to be a corruption of *loha* (mines and minerals). The Pāṇḍyan king Neḍun-Chēḻiyan ordained that the treasure-trove belonged not to the state but to the finder.[2] *Tirai* refers to roving the seas, with special reference to fisheries. The evidence of survivals shows a special tax known as *aṅka*, which was the fee paid to the state for permitting a trial by combat, the contending parties to the suit either engaging personally in the conflict or hiring mercenaries for the purpose.[3]

Administration of justice was free in the Tamil country, and there was no exception from the law taking its course, even against those in high places. A king's chariot having crushed an animal's

[1] In the plates of Śivaskandavarman Pallava we have the eighteen kinds of dues levied on villages :

L. 31. *akara yollaka vinesikhaṭṭāvāsam adūdha dadhigrahaṇam*
L. 32. *araṭṭasamvinayikam aloṇaguḷachchobham akaraveṭṭhi*
L. 33. *konjallamapāramparabalivadda gahanam alana kaṭṭhagaha-*
L. 34. *nam aharītaka sāka pupha gahanam evamādikehi aṭṭhā*
L. 35. *ra* (*da*) *sa jāli parihārehi*. (*Ep. Ind.*, Vol. I, No. 1.)

Bühler has discovered in this list levies on milk, curds, salt, sugar, vegetables, flowers, grass, wood, and oxen and forced labour. I find references likewise to tribute (*kara*), proceeds from mines (*ulaka*), gains from the quartering of troops (cf. *achāṭṭa bhaṭapraveśyam* in Gupta inscriptions), and a tax on grass (*śāka*).

[2] *Śilap.*, XXIII, 128. [3] Graeme : Report on Malabar, 1822, p. 26.

hand, amputation of the prince's hand was ordered forthwith. Sometimes innocent people were brought to grief by the iron rigour of the law. On these occasions the poets interceded, and saved them from the clutches of the law.[1]

Warfare was a constant occupation of the Tamils, and rules of war are described in many places. Palyāgaśālai Pāṇḍya[2] warns cows, Brāhmans, women and the sick and infirm to flee from the field of battle ere it begins. Fortresses were levelled to the ground or set on fire.[3] 'The beautiful homes are levelled with the dust. Asses are yoked to plough the soil with spears, and worthless plants are grown on the foundations.'[4] Karikāla Chōḷa made the invaded country a desert and ravaged it with fire. Elephants in rut were set to pull down massive pillars in picturesque halls.

War began with the capture of cattle on the hill, and was carried to the pasture region, where there were forts, and to the littoral, where the fleet operated. When the capital in the estuary region (*marutam*) was besieged, the opposing forces were ranged on the plain (*pālai*) and victory was won with the *vāgai* flower as the emblem.

Local Institutions

Inscriptions which belong to the time of Parāntaka I give details of Chōḷa administration. The village assemblies were well organised. There were three classes of them: *sabhā* of Brāhmans, *ūrār* of village residents, and *nagarattār* of merchants. Membership

[1] *Puṟam.*, 46-47.
[2] *Ibid*, 9.
[3] *Ibid.*
[4] *Puṟapporuḷveṇbāmālai*, V, 120.

of the *sabhā* was confined to shareholders in the *agrahāra*, if they knew some one of the *dharmaśāstras*. But in the case of new members knowledge of a whole Veda was insisted on. There were rules against the persistent opposition of refractory members. Nothing is definitely stated about the working of the other assemblies. The temple was the meeting place, or some tree with a platform round it. Sometimes men of other castes had seats in the *sabhā*, at the meetings of which the royal or local officers were also present. Affairs of the temple were also considered here, and the various classes of temple servants were present.

The assembly had both deliberative and executive functions. They were the custodians of all charitable endowments. They collected the taxes and granted exemptions, chiefly to temples. In default of payment there was confiscation, as also when lands had been given up, or their holders had departed. If a canal overflowed its banks, it was the assembly that took prompt measures through its committee. They kept the accounts of transfers of land and revenue receipts. The *tirai kaṇakkan* was their officer of rents, rates and taxes. Charitable grants, which were tax-free, were registered in the *vari-pottagam*, and money accounts were recorded in the *baṇḍāra-pottagam*. All these accounts were periodically subject to audit by the king's officers or inspectors. In 932 A.D., for instance, a writ was issued by Parāntaka I to re-check the accounts of the temple of Tiruneyttānam. Suspected delinquents were liable to undergo the ordeal by the red-hot iron.

The assembly worked in committees for general management, the supervision of tanks, gardens, temples, charities, and the currency, and other purposes. A special committee at Uttaramallūr consisted of four men from the heart of the town (*māḍaviti*), two from the army and three from the boatmen's quarters (*saṅkarappāḍi*), all appointed by election. There was representation by wards, of which there were 30 at Uttaramallūr (Chingleput) and 60 at Śēndalai (Tanjore), and the representatives were chosen by lot, each voter putting a palm-leaf ticket into the election pot. The committee for general management was regarded as the most important, and was recruited from the ex-members of other committees. Only honest men were chosen as accountants. Dishonest men and their relatives were declared ineligible for membership in the future. Elections were annual. Re-election was permitted after three years from the expiry of office, and the re-elected was then to serve on another committee. The main principle was that every villager should have his turn for serving the village on its assembly. This was made easy by payments of some kind to the members, as well as by the holding of the sessions during night.

Certain qualifications were demanded for membership of the assembly, such as knowledge of business, honesty and good character. The relatives of dishonest officers were all disqualified, as also those guilty of the cardinal sins, outcastes, and even eaters of forbidden food. The property qualification needed was a quarter *vēli* of land and a house in the village.[1] No one was fit for membership if he was below 35 years, or above 70 years, of age.

[1] Knowledge of one Veda with *bhāshya* and ⅛ *vēli* of land, in the alternative.

Misappropriation of charitable endowments was detected by royal commissions. The Agnīśvara temple at Tirumālpērūr in North Arcot was subjected in 989 A.D. to such inspection, and the men in charge were heavily fined. A similar defalcation was noticed in Tiruvallam in 992 A.D. by the panchāyat of inspection with prince Gaṇḍarāditya as Chairman. The emperor insisted on regular accounts being maintained of the *brahmadeya* and *devadāna* lands. Thus it is clear that the village assemblies were under effective royal control, when circumstances called for intervention.

The district assembly was styled *nāṭṭār*. We may presume that it met to discuss matters concerning the whole district. A number of *nāḍus* were included in the *vaḷanāḍu*, and a number of these again in the *koṭṭam* or *maṇḍalam*. The last, originally an independent tract, became a province in the Chōḷa empire. Rājarāja's empire included several such provinces.

VIII

POLITICAL THOUGHT IN WORKS ON POLITY

The political thought of the *Kuṟaḷ* is based on Sanskrit texts. The six elements of sovereignty other than the king are detailed and described; but troops take the first place, council the fourth, and fortifications the last place, in the enumeration,—showing a shifting of the emphasis. Tamilians were in a state of almost chronic warfare. Boldness, learning and strength of will were the virtues of the king, and liberality also was expected of him. He was to be always accessible to his subjects, and never to use harsh words; he was to rule by love and not by fear, to develop the economic resources of the state, to administer justice impartially, and to tolerate advice, however unpalatable. He was to tend the people with care.[1] Ministers were the eyes of the king; so they were to be chosen wisely for their worth, and to be always consulted. They were not to be chosen by favouritism, but for expert knowledge and capacity for action. The king was to supervise everything, and be ever wakeful. He was to be helped by spies, but to take action only when three independent reports from different classes of spies were found to be in agreement. The *mantriparishad* of the Chēra king is mentioned in the *Maṇimēkhalai*.[2]

The polity of the *Kuṟaḷ* is evidently based on Sanskrit tradition, but it is earlier than the Śānti Parvan of the *Mahābhārata* in its existing form. The *Kuṟaḷ* has, like the *Kauṭilīya*, only four tests of ministerial qualifications (*upadhā*), whereas the *Mahābhārata* adds a fifth.[3] But the political ideas of the *Kuṟaḷ* appear to be based rather on Kāmandaka's version of the *Kauṭilīya* than on the latter itself. The *Nītisāra* of Kāmandaka is professedly based on the work of Kauṭilya, and must be assigned to the Gupta age, as there are quotations from it in the *Pañchatantra*. There are few original contributions of the author to political thought. He exalts the importance of *daṇḍanīti* by saying that righteousness, wealth and satisfaction flow from it alone.[4] In this matter he

[1] Sections 39 and 45. Similar ideas are found throughout the Śangam texts.

[2] *Maṇimēkhalai*, ch. 28.

[3] Śānti, 83, 52.

[4] Kāmandaka, II, 38.

appears to agree with the school of Śukra, who had considered *daṇḍanīti* as the only *vidyā*,[1] and whose *Nītisāra* was codified for the most part in this age, judging from the modification of the original position[2] along the lines of Kāmandaka. The impress of the Gupta age is discernible in these works in the exaltation of *dharma* as leading to *artha* and *kāma*, and as the paramount one among the three objectives of human endeavour.

Kāmandaka has more elaborate descriptions of the *maṇḍalas*. He cites two authors not mentioned by Kauṭilya—Puloma and Maya, and a third author named by his commentator Śaṅkarārya as Satya, whom we may possibly identify with Satyāchārya quoted in the works of Varāhamihira. He considers hunting and gambling as the vices of the ruler which are politically the most reprehensible. In this view he follows the older school of Kauṇapadanta rather than that of Kauṭilya, with whom sexual weakness and addiction to drink are the worst among the vices.[3]

Bṛhaspati represents a later stage, probably the early Pallava period.[4] Kāmandaka had added trickery and deception (*māyā* and *indrajāla*) to the classical list of political expedients, and Bṛhaspati expressly forbids these.[5] But he allows the king to ferret out the secrets of his rivals by association with gamblers, revilers, and wicked men who might let things out in sport. He would have the king divide and sway the ministry,[6] which shows that ministers

[1] Kauṭilya, I, 2.

[2] Śukra, I, 5.

[3] Kāmandaka, ch. XIV ; Kauṭilya, Bk. VIII, ch. 3.

[4] Cf. references to the Pallavas, *kusumānta*, *kāpālikas*, *Gaṅgādvāra* or Haridvār ; Kāñchī, and the hills and rivers of the Dekhan.

[5] I, 8.

[6] *Sāmabhedadānāni mantrishu*.

were powerful. The king's men were to proclaim the reverse of the truth before those people who were likely to advertise what they heard. He was to give audience at 8 a.m., sit in the hall of justice till noon, and have only three hours' sleep every day.[1] There was no objection to his telling untruths when prestige was at stake.[2] He was to engage in sports till he was 25 years of age.[3] He was to refrain from patronising new army leaders or *kusumāntas*, for they instigated civil war and loss of life.[4] He was to protect the four castes and watch the 18 *tīrthas*. Among the public places which were subjected to espionage were temples, dancing halls, sacrificial halls, watering places where people assembled at twilight, roads, quarters of heretics, bazaars, elementary[5] schools, military schools, fields and elevated places, sites of festivals, prostitutes' dens, baths, the residence of ascetics, drinking houses, serais and inns for travellers. Travellers were to be examined at the gates of the city. Village headmen and city magistrates were to be held in esteem; and villages, cities and temples were to be free from oppression.

Ministers were consulted on matters of policy. That counsel was the best in respect of which they were all agreed, from the standpoint of practical action as well as of policy. If differences of opinion resulted in some sort of compromise, it was to be considered. Where feeling ran high, the proposed line of action was to be avoided. The king was to initiate the discussion and the ministers, in order of precedence, were

[1] I, 66.
[2] I, 86.
[3] I, 89.
[4] I, 98 and 105.
[5] *Bālavidyā pāṭha deśa.*

to be heard and their views considered. They were to give their opinions honestly and fearlessly, and try to win the master over to their side. They were to devise measures for averting impending disasters. The king was to entertain people in his service according to merit and efficiency, and character was much more important than mere learning.[1] But counsel was always to be taken with men of intelligence. The test of intelligence was the capacity to discuss possible difficulties, however displeasing their divulgence may be to the master.[2]

The extant text of Śukra appears to reflect political conditions of the later Hindu age. The purpose of *Nītiśāstra* is described as securing the peace and prosperity of a state by the union and contentment of the subjects, harmony in the relations of rulers and subjects, and peaceful intercourse with other states.[3] The character of the king is described as *sātvika*, *rājasika* or *tāmasika*[4], according as he was actuated by disinterested regard for duty, was ambitious and fond of power and resorted to intrigues and quarrels, or was tyrannical and oppressive. The king was to enforce obedience to *dharma* and was to rule according to equity.[5] He was to consult his ministers on all matters of policy. These were the *Purohita*, *Pratinidhi*, *Pradhāna*, *Senāpati*, *Mantri*, *Prāḍvivāka*, *Sachiva*, *Sumanta*, *Amātya* and *Dūta*. The salary of each was to be 10 per cent more than that of the succeeding one in the list. The *Purohita* was the mainstay of the kingdom, an expert in religion and

[1] V, 18 and 20.
[2] *Ahitamapi kāryaṁ yasya pratibhāti sa mantrayogyaḥ* : VI, 6.
[3] Ch. I, v. 36. [4] I, 57. [5] 4, 5, and 52.

polity as well as in military science, one who could be relied on to give disinterested advice, and had so much influence that he could bring his master round from an erratic or angry mood to virtuous ways of life. They alone were good ministers who were held in esteem by the king and who could control him. The kingdom could not be prosperous if there were ministers whom the ruler need not fear.

The *Pratinidhi* was the king's *alter ego* and the *Pradhāna* was the prime minister. The *Sachiva* was in charge of the army, and the *Mantri* of diplomatic relations. The *Paṇḍita* was well up in local history and custom, and the *Prāḍvivāka* likewise in civic matters, as he was the Chief Justice. The *Amātya* was in charge of lands and records, and the *Sāmanta* of receipts and disbursements. The *Dūta* was the ambassador, clever, eloquent and fearless. The king was to appoint ministers to each post in rotation. Each was to have two colleagues in his department. Every officer was transferred once in three, five, seven or ten years. Promotions were to be awarded on merit. All business of the Council was to be conducted in writing. No officer or servant was to do anything without a written order; nor should the king issue any command orally on any matter, however small. 'A written document is the best guide, for, oral orders are liable to error.'[1] The ministers and officers were to submit written reports of their work. These reports were to be made daily, monthly, yearly or once in many years, according to circumstances. The business of state was done in the Council Hall, near which ministers and officers had their dwelling houses.

[1] II, 582, 587.

No paper was to be submitted for the king's orders until it had passed through every member of the ministry. Thus we have the ministry constituting a sort of Cabinet, in which each member knew every important matter of administration.

One interesting development in this period is the formulation of rules relating to the public service. These read like a chapter taken from the modern Civil Service Regulations: 'The king should pay a quarter less than the usual salary to the servant when ill, give three months' leave on full pay to one who has served for five years, six months' leave to one who has long been ill, but not more to any.' No portion of the pay was to be deducted from the full remuneration of a servant who had been ill for only a week. If a sick servant was a highly qualified expert, he might be granted leave for any length of time on half his salary. The king was to give every servant fifteen days' respite from work in the year. He was to grant a life-pension of half the salary to the man who had spent forty years in his service and, when he died, a compassionate pension of half the amount to his son, if a minor, or to the widow or her daughter. He was to give the servants a bonus of one-eighth of the salary by way of reward every year and, if one's service revealed exceptional ability, one-eighth of the entire salary drawn during his tenure of office. He was to give, as bonus to the son of the man who died at his work, such a sum as his qualifications might justify.[1]

We have some evidence of political education in the literature of the period. In the *Pañchatantra*[2] it

[1] Śukra., Ch. II, 819–835; pp. 99–100. [2] Kielhorn's Ed., p. 11, L. 11.

is mentioned that *nītiśāstra* was taught to children, while yet in the lap of the parents. The Gaṅga king Mādhava prides himself on being an expert in the science of polity, even including its secret doctrines.[1] The *Pañchatantra* considers Chāṇakya as the most popular authority, but Bāṇa mentions Bṛhaspati, Kālidāsa, and Śukra. In the 7th century there was a revolt against the political doctrines of Kauṭilya, headed by Bāṇa and Daṇḍin.[2]

In General Literature

The political thought enshrined in Kāḷidāsa follows in the main the traditional conception. His ideal is not that of a puppet king. Kauṭilya had emphasised the importance of diplomacy (*mantraśakti*), which he considered as immensely more important than the other two *śaktis*.[3] But according to Kāḷidāsa, *utsāhaśakti* when properly applied, and *prabhuśakti* enabled the king to augment his resources and to win his rivals over.[4] The ideal king was one who pleased the people by doing what was good for them.[5] He was to be neither too harsh nor too mild, like the sun on his southward course. He was to be always alert, and to this end have hunting and other exercises.[6] His duties are thus described:[7] watchfulness and service to the people irrespective of personal convenience, checking those on the path of unrighteousness,

[1] *Sopanishadkasya nītiśāstrasya vaktṛprayoktṛkuśalaḥ.*

[2] *Atinṛśaṁsaprāyopadeśanirghṛṇaṁ Kauṭilyaśāstraṁ :* Bāṇa : *Kādambari*. Cf. *Mudrārākshasa*, which explains Kauṭilya as *kuṭilamati*. (Act I).

[3] VIII, 5.

[4] *Kumārasambhava*, I ; *Raghuvaṁśa*, VIII, 19.

[5] *Rājā prakṛtirañjanāt.* [6] *Śākuntala*, II, 4 and 5. [7] *Ibid*, V, 78

and protecting the good. It is interesting to notice that Kāḷidāsa adds that the king was to bring about a compromise and secure harmony among his subjects, whenever there were rancorous dissensions,[1] and to be in *loco parentis* to those who were helpless, such as orphans.[2]

The king got up early in the morning and sat in the hall of justice (*dharmāsana*), sometimes till mid-day. He had his bath and food only in the afternoon.[3] On the arrival of Śakuntaḷā at Dushyanta's court, he was found at his *dharmāsana*, and the poet notes that it was already mid-day.[4] When the king got up late and felt unwell, he deputed Piśuna to preside at the *dharmāsana*, and enjoined him to put in writing whatever business was disposed of by him,[5] whether in the Hall of Audience or in the Court of Justice.

There are clear statements in regard to the working of the ministerial council. In the *Mālavikāgnimitra* the king is seen to confer with his *Mantrin* on confidential business.[6] But the consultation was sometimes through messengers. In Act V of this drama we have the king sending the *Amātya* to consult the other ministers, and his returning to say that the *Mantriparishad* had agreed with the king. Thereupon the king directed them to instruct the

[1] *Praśamayasi vivādam* in *Śāk.*, Act V.

[2] *Yena yena viyujyante prajāḥ snigdhena bandhunā | sa sa pāpādṛte tāsām Dushyanta iti ghushyatām.*

[3] *Shashṭhe bhāge divasasya ātmanaḥ chhandavartī* in *Vik.*, Act II.

[4] *Śāk.*, Act V.

[5] *Yat pratyavekshitam āryeṇa paurakāryam tat patramāropya dīyatām* in *Vik.*, Act II.

[6] *Lekhahastena mantriṇā* and *ekāntasthaparijanaḥ.*

Senāpati to carry the order into execution.[1] Sometimes the ministers were left in charge of the kingdom, as when Dilīpa was out for three weeks at Vasishṭha's hermitage,[2] or when king Agnivarṇa became indifferent to public duties and gave himself up to pleasure.[3] On the latter king's death, the ministers set up the pregnant Queen on the throne.[4] Consultation with the ministers was obligatory,[5] and orders were to be in writing. These rules are laid down in the *Śukranītisāra*, and Kāḷidāsa explicitly mentions Śukra.[6] If the *Kuntaḷeśvara dautyam* be a work of Kāḷidāsa's, it shows that there was an order of precedence at the Durbar and that foreign envoys were usually assigned dignified seats, above the *Sāmantas* or Chieftains.

Bhāravi represents political thought of about a century later. He includes *māyā* among the *upāyas*,[7] apparently after the school of Kāmandaka, who added *māyā, upekshā* and *indrajāla* as three expedients in addition to the classical four. There is also a reference to policy overcoming the bounds of honesty. Treaties were broken when it suited ambitious princes.[8] It was impossible to govern without the help of ministers,[9] as the art of politics had become complicated (*vishama*). A state was to be ruled on the basis of army and finance.[10] The most important

[1] *Deva amātyah vijñāpayati mantriparishadah api evameva darśanam | Rājā :-tena hi mantriparishadam brūhi senāpataye Vīrasenāya lekhyata ēvam kriyatām iti* ||

[2] *Raghu.*, I, 34.

[3] *Ibid*, XIX, 4.

[4] *Ibid*, XIX, 52.

[5] *Anumatassachivairyayau.*

[6] *Adhyāpitasyauśanasopi nītim* in *Śāk.*, VI.

[7] *Māyinah māyāvishu* in *Kirāta*, I, 30.

[8] *Kirāta*, I, 45.

[9] *Ibid*, II, 3.

[10] *Kośadaṇḍayoh* in II, 12.

thing for the king was to see that his rule was popular and that his subjects did not resent his measures.[1] It was difficult for a king to overcome the wrath of his subjects.[2] Duryodhana's state was safe and stable and could not be easily shaken so long as he had a hold on the affections of his people.[3] There were meetings at which royal authority was questioned, because measures had been undertaken without proper consultation and previous sanction. A vote of censure could be passed, if there were a certain number attending such meetings.[4]

IX

INTER-STATE RELATIONS

Aśoka's *Kalinga* inscriptions show that the people of the conquered country had rights, which were respected. The Gaṅga king Avinīta claims to have maintained these rights in the country he conquered.[5] It was a political doctrine that no war should be waged without a previous declaration of hostilities, that unfair methods of fighting should not be resorted to, that non-combatants should not be molested, and that in the settlement following war, local rights and

[1] II, 37. [2] *Antahprakritikopah* in II, 51.

[3] II, 49.

[4] This is my explanation of III, 51, which the commentators do not explain clearly. The verse is: *Karoti yo aśeshajanātiriktām sambhāvanām arthavatīm kriyābhih | samsatsu jāte purushādhikāre na pūraṇītam sam upaiti samkhyā ||* *Samsat* evidently is *janasamsat* or assembly. *Aśeshajana* has a variant reading *sarvajana* and denotes a mass meeting of the assembly or *gaṇa*. To make up the quorum was the duty of the *Gaṇapūraka* in the Pāḷi texts. Mallinātha with his shrewd political sense defines *pūraṇī* as *pūryate anayā iti*, but, of course, misses the point of a quorum.

[5] *Ep. Car.*, Vol. IX, Db. 68.

usages were to be respected. Inscriptions bear witness to the application of these principles. Samudragupta tells us that wherever he conquered, the defeated kings were restored to their places. Sometimes tributes were exacted from them, but seldom was their dynasty superseded. Kāḷidāsa echoes this usage of his time in his description of Raghu's *digvijaya*. The campaigns began with *pratāpa* (ultimatum), the frontiers *(pratyanta)* and the rear *(pārshṇi)* were well guarded, and the defeated chieftains lost their fame but not their lands. Those who submitted lost little, and those who resisted were deposed and subsequently restored to their places.[1]

There was some sort of gradation among the kings of the period in accordance with their greatness and resources. The *Śukranītisāra* introduces a mathematical basis of calculation, which is the more curious on account of its definiteness and accuracy: it was according to the state revenue that a king was styled *Sāmanta*, *Māṇḍalika*, *Rājā*, *Mahārāja*, *Svarāṭ*, *Samrāṭ*, *Virāṭ*, or *Sārvabhauma*. While this is little more than pure political speculation, we have terms on coins and in inscriptions which obviously point to different degrees of kingly power—Rājā, Mahārāja, Rājādhirāja, Maheśvara, Kshatrapa and Mahākshatrapa.[2]

The general importance of diplomacy may also be gauged from the fact that the study of *nītiśāstra* was considered obligatory to princes in this period. We have references to this in the inscriptions of Dekhan

[1] *Udghāṭapratiropitāh : Raghuvamśa*, IV.; *Allahabad Pillar Inscr.* of Samudragupta, Fleet : *Gupta Inscr.*, No. 1.

[2] Rapson : *Coin Catalogue.*

dynasties like the Gaṅgas and the Kadambas. One Gaṅga king prides himself on being a scholar and teacher of scientific and practical politics. Another comments upon Bhāravi's *Kirātārjunīya*. A third, as late as the tenth century, maintains this tradition of his family. The Kadamba king, Kākutsthavarman, is said to have brought round, by diplomacy, his *sāmantas* who could not be won over by any of the other expedients *(upāyas)*. His doctrine was that a state should be in a condition of constant preparedness for war, but should be reluctant to enter on actual hostilities.[1] Mahendravarman speaks of his father Siṁhavishṇu as having won kings over by diplomacy.[2]

The *Pañchatantra* opens with a story of how polity and diplomacy formed necessary items in the curricula of a prince's studies. It was to popularise the subject that the book was written in the form of stories. Similar motives of popularisation are traceable in the case of *Śukasaptati*, the *Vetāḷapañchaviṁśati*, the *Bṛhatkathā*, the *Daśakumāracharita* and other story books. At the same time there were precepts of polity taught in the form of poetical pieces like Bhartṛhari's *Nītiśataka* and in the form of *sūtras* like *Chāṇakyanīti* and *Bṛhaspati Sūtras*.

X

INFLUENCES OF THE FOREIGN DYNASTIES

It has been contended by some that the contact with Persia, and Persian rule in the Indus region, profoundly influenced Indian life and institutions.

[1] *Saktitrayopetamathāsanastham* : *Ep. Ind.*, Vol. VII, No. 5.
[2] *Nayavijitasamastasāmantamaṇḍalasya—Mattavilāsa*, p. 2.

Leaving aside the extravagant claims set up by Dr. Spooner, there is still a school which would trace to an Iranian source Aśoka's ideas of issuing proclamations to his subjects and inscribing them on rocks and pillars, like the Achæmenid kings. There is some justification for this view. V. A. Smith claims as Persian the *panchāyat* at Pāṭaliputra which may have had consular functions and certainly looked after foreigners, the system of hair-washing of the emperor, and the cropping of the hair as a penal measure. There is nothing to prove or to disprove this view. The attention to foreigners in a city is enjoined in many a *Sūtra* text, and some of these are accepted as of earlier date than the Maurya period. The main directions in which foreign influences are to be traced on the public life of India are social, economic and religious.

The crude punch-marked coins of India are apparently descended from the pre-historic seals of the Indus valley. The Greek contact with India improved our system of coinage and adapted it to the conditions of external commerce and internal trade. This is clear from the coins of Sophytes (Saubhūti). The silver coin of Kadphises II resembles the Indian *kārshāpaṇa* in weight (56½ grs. = 32 *rati*), and his head on the coins resembles that of Augustus. Coins of Kanishka are found as far away as Scandinavia and Wales,[1] and a silver coin of Huvishka agrees in weight with the Indo-Parthian silver.[2] The Kushāṇas adopted the Roman standard and re-coined the *aurei*. This resulted in the extension of Indian commercial

[1] *J.R.A.S.* for 1912.

[2] *Arch. Sur. Rep.* (W.C.) for 1915–16, p. 59.

activity to the remotest parts of Europe. The service of the Kshatrapas was in another direction. They put more of the precious metal in the coin *(kusana)*, possibly to restore the ratio of gold to silver in the currency. We find the *kusana* of Ushavadāta an eighth higher in value than the old *kārshāpaṇa*. Here was an attempt to purify the currency. The *kārshāpaṇa* shows alloy up to one-fifth.

Sophistication of the currency was unknown in India till she came into contact with the Greeks and the Parthians. Jaina traditions speak of Kauṭilya as making money by re-coining every *kārshāpaṇa* into eight. This was an expedient in times of stress, if the story is to be believed, for Kauṭilya allows alloy only to the extent of 31·25 per cent. There is evidence that when normal conditions were restored, the weight of the coin was pushed up to the standard by various devices. In the hoard of coins discovered by Walsh at Patna,[1] molten copper was added to the punch-marked surface to make up the lost weight.

The Græco-Bactrians of the Punjab used debasement of the currency as a financial expedient. They used copper pieces thickly coated with silver,[2] and they and the Indo-Parthians issued lead coins. The first lead coins of India are those of Strato, Azes and Rajubala. Lead coins were issued by the Indian dynasties of the Sātavāhanas and the Kadambas, apparently after the example of these foreign dynasties. In the latest (introductory) portion of the *Jātaka* literature we find mention of *sīsa kahapana* (lead *kārshāpaṇa*). The Greeks did not introduce the

[1] *J.B. & O.R.S.* for 1919. [2] *J.A.S.B.* for 1890.

drachma into India. That was the gift of the Gurjaras in the Gupta age.

In their currency arrangements the Gupta emperors followed local custom and usage. They struck gold coins in the Kushāṇa dominions, silver in the Kshatrapa, and copper in eastern Malwa. Samudragupta's earliest and commonest type of coins[1] closely resembles the Kushāṇa coins of eastern Punjab. On his conquest of Surāshṭra, Chandragupta II issued silver coins copied from the Kshatrapas. They show on *obverse* the king's head with Greek inscriptions surviving, and the date, and on *reverse* the *garuḍa* bird instead of the *chaitya.* Gold coins of Kumāragupta are rare, but the silver coinage was considerably extended, and the peacock replaces the *garuḍa* on the *reverse.*

The extent to which the foreign dynasties were indianised may be gauged even from their political systems approximating to the Indian and actuated by Indian conceptions. The Sanskrit inscription of Rudradāman at Junāgaḍh says that he provided the Girnar lake of Mauryan times with conduits, drains and provision against overflow.[2] The breach was 630 feet long and 108 feet deep, all the water escaped, and the lake became a bed of sand. The ministers in council and the executive despaired of healing the wide breach and objected to the work[3] being begun.

[1] The 'standard' type in Allen : *Gupta Coins.*

[2] *Suprativihitapraṇālīparivāhamīḍhāvidhānam.* Kielhorn (*Ep. Ind.*, Vol. VIII, p. 45) renders the last expression as 'provision against foul matter' on the strength of Prākrit passages. But *mīḍha* simply means 'raining in torrents' (Vedic *mīḍhush* means *varshaka* as in *T.S.*, IV, 5, 1), and naturally refers to the arrangements for conducting the surplus water away in times of excessive rain.

[3] *Pratyākhyātārambham.*

But Rudradāman persisted, upon the advice of his *Amātya*, the Pallava Suviśākha son of Kulaipa, spent his own money,[1] and pushed through the work expeditiously in the interests of the people, urban and rural (*paurajānapada*), of the province of Ānarta-Saurāshṭra. The inscription is interesting as showing that the framework of polity in the Kshatrapa country was Indian. We have *Karma-sachivas* and *Dharma-sachivas* among ministers, corresponding to the executive *Amātyas* and consultative *Mantrins* of the polity described by Kauṭilya. The sanction of the ministry was required for expenditure from public funds. The ideal of kingship implied in Rudradāman's titles and attributes is likewise Indian: the king set conquered princes back on their thrones,[2] as he followed the path of *dharma*, and saw to the safety of cows and Brāhmans. He would not oppress the people by taxes, forced gifts or impressed labour.[3] He took from his subjects only such revenues as accrued in the natural course of economic life.[4] He took his wife at *svayamvara*, i.e., such as chose him for husband of her own free will. His rule was for the protection of all the castes, and inaugurated a reign of peace as indicated by his coronation oath.[5]

[1] *Svasmāt kośāt mahatā dhanaughena.*

[2] *Bhrashṭarājapratishṭhāpaka.* [3] *Kara, vishṭi* and *praṇaya.*

[4] *Yathāvatprāptairbaliśulkabhāgaih.*

[5] *Purushavadhanivṛttikṛtasatyapratijña* (*Ep. Ind.*, VIII, No. 6).

CHAPTER V

TYPES AND SYSTEMS IN THE MIDDLE AGES

I

RAJPUT POLITY

RAJPUT kingship was patriarchal. The vassal chiefs claimed kinship with the Rāṇa. Prominent among these were sixteen, and every one of them was the master of his men. They had to attend the Court of their chief, and could not be absent without leave. They had to ride with him when he went out hunting, follow him to war, and accompany him to the Court of his Sovereign. If the chief's person was in danger, his men were to offer themselves as ransom for his release.[1] Devotion to the chief was stronger than loyalty to the Sovereign; Nimaj of Marwar laid down his life in fighting for his chief against the Sovereign. The chief of Deogarh sent one of his vassals to his king, who found favour at Court, but thereby offended his old master. The Sovereign was appealed to only in cases of oppression, for protection against injustice, or where the chief found a vassal refractory and overstrong. A good instance in point is the appeal to the Rāṇa by the Rāja of Bunera against the Rahtore Chief of Dabla.[2]

[1] Tod, Bk. III, Ch. 2. Crooke's Ed., p. 184.

[2] *Ibid*, p. 144. The Rajputs' reverence for hereditary right stands in contrast to the preference among their kinsmen, the Jāts, for elected headmen. Rajput polity is less democratic than the Jāt. (Qanungo: *History of the Jāts*, p. 4).

The Rāṇa's authority over the chieftains is clear from a charter, dated 1818, which is cited by Tod as it embodies ancient usage. His was the sole right to transit duties throughout the state. No chiefs were to commit deeds of violence within their estates. They were to entertain no *thugs*, thieves or robbers. All property stolen was to be made good by the proprietor of the estate concerned. Merchants were to be protected. The chiefs were to be in attendance on the Rāṇa regularly for three months each year, and during the Daśara festival, when the muster of all feudal retainers was taken by the Rāṇa in person, and honorary dignities were bestowed on them. They were also to wait upon him on urgent occasions whenever summoned. The vassals of each chief were to serve their immediate master, and the Rāṇa was to see that the dignities of each chief were maintained[1] according to his rank. But the tillers of the soil were not to be oppressed by exactions or arbitrary fines. The chiefs paid *nazar* at the accession of a Rāṇa, and a fee (*kaid*) on succeeding to their estate, when the grant was renewed.[2] Military service was to be rendered by every one of them when demanded, whether at home or abroad. Every one who got an annual rent of Rs. 1,000 had to furnish three horsemen. Failure entailed a heavy fine or confiscation of the estate, in whole or in part.

The Rāṇa was helped by four great officers of state. The *Pradhāna* was Prime Minister. He was in charge

[1] 'Government is only maintained by good feeling, and by respect for the various dignities of the state.'—(Al Maśudī in E. and D., Vol. I, p. 20).

[2] The Knight's fee of Mewar was about Rs. 250.

of all the territorial and financial arrangements, and of all the fourteen departments of expenditure. The *Bakshi's* duties were partly civil, partly military. The nobles assembled at his muster, and he paid for the extra services rendered by feudal tenants. His deputies were *Faujdārs* in military charge, and his four secretaries maintained records and registers of deeds and accounts. The *Suratnāma* was in charge of the household expenditure and establishments, of which daily accounts were maintained. The *Sahāi* was secretary, both for home and foreign affairs.

There were three kinds of protection against any abuse of power by these officers. The *Pradhāna* and the *Bakshi* belonged to non-militant tribes, and were chosen from different localities. All grants of money or land were to be signed by every minister. All the thirty-six *kārkūns* or superior officers were appointed direct by the Rāṇa, and had charge of the armoury, the regalia, the mint, the stables and other departments. The growth of ministerial power was sought to be prevented in these ways, but the central government was weakened by this very process, and the centrifugal forces asserted themselves whenever the Rāṇa's personality ceased to be a strong cementing influence.

The country was partitioned into districts of 50 or 100 villages each. Their classical number was eighty-four;[1] hence they were known as *chourasi*. The government of each district was under a civil and military officer. But the Lord of the Frontier was

[1] According to the bard, cited by Tod (Vol. I, pp. 348-9), Rāṇa Sangrāma was followed into the field by 7 Rājas, 9 Raos, and 104 Rāwal and Rāwat, who had mustered a force of 80,000 horse and 500 war elephants.

appointed direct from the court, and had judicial, military and civil functions. Theoretically the frontier chieftains were expected to attend his court, but in practice the higher vassals deputed a member of their family for this function. Every one of the 84 chieftains claimed the right of administering justice in his own domain, in civil matters. In criminal cases it required the special sanction of the Crown. But in practice, civil administration was largely in the hands of the panchāyats.

The chiefs were divided into distinct grades. First we have the sixteen, whose estates fetched an annual rental of more than 50,000 rupees. They appeared before the Rāṇa only when invited, and on occasions of festivals and ceremonies. They were the hereditary councillors of the Crown. The second class had incomes ranging from five to fifty thousand rupees. They were always in attendance, and the *Faujdārs* and military officers were selected from their number. The third class had incomes under Rs. 5,000 and were attached to the person of the Rāṇa, who used them against his over-grown vassals. The last class consisted of the off-shoots of the younger branches of the Rāṇa's family who had appanages bestowed on them.

In every Rajput state the Premier was the military minister, and civil administration was under a separate minister. The two, however, acted together in most cases. The Premier's post was hereditary,[1] though he could not usurp the throne, thanks to the law of succession. At Udaipur he was called the *Bhanjgurh*, and the place belonged to the Saloombra chief, who

[1] Noted by Al Maśudī (E. and D, Vol. I, p. 20).

was in charge of the palace and of the government, when the Rāṇa left the capital. The ministers of Mewar were mill-stones round the neck of their prince, who could not govern without their co-operation. In Kotah and Jasalmir the power of the minister was supreme.

Each chieftain was bound to respect the customs and privileges of the fief and the land-rights of his vassals. His *Faujdār* had to account for any robbery in his estate. He was to maintain a separate civic magistracy in each town consisting of the Chief Citizen (*Nagarseṭ*) and his four colleagues. He was to consult his vassals at a council on important matters, and to arrange that any crime committed by any of them was adjudged by four of his peers. He was to see that the local merchants kept the dams of lakes in proper condition.

The Rāṇa with the aid of his council, the four ministers, and their deputies promulgated all legislative enactments. The Rajput *Pradhānas* were tenacious of their rights. Judicial authority was wielded by rulers of districts as well as by a special officer at each frontier post (*thāna*). The last-named officer assembled the village jury or assessors in each village or town, who were elected by their fellow-citizens. The jury invariably included the *Paṭel* and *Paṭwāri*. Where there was delay in the execution of a decree, payment was collected by the *rozina* system, by which a force was stationed in the house of the debtor till the payment was made. Government officers seldom interfered with the working of the panchāyats.

'To be excluded from the Council of the Rāṇa is to be in utter disgrace. The Council of each Chief is a miniature representation of that of the Sovereign. The greater sub-vassals, his civil *Pradhāna*, the Mayor of the household, the *Purohita*, the bard and two or three of the most intelligent citizens form the minor Councils, and all are separately deliberating while the superior Court is in discussion. Thus is collected the wisdom of the magnates of Rājwarra.'[1]

There were some of the feudalistic incidents familiar to us in the history of mediæval Europe. The feudal *relief* was exacted at the rate of one year's revenue in Mewar. The estate was taken possession of as soon as a man died, and was again put in possession of his heir at an imposing ceremony. This resumption of the estate was clear in Mewar, but may have extended also to the adjoining parts of Rajputana. Tod draws this inference from the remonstrance of the vassals in Deogarh against the alienation of their sub-fees to strangers. The incident of *escheat* likewise existed, but it was mitigated by the practice of adoption. *Forfeitures* for crimes are illustrated in the annals of Marwar, where most of the fief-holders were exiles from their homes. Among the *aids*, the most important was that levied in Mewar, which amounted to an eighth at the marriage of every daughter. The war-tax could be taken on occasions when the head of the clan was in trouble. In Amber an *aid* was taken at the marriage of the heir-apparent (*Rājakumāra*). The gains from *wardship* were, as usual, abused; but a safeguard was provided against this abuse by custom, which regarded the mother as the natural guardian of the minor. She was helped by the elders of the family in bringing him up. The feudal

[1] Tod, Vol. I, p. 127.

incidents of *marriage* and *alienation* were altogether unknown in the Rajput system. In theory the grant of an estate was for the life of the holder, with the right of inheritance for his off-spring, whether in lineal descent or by adoption. It was resumable for crime or incapacity; but the resumption of an old established grant was rare in practice, and risky in most cases. There was a marked tendency to a minute subdivision of holdings on account of the Hindu principle of heredity, re-inforced by that of adoption.

It is clear that Rajput polity was based on military considerations, and approached in some respects the feudalism of mediæval Europe. This is shown by the liability to military service, to attendance at the lord's Court and Durbar, and to *relief*, fines, and contributions towards marriage expenses. But Tod draws the comparison too close. The right of adoption was an ancient Hindu right of the childless man as well as of his widow, and could not be denied. This served as a protection against the abuse of the feudal right of wardship. The right of marrying a minor to whomever he chose pertained to the feudal lord in Europe, but was unthinkable in the Indian social system. On the other hand, the liability to military service was extended in India, whereas in Europe it meant merely an obligation to follow the lord in war. Another essential point of difference was that local customs were respected, and local self-governing institutions like the panchāyat were retained, even in feudal demesnes. There was also a body of agricultural tenants who held their lands on other than this sort of feudal tenure. We are no doubt reminded of the socage tenants of mediæval England, but these were swept away by the tendency to make tenures uniform after the Norman Conquest. The conservative spirit of India was a safeguard against such a culmination.

Rajput genius gave a military colour to Indian polity which had become mild and pacific and was wanting in virility and power. The paintings of the period give us a picture of society 'simple, aristocratic, generous and self-sufficient.'[1] Rajput ideas of chivalry and *jauhar*, the emphasis on forts, and the general clannish feeling among the tribes, had a reaction on polity. But the forces of gravitation in the Rajput state tended to shift from the centre to the circumference, and this facilitated the piecemeal conquest of India by Muhammadan invaders.

II

AFGHAN POLITY

During the period of Afghan rule there was a new form of Government at Delhi. The Afghan king was an autocrat, but the autocracy was tempered by political difficulties. There was no principle of primogeniture, and no settled scheme of succession. The kings were placed between two grindstones—invasions from without, and revolts within. The times, therefore, demanded a government efficient as well as popular. During the formative period of the Delhi Sultanate, succession to the crown passed from a Slave king to the ablest of his slaves. Absence of hereditary

[1] This is clear 'from these heads, so severe, so confidently poised, from these sensitive, expressive hands, these white and gold and coloured muslins.' (A. Coomaraswamy: *Rajput Art*, Vol. I, p. 15).

succession led to a struggle for the throne and the survival of the fittest among the candidates.

Every subject had the right of petition to the king, and the right of appeal too. Ahmad tells us that Muhammad-Ibn-Taghlak gave audience twice a day, served a repast for 20,000 men, and had talks with 200 learned men at every meal.[1] The political principle was thus established, of the king's coming into direct touch with public feeling and with the opinions of the learned. Another principle was the differentiation of the king's privy purse from the state revenue. Nasir-ud-din lived on the sale of copies of the *Koran*, of which two were made every year, and Zain-ul-Abidin of Kashmir was satisfied with the produce of the royal mines. Balban advised his son to use public money only for purposes of administration and religion. Lastly, the emperor personally supervised the work of his officers. Firuz Shah was addicted to drink, and the government was actually in the hands of a Hindu minister converted to Islam. The efficiency of government was at its best under Sher Shah, during the declining period of Afghan rule. He got up at 2 a.m. and his daily routine shows a strenuous life. His maxims also are noble: 'it behoves the great to be always working,' 'justice is the most excellent of sacred rites,' 'a king should not have corrupt *Vakīls* or *Vazīrs*.'[2]

Central Government

The central administration was modelled on the Persian in civil government, and on the Turkish in

[1] Shahabuddin Ahmad, cited in Elliot and Dowson: *History of India*, Vol. III, p. 579.

[2] Elliot and Dowson, Vol. IV, pp. 314, 409.

military. The Council was entirely consultative. There were four departments[1]: those of revenue, commerce, war and general administration in the order of importance.

The officers were paid in cash. Ala-ad-din condemned the system of paying public servants by grants of land, on the ground that it might promote feudalistic tendencies to rebellion. But Firuz Shah assigned posts to eminent nobles for defending the frontiers or managing the internal affairs. This hastened the disintegration of the kingdom, though the Sultan tried to purify the administration by forbidding presents being brought by the nobles, and by paying them for every present already brought by them.

Hindus were appointed to offices only in the lower ranks of the administration, but not in the central government at Delhi. Association of Hindus with the central administration was a feature not of the Sultanate but of the kingdoms into which it broke up: 'It is generally believed that Gangoo was the first Brāhman who accepted office in the service of a Muhammadan prince, before whose time the Brāhmans were never engaged in public affairs . . . . conceiving the service of princes as destructive of virtue . . . . They never consented to wear the chain of servitude, though courted by gifts and promised the highest distinctions. Since Gangoo's acceptance of employment, however, the management of the

[1] There were two well-organised departments in the 13th century—the Exchequer and the Army. The Intelligence department was founded by Balban and perfected by Ala-ad-din. Firuz Shah's *Vazīr* controlled the Mint, Public Works and Industries. (E. and D., Vol. III, pp. 355, 357–359).

revenue has been committed generally to the Brāhmans by all the princes of the Dekhan.'[1]

Of the officers of state those of the highest rank were called *Khāns*. Then came the *Māliks*, *Amīrs*, generals (*Isfah-salārs*) and lastly the officers (*gend*). There were 80 *Khāns* and 900,000 horsemen consisting of Turks, Persians and Indians. A feature of the administration was the existence of a large number of slaves, as many as 20,000 at Delhi alone. The *Khān* was commander of 10,000 horse, *Mālik* of 1,000, *Amīr* of 100, and *Isfah-salār* of a smaller number. They received from the state salaries of two lakhs of *taṅkas*, sixty to fifty thousand, forty to thirty thousand, and twenty thousand respectively. Civil officers got salaries ranging from 1,000 to 10,000. Soldiers received their pay in money, but their officers had villages of which they received the revenue.

The chief minister of the Sultan was the *Naib* or *Amriya*, who had a large province as his official appanage. There was also a *Vazīr*. Four Deputy *Vazīrs* were in charge of the departments of state, and got salary in cash ranging from 20,000 to 40,000 *taṅkas*. But the four *Dabīrs*, or secretaries to the *Vazīr*, each got the revenue of a large maritime town. Each secretary had under him 300 clerks. The Chief Justice was known as *Sadr-i-Jahan* and received the revenue of ten towns, about 800 *taṅkas*. The *Shaikh-ul-Islam* was in charge of *Fakirs* and had the revenue of ten villages. The *Sadr* had the learned men in his charge and there were 1,200 physicians, 10,000 falconers, 1,200 musicians and 1,000 poets.

[1] Ferishta: Briggs' trans., II, p. 292.

The officers were consulted in a sort of Council.[1] Though they had no right to be consulted, a convention had grown up to the effect. There was no constitution, the emperor summoning such officers as he liked. The meetings were secret, and the deliberations not open to the public. The initiative on all matters rested with the emperor. There appears to have been a free and frank statement of opinion on those matters in regard to which the Sultan had not previously made up his mind. The decision of the emperor was given then and there, before the Council dispersed. There were, besides, social gatherings of the senior officers and of such others as might be invited, which enabled the Sultan to know their opinions in an informal way. The imperial Court or Durbar (*Bar-i-am*) was a public assembly at which all could lay their complaints before the Sultan. Here every kind of public business was transacted. Appeals from the *Kāzi's* Court went to the Sultan, and he examined witnesses when necessary. Judgment was speedily delivered, and the sentence carried out, especially in criminal cases. The sittings were long and tiresome.

As regards the confidential ministry, its members were different from the courtiers and favourites, and were not in too intimate relations with the Sultan. Even the *Vazīr* was not regarded as much above the others. The advice of Bughra Khān to Kaikubād shows this: 'Keep all the four equally near to yourself, and make them your advisers in all political

[1] Sher Shah's ministers were mere Secretaries, who rendered accounts and made reports every day, and recorded the orders of the emperor for future guidance. (E. and D., Vol. IV, p. 410).

affairs of which they know the difficulties and dangers. Do not throw the business of the government into disorder by entrusting everything to one man. Do not let any one of your ministers or courtiers have too much influence over yourself or the administration. Further, every scheme you may have thought of, and every order you pass concerning the business of any of the ministers, and all confidential secrets of the state, must be discussed in the presence of all the four ministers. Though the position of the *Vazīr* is higher than that of other ministers, it will not be prudent for you to favour any of the four pillars of your kingdom to such an extent as to wound the feelings of others and to alienate their hearts.'[1]

The government of the Dekhan was similarly organised by the Bāhmani Sultans. Muhammad I had eight ministers. At their head was the *Vakīl* or Sultan's lieutenant in all matters, and with him was associated a *Pīshva.* Next came the *Vazīrs*, one in charge of the internal and the other of foreign affairs. Then came the *Amīr* in charge of finance (*Jumla*), and his assistant the *Nāzir.* Lastly we have the *Kotwāl*, the Magistrate and Police Superintendent, and the *Sadr*, who was in charge of the departments of Justice and Religion.

Provincial and Local Administration

Every old kingdom absorbed in the expanding Sultanate of Delhi became the nucleus of a province, and there was a tendency to the subdivision of provinces as time went on. Muhammad-Ibn-Taghlak

[1] Habib in *Pro. of the 3rd Or. Conf.* (1925).

ruled over twenty-five provinces. The Bāhmini Sultanate had four, but Firuz constituted the Raichur Doab into an additional province, and Muhammad Gawan split up every one of the old four provinces into two. The powers of the governor were reduced further by withdrawing from his jurisdiction the *parganas* where there were state lands and by the central government's assuming direct control of the military appointments. Each governor was ranked as a Commander of 2,000 horse and got about four lakhs of rupees, which was raised by Gawan to five lakhs; but the increase in pay was not appreciated, as the inspection and control—now introduced—deprived the governor of his customary illicit gains. Both in Delhi and in the Dekhan the provincial governors laughed at control, and the tendency to decentralisation and dismemberment proved irresistible.

The Indian village system was retained, and life in the village was allowed to run its usual course. But the work of collecting the land-tax was entrusted to *Amīls* appointed and dismissed by the Revenue Office. The *Paṭwāri* had to send to the Central Revenue Office an account of the tax paid in cash or kind, and another statement was received from the *Amīls*. The governor of the province had to send a consolidated statement. These three were compared. But the Afghan rulers did not care very much for village administration. Whenever they did, like Zain-ul-Abidin of Kashmir, it was in the direction of extending irrigation facilities to the remotest villages, and of enforcing the joint responsibility of villagers for thefts and robberies committed within the borders of the village.

Public Finance

The most important department of administration was that of revenue, and land tax was the principal source of revenue. During the thirteenth century the revenue was realised direct from the headman and from local chieftains, who were allowed a commission on the collection. But discipline could not be enforced nor taxes collected in the reign of Ala-ad-din Khalji. Hence his appointment of *Amīls.* There was no classification of lands, and the state demand is estimated by Barani at one-half, whether of the gross or of the net produce. The state department of agriculture tried to improve the yield, thus increasing the revenue. The most important of these improvements are associated with Firuz Shah who is credited with 845 public works including canals, dams, reservoirs, bridges, baths, forts, mosques, colleges, inns and monasteries. Roads are conspicuous by absence. He cut the famous double system of canals from the Jumna and the Sutlej, which supplied water for irrigation, the canal which now brings water to Delhi and irrigates about 200 miles, giving the people two harvests instead of one. He imposed a water-rate of ten per cent., which brought the state a revenue of three lakhs a year.

Sher Shah introduced the system of measuring the land and taking a third of the gross produce. He gave the cultivators the right of choice as to the mode of payment of the revenue. Some of the headmen asked for written engagements for a fixed money rent. Others preferred payment in kind. Sher Shah fixed the payment in every case so that there might be no oppressions or exactions.

The Afghan kings tried to control the economic operations in the state. Ala-ad-din introduced some regulations for the fixing of prices.[1] He forbade regrading and engrossing of supplies. Corn was to be sold in the fields. In times of drought people were to buy only according to their needs. A daily report of prices was to be sent to the Sultan. There was an Inspector of the grain-market. Piece-goods were to be sold only in a special building erected for the purpose and at the fixed rates, and licence was to be purchased for selling fine pieces. The Sultan is said to have fixed the prices of even needles, combs and shoes, earthen pitchers and cups. Brokers were forbidden to trade in horses. At the same time, trade was encouraged in articles that were necessaries of life, and money was advanced to merchants to buy goods abroad. This principle of price-regulation continued in later reigns. Afif notes that under Firuz Shah 'orders were given for the reduction of the price of sweetmeat in unison with the general fall of prices.'

Muhammad-Ibn-Taghlak's currency experiments are well-known. But his currency regulations also are interesting. His mintages 'are instructive both in the novelty and variety of their types, admirable in the artistic perfection of their design and execution, and especially significant in their reflex of the individuality of the monarch himself, marking, as they do, the various phases of his career—his early wealth and reckless profusion, its resulting poverty, which he attempted to meet by a forced currency, and equally

[1] Ahmad : *Tabakat-i-Akbari* (Trans.), p. 175.

his ready return to money payments on its ascertained failure.'[1] He tried so to control the currency as to retain its bimetallic character. As a result of his campaigns in the Dekhan he got large quantities of gold, and there was a fall in the silver value of gold. He therefore issued a gold *dinār* at a weight of 200 grains, and a silver coin of 140 grs. The latest of these issues belongs to 729 A.H. when the old *tanka* was revived (175 grs.) and heavy coins of mixed metal (140 grs.) were issued.

The greatest achievement of the Sultans of Delhi was the provision of a suitable system of currency. Altamish issued copper coins of minute weight, some weighing only 10 grs., for the requirements of retail trade. His early coins were continuations of those of Muhammad of Ghor, who had issued coins on indigenous lines. His silver *tankas* were 175 grs. in weight and, remodelled by Sher Shah and Akbar, became the ancestor of the modern rupee. But fractions of the silver *tanka* of his time are rare. Under his successors we have a few anna-pieces, two-anna pieces, and half-rupee pieces. Altamish's only gold coin weighs 70 grs. Balban supplied the required amount in this direction, and his gold *tanka* became the standard later. Ala-ad-din Khalji calls himself on his *tankas* 'the second Alexander.' He struck a few square gold coins. The coins of Devagiri in South India also appear now for the first time. Muhammad-Ibn-Taghlak captured Warrangal and made it a mint town. The finest coins of the period are those of Mubarak Khalji who proclaims himself the 'Supreme Head of

[1] Thomas: *Chronicles of the Pathan kings*, and H. N. Wright: *Catalogue of Coins in the Indian Museum, Calcutta*, Vol. II, Pt. 1.

the religion of Islam,' thus realising the abandoned ideal of his father, and anticipating Akbar. The weakening of the force of Islam is illustrated also in Sikandar Lodi's shaving his beard. Sikandar Lodi artificially brought the prices down by reducing the demand for currency. He ordered that nothing but corn should be taken as rent. Gold and silver were dear, and prices and wages low. One *buhloli* of 145 grs. could purchase 10 mds. of corn, five seers of ghee and 10 yds. of cloth; and a single *buhloli* could take a man, horse and guide from Delhi to Agra.

Conditions of insecurity during the period led to a great deal being hoarded. An earthen jar of 500 gold mohurs was unearthed in the reign of Sikandar. These were coins of Ala-ad-din Khalji. The treasure-trove was left to the finder, as a rule.

Sher Shah systematised the revenue and fiscal departments, and thoroughly reformed the coinage.[1] The mixed-metal currency preserved from Muhammad I's time, disappears now. The *dām* is issued with its subdivisions of $\frac{1}{2}$, $\frac{1}{4}$, $\frac{1}{8}$ and $\frac{1}{16}$. The silver *tanka* was altered in weight and given a wider circulation. Its weight was probably 180 grs., more or less the same as the *tōla* of to-day. Sher Shah also developed largely the custom of establishing mints at the more important centres in his dominions.

Under Firuz Shah Taghlak there was a unique experiment for solving the problem of unemployment. The Sultan had a large number of men employed on his own reproductive public works, such as canals, reservoirs, bridges and gardens. He sent the unemployed round to his nobility, who had to provide work

[1] Thomas: *op. cit.*, p. 392.

for a certain number of them. Some were employed on the estates, some in the army, and some in the mechanical trades. We are told that 12,000 were employed as artisans at Delhi. Our chronicles call them slaves, which probably means only that they were entirely dependent on the government. Sher Shah gave stipends to widows, the sick and the infirm, the old and the destitute, from the treasury of the adjoining town. This primitive poor-law experiment was, however, given up after his time.

Defence

The rule of the Afghan kings witnessed at least one experiment in the problem of defence. This is associated with Balban whose policy was to organise a province on the vulnerable north-west frontier. The frontier provinces and tribes were kept in order, and their military incursions kept in check by the imperial army under the king's cousin Sher Khan. The arrangement was premature, as it placed too much power in the hands of this governor, who wielded almost royal authority and had to be removed by poison. But the experiment is an interesting one. It was repeated in Akbar's time by Todar Mal in Baluchistan, anticipating the formation of the North-West Frontier Province under Lord Curzon.

The military arrangements were based on the Turkish system. There was no Commander-in-Chief in general: one was appointed for every occasion. The War Minister was in charge of the organisation, and sometimes, of the discipline in the army, but he was not necessarily great as soldier and general. The horsemen were paid by the state, and there was an annual review of the forces. There was foul play and dishonesty in the muster, and the Sultans of Delhi introduced the system of branding horses. It is found mentioned in the times of Mahmud of Ghazni, Ala-ad-din Khalji and Sher Shah. The branded horses belonged to the state and were paid for in cash. The state army, whether in the capital or with the nobility in the provinces, was under the War Minister. The old custom was that, in war, four-fifths of the spoils went to the army and one-fifth to the state. Now that the troops were paid by the state and got fixed salaries, this custom was discontinued.

Justice

The Afghan government was remarkable for dispensing speedy justice. Conspiracy against the king, and disobedience to state orders were the highest political offences and were visited with capital punishment. The *Kāzis*, of whom there was one at the capital and one in every large city and town, acted as judges and Justices of the Peace. They were appointed for life, heard parties and witnesses, and pronounced decisions on the spot. Early in this period they were independent of the state. They were the sole exponents of the law, as there were no lawyers. Ala-ad-din Khalji invaded the independence of the judiciary, and his successors[1]

[1] Except Sikander, whose chief justice was styled *Mir-i-Adil* (Ahmad : *Tabakat-i-Akbari*, (Text), p. 173).

went further in this direction. The Islamic system required revision, especially in the department of criminal law. The emperors had Hindu pandits to advise them on questions of Hindu law. In the villages they retained the Panchāyat, subject to an appeal to the provincial governor.

Judicial power seems to have been wielded fairly by the Sultans. Many of them had a name for the prompt and impartial administration of justice. It has been said of Sikandar Lodi that 'so strict was he that no man could even look sternly at another.' His *Vakīl* remained all day at the seat of justice, and the *Kāzi* with twelve of the *Ulema*, was always present at the king's palace. 'All cases brought before the Court of Law were tried before these 12 wise men who decided them and wrote out decisions, of the nature of which the Sultan received immediate information. He insisted on speedy justice.'[1]

Sher Shah enforced the old principle of responsibility for thefts and robberies as well as for murder. Thieves and robbers were to be traced by the *Mukkadams* of the surrounding villages, who were compelled to make the losses good. Similarly in cases of murder, the *Mukkadam* of the village was hanged if the culprit was not found: 'for it has been generally ascertained that thefts and highway robberies can only take place by the connivance of these headmen.' The *Tarikh-i-Daudi* mentions two instances—the theft of a horse from the Sultan's camp at Thaneswar, and a murder near Etawa. Of course, a culprit was soon found in each case!

[1] *Tarikh-i-Daudi* in Elliot and Dowson, Vol. III, p. 454.

III

SOCIO-POLITICAL RELATIONS

There is some exaggeration of the tyranny and exclusiveness of the Muhammadans of Delhi. Lane-Poole quotes Barani's *Tarikh-i-Firuz-Shahi* to the effect that Firuz Shah 'sternly forbade public worship, whether of idols or of portraits, and introduced the system of taxing the Brăhmans.' The Muhammadan tax-gatherer is said to have had so much authority that 'if he asked the Hindu to open his mouth to spit into, the latter had to submit to it meekly and promptly.' Ala-ad-din Khalji is described by Barani as having persecuted his Hindu subjects so badly, that they were taxed to the extent of 50 per cent of the gross produce, that no gold or silver or even betelnut was seen in Hindu families, and that even wives of native officials had to take service in Muslim families.

In the first place, these oppressions were not confined to the Hindus, even according to the chroniclers. Among the Islamites there were divisions like Sunni and Shiah, the Deccani and the foreigner, which were at war with one another. The political difficulties of the Sultans further embittered sectarian differences. Barani says that Ala-ad-din used poison to get rid of the suspected nobles, and punished brutally the wives and children of those who had caused disturbances. So repressive were his measures that even convivial gatherings were forbidden, and hospitality fell into disuse. The system of espionage was so universal that even bargains in the bazaar were kept under control. Secondly, some of the rulers had as ministers Hindus converted to Islam, who did not give up relations with their kith and kin. Firuz Shah's mother was a Rajput princess Bibi Naila, daughter of Rāṇa Māl Bhaṭṭi, who married Rajāb the younger brother of Ghiaz-ad-din Taghlak to save the Rajputs from the threat fulminated by him as the Warden of the Marches. The prosperity of Firuz Shah's reign was due to his minister Makbul Khan, a Hindu converted to Islam.

Thirdly, there were social relations between Hindus and Mussalmans, and these reacted on the sphere of politics. Even Mahmud the Iconoclast maintained a corps of Hindu horse. Perhaps the first Hindu in high office was Tilak, son of Jayasena, employed by Mahsud of Ghazni in equal rank with his Muslim nobles. Muhammad of Ghor allied himself with the Hindu Rāja of Jammu against the Muslim Malik of Lahore, and employed Hindu legends on his coinage. Balban's nephew and other nobles had Hindi nicknames. A Hindu named Ratna occupied a high position under Muhammad Taghlak, like the Brāhman astronomer Gaṅgu.[1] Firuz Shah arranged for the translation of Hindu books into Persian. The *Mahābhārata* was translated into Persian by order of Hussain Shah and Nusrat Shah of Bengal. Fourthly, village administration, revenue and judicial, was entirely in Hindu hands. Muslim nobles were not allowed to plunder the Hindus or to withhold from them their just dues.

[1] See p. 147 *supra*. Sir Wolseley Haig (*Camb. Hist. of India*, III, p. 170*n*.) disbelieves Ferishta's 'absurd' legend to this effect, but without proper reasons. Ferishta was by no means well disposed towards the Hindus, and had to record the tradition about the Brāhman ministers because it was universally believed and had become incontrovertible. It accounts for the surname *Gaṅgu*.

Muhammadans adopted Hindu customs in the reign of Firuz Shah. The emperor had to suppress the *tāntric* practice of drinking and promiscuity, characterising the nocturnal intercourse of Hindus and Mussalmans in some places. In one instance Muhammadan women worshipped Hindu idols, and Firuz Shah ordered the Brāhman in charge to be hanged, and the wooden tablet covered with images to be destroyed. Muhammadan women followed the example of their Hindu sisters, and went out of cities in large parties, on pilgrimages to tombs, on foot and on horse-back. Firuz Shah sought to suppress these practices. A son of the Governor of Lucknow was accused of becoming a convert to Hindu doctrines. Poets like Amīr Khusru were ardent admirers of Hindu philosophy and learning, and not merely of Hindu fables like the *Kalīlah* and *Dimnah*, which were circulated in their Persian translations. Music formed the bond of friendship between the Muhammadan king of Kashmir and the Hindu Rāja of Gwalior. Sūfism, re-inforced by Hindu Vedānta, gave rise to the *Mahdi* movement. Even in Firuz Shah's reign *Mahdis* appeared in Gujarat, and one of them wrote a book which was promptly burnt under the Sultan's orders.

Such influences were the natural results of social intercourse and could not be extinguished by political authority. The practices appear again under Sikandar Lodi, in whose reign a holy Mussalman protested publicly against the Sultan's interference with the religion of his Hindu subjects. This was not the only instance. When a Brāhman claimed equality for all religions, the *Kāzis* of Lucknow were divided as to

11

his guilt. Mussalman poets enriched the Vaishṇava literature of Bengal, and Afghan art in the 15th century is redolent of Hindu influences in many minute details. On the Mussalman side, we have the prominence of the *Nūr Bakshis*, who considered the path of devotion as much more important than adherence to the Law of the Prophet. Hindus as well as Mussalmans formed the following of the *Pachapiriyas*, a sect which claims to date from a nephew of Mahmud of Ghazni.[1] On the Hindu side, we have the formation of the schools of *bhakti* in Kashmir and Bengal, which culminated in Lallā, Kabīr and Chaitanya.

The Time-Spirit influenced some of the Mussalman rulers of India. Zain-ul-Abidin of Kashmir (1420-70) deserves special mention. He loved the society of Hindus of learning and culture, restored temples, abolished the *jiziya*, restored those exiled by fanaticism, and ordered a translation of the *Mahābhārata* into Persian. Sher Shah's arrangements in every *sarai* show regard for the convenience of the Hindus, who were assigned separate lodgings. Brāhmans were settled there, to entertain them and provide hot or cold water, food and other conveniences. We learn from inscriptions that there were separate wells for the use of Hindus, as well as for Mussalmans.

IV

SOUTH INDIAN POLITY

The political traditions of the Kadambas, Gaṅgas, Chāḷukyas and Rāshṭrakūṭas are found preserved

[1] Elliot and Dowson, Vol. II, p. 513 ff.

in the polity of the Hoysaḷas. The king's powers were limited by the Council of five ministers (*Pañcha-Pradhāna*). This Council carried on the administration during the minority of kings like Narasiṁha I. Ministership was hereditary except in the case of these five. Foremost among the latter was the *Yuvarāja*, who sometimes had a province in his independent charge, and sometimes acted as viceroy. The queen also held political power, and appeared by the side of the king at Durbar. An interesting frieze of Vishṇuvardhana's Durbar, the queen sitting by the side of the king and his ministers, appears in front of the Beḷūr temple. Another queen, Bammaḷādevī, was ruling over a district or *nāḍu*. Umādevī the queen of Ballāḷa II took part in expeditions, and regulated temple administration.[1] There was a minister of public benefactions, a master of diplomacy, a royal Steward and some sort of 'minister of labour.'[2]

The officers of state were differentiated from those of the palace. But sometimes there were transfers from one department to another. The *Mahāpāsāyita* of the palace is thus found governing different parts of the country. The other officers of the palace were the Chamberlain, the Durbar Bakshi, the Betel-carrier, the Secretary and the Treasurer.[3]

The Council of ministers (*amātyas*) was recruited entirely by merit, and membership was for life.

[1] *Mys. Arch. Rep.*, 1926.

[2] These were in order :—*Lokopakārakaraṇa*, *Tantrādhikāri*, *Chaturvidhapraṇītantīti Chāṇakyatantrādhikāri*, *Mane Heggaḍe*, and *Bahaṭṭāraniyogādhikāri*.

[3] The names of these are given as :—*Padiyāra*, *Sajje-Vaḷḷa*, *Haḍapada*, *Mantri* and *Nidhikāra*.

There were the Minister of Diplomacy, the Finance Minister, the Army General, the Keeper of the King's Seal and the Chief Officer of the Palace. Probably, the ministers were consulted individually by the king, but we have also instances of their settling matters in Council, as in A.D. 1182. They sat with the king as the highest Court of Justice, and accompanied him on his tours and expeditions. The power of the Council weakened in the thirteenth century, when the military officers about the person of the king were his actual advisers.

It is difficult to estimate the relative importance of the five ministers even in the earlier period. Their functions were not always clearly differentiated. In the 13th century there are several instances of combination of offices. Sometimes titles like *Sarvādhikāri* or *Daṇḍanāyaka* were bestowed on officers of merit, and did not denote any political authority.

The provincial government was organised on the usual lines. Some governors were hereditary *Sāmantas*, others were appointed by the king. The Hoysaḷas continued the Chāḷukyan system of having a Superintendent over the feudatories,[1] who was an influential officer especially on the northern frontier as the local Chōḷa chieftains were retained in their former places. The governors were transferred from one important charge or province to another. But this system was given up in the 13th century, and the provincial governors tended to become independent of the central power.

1. In a record of 1192 he is styled *Manneya Mahāsāmantara Ādhishṭhayahāra*.

Every governor was the head of both the civil and military departments, and he had a permanent body of troops under him (*paḍai*). He was responsible for the collection of taxes and for the administration of justice; but he could not make remissions of revenue without the consent of the king.

Districts were in charge of *Heggaḍes*, who likewise combined civil, military and judicial functions. But in financial matters they were subject to the control of the *Śrīkaraṇa Sarvādhikāri*[1] or Accountant-General. Special officers collected particular taxes in the tracts which were not given exemptions. Each of these financial *Heggaḍes* had an accountant under him. Similarly the officers in charge of forts and military stations were in command of forces, which were under the control of the *Daṇḍanāyaka* of the Central government. The forces of the time consisted of cavalry, infantry and elephants. The elephants formed a very important part of the army, and they were given special training in killing warriors, being made to trample under foot stuffed objects of human shape. The leader of the elephants was *Gajasāhani*. As elephants were captured in the country, every chieftain was required to maintain a number of them. Sometimes villages were assigned to chieftains in perpetuity for the purpose. Horses were mostly imported by sea. The Hoysaḷa king enlisted local robber tribes of the Bēḍas in the army. But the army contained men of all castes including goldsmiths and barbers. Sometimes there were caste contingents separately organised. Some of the *Daṇḍanāyakas* were Brāhmans. Many of the men swore to die with their master in

[1] Śrīkaraṇada Heggaḍe—*Mys. Arch. Rep.*, 1912, p. 43; 1913, p. 37.

the field or to accompany him on the funeral pyre. These were known as *garuḍas.*[1] When Ballāḷa II died, one thousand *garuḍas* died with him. This practice was apparently discontinued under Vishṇuvardhana, some of whose *garuḍas* are seen holding places after his death.

Each village had its assembly, meeting in the temple or elsewhere. The assembly had the right of purchasing or selling lands, granting remissions of revenue and arranging for the administration of village affairs. Its governing body (*Mahāsabhā*) had the power of taking or granting loans and making free gifts of land for public work done (*koḍige*), for menial services rendered (*umbaḷi*), or for safeguarding the properties of the villagers (*gauḍike*). The assembly levied taxes such as *bittuvaṭṭa* (on every unit of seed sown), *talārike* (watchman's fees), and *kasaruvaṇa* (tax on silt).

The *Gauḍa* or *Masaveggaḍe* was the head of the village, and his assistant was the *Sēnabōva.* The watchman or *Talayāra* was appointed by the king in the case of important towns. Among the other officers of the town the most important was the Mayor (*paṭṭaṇaswāmi*), one of the foremost merchants.[2]

The *Gauḍas* of a particular locality were members of the *nāḍu* or assembly of the division, and were known as the *nāḍu-Gauḍas.* The *nāḍus* which were of commercial importance included the representatives of guilds (*samayas*), of which 18 are mentioned in many records. The president of the *nāḍu*

[1] Compare the *Vēḷaikkāṟas* of the Tamil inscriptions and the *Chāvēr* of Malayāḷam. The practice is referred to by Abu Zaid (E. & D., I., p. 9).
[2] *Ep. Car.*, II, No. 407.

assembly was the *nāḍu-Prabhu* or *Nāyaka* who had a *nāḍu-Sēnabōva* as assistant. The officers were paid by hereditary gifts of land (*koḍige*). The main function of the *nāḍu* assembly was to settle boundary disputes between villages.

V

VIJAYANAGARA POLITY

The emperors of Vijayanagara based their polity on the model of the Hoysaḷas and the Kākatīyas. The king was absolute, but his power was practically limited by military necessities, which brought rising generals into prominence and led to the foundation of hereditary offices. We thus have the rise of the Sāḷuvas under the first dynasty of Vijayanagar, and of the Tuḷuvas under the first and second dynasties. Even during the reigns of powerful kings like Devarāya II much power was wielded in practice by ministers like Lakkaṇṇa Daṇḍanāyaka. Early in the 16th century the minister Sāḷuva Timma appears as king-maker, and towards the end of the century the do-nothing king Sadāśiva was superseded by the three brother-ministers, who were in charge of the Army, of Justice and of Finance.

The provincial system of Vijayanagara discloses some new features. Nuniz [1] says that the provincial governors farmed the revenue to their own advantage, paying a fixed sum every year to the king; and that the king had no Comptroller of the revenues, or other officers of the state or of the household. The provincial governor had to give a third of the collections to the king. He could keep the two-thirds for his

[1] Sewell : *Forgotten Empire*, pp. 384–90.

expenses, including the maintenance of a body of horse, elephants and infantry, which he had to keep in readiness for the use of the state. He made extra profits by maintaining a smaller number than was required. In this way the provincial governors grew very rich. But Nuniz adds that their property could be confiscated by the state. They rendered their accounts during *Dasarā*, and paid the amounts due from them. The provinces were arranged in different sizes and according to no definite system, if Nuniz's account can be believed. But we know from the inscriptions that the older kingdoms within the empire were retained in their integrity, and placed in charge of viceroys who were related to the emperor. The provinces detailed by Nuniz were in charge of ministers or advisers of the emperor, who were not necessarily next of kin to him. Some of them had territory scattered over various parts. Timmappa is described as the Lord of the cities of Udayagiri (Nellore), Koṇḍavīḍu, Penukoṇḍa (Anantapur), of some cities in Orissa and some near Cape Comorin. Similarly Sāḷuva Nāyaka was lord of the Coromandel Coast, Negapatam, Tanjore and Quilon. It is not easy to reconcile these statements unless they be taken as denoting that the former viceroy had the Telugu country in addition to the sea-coast as far as the Cape, and the latter viceroy all the fertile Tamil districts in the interior. If so, the arrangement would seem to be due to the emperor's desire to prevent either of them from becoming too powerful, as these were the foremost of the governors in charge of provinces. The other governors were those of Goa and the neighbouring lands, Bankapur and the interior Kannaḍa districts, the lands round about the capital, the western Kannaḍa country, Mysore, Malabar, Gutti, and the northern province adjoining Bijapur. The governors were of different ranks. The first class had a large province yielding 3 lakhs, and the other provinces whose revenues ranged from 2 lakhs to 15 thousand rupees.

The description of Goa by Mexia shows how the local government worked during the period. The 31 villages comprising that territory were self-governing institutions, and the ancient usages were allowed to prevail until Goa became a city under the Portuguese. In the empire of Vijayanagar attention was concentrated on villages. The empire of Pulakeśin II, according to Yuan Chwang, consisted of 99,000 villages. The empire of Sadāśiva Rāya had 126,000.[1] It was the aim of the later emperors to induce people to remain on the land, by remissions of various kinds of taxes—such as those on marriages, on music and on Brāhmans. Special encouragements were given to settlers in new tracts and in depopulated villages.[2] But there were also some instances of sales of villages for non-payment of taxes.

The system of taxation is described in detail in the inscriptions. The land tax was based on a classification of lands according to the nature of the dues to the state, as well as according to fertility and the estimated produce. Numerous exemptions were given when the produce suffered damages in the course of cultivation or the harvest. The assessment on dry land is estimated at 85 per cent. of that on wet land, in the Tamil districts of the empire,[3] which

[1] *Ep. Car.*, Vol. vii, Ci. 62. [2] *Ep. Car.*, Vol. xi, Hk. 112.
[3] *Mad. Ep. Rep.* for 1914, No. 59.

shows that land had become more attractive than before, and that dry lands were taken into cultivation. This was probably on account of the pressure of population in the Tamil country. But inscriptions in the Kannaḍa districts of the empire show that some villages there were deserted.

The assessment on arable land was calculated on the cultivable area. Lower rates of assessment prevailed on lands irrigated by wells, and those newly brought into cultivation. The full assessment was 50 *kalam*[1] of paddy on every *vēli*,[2] and 20 *kalam* on land irrigated by baling water. The other taxes on land amounted to between 20 and 10 *paṇam*[3] per *vēli*. Some of the garden lands paid 50 *paṇam* when they were under plantain and sugar-cane, but gardens growing other produce or vegetables were charged at much lower rates. The taxes on trees like cocoanut and areca were based on the amount of the produce. The house-tax was calculated not only on the size of the houses, but also on the profession of the people living in them. It ranged from 3 *paṇam* to ¾ per year. There were regular profession taxes. Merchants paid three *paṇam*, weavers 4, if they had only one loom, and 9, if they had more than one; shop-keepers 3, lace-makers 3, artisans 5, barbers and washermen 4, oil-mongers 20, members who acted as judges on the panchāyat 5, members of the village Council ½, *Pariahs* ½. It would appear from this table that the manufacture of oils was a prominent industry at the time, like weaving. The judges at the panchāyat must have been in receipt of fees, to justify the heavy

[1] *Kalam*—24 measures.

[2] *Vēli*—6⅔ acres.

[3] *Paṇam*—2⅓ annas.

tax on them as compared with other villagers. Many inscriptions refer to the remission of taxes on barbers and on *Pariahs*. This can be understood if we remember that the popular music of the time was almost entirely in charge of these classes. It is clear that even the humblest man had to make his contribution, however small, to the public exchequer.

VI

THE PORTUGUESE SYSTEM

When the Portuguese came into contact with Vijayanagar and established their hold on some of the coast-lying regions, they continued the Vijayanagar system. Albuquerque [1] was under the necessity of employing Hindu clerks in offices, and established schools for educating the natives. He carefully maintained the constitution of the village communities and their peculiar usages and customs. He left the civil administration in the hands of Indians, but made it a rule that Portuguese India must pay for its own administration, out of the tribute from vassal states, the fees for safe conduct and licences to trade, the proceeds of crown lands, and local taxation. He found that the natives of Goa were splendid ship-builders and workmen, and utilised their services. He established the system of farming out the lands as, for instance, those of Goa to the pirate Timoja. Portuguese historians say that he reduced the revenue to what it had been under Hindu rule, which shows that the revenue had been increased under the Bijapur Sultans. The only change he made was the establishment of a mint in

[1] Albuquerque: *Commentaries*.

which gold, silver and copper money were coined, and the prohibition of the use of the older currency. He placed the government of forts in charge of three officers, the Factor, the Captain, and the Treasurer. The Factor was in charge of commerce and correspondence, the Captain of the troops; and the Treasurer received the revenues, tributes paid by sea-side states, the proceeds of safe-conducts sold to trading vessels, and the income from the territory round Goa, as well as the customs dues. The three officers formed a Council and conducted a general business in consultation. The arrangement was apparently based on the ancient Hindu system, and was adopted by Śivāji in later times.

VII

INTER-STATE RELATIONS

The general trend of polity in this period was to lessen the horrors of war, and to humanise relations in peace. The testimony of the Portuguese shows that Indian warfare was humane and governed by proper principles, as late as the 15th century. Instances are not wanting of kings making prodigious sacrifices in order to maintain a political compact with honour, like those made by the Rāja of Anegondi in his unwillingness to give up a Mussalman refugee. Of course, there were exceptions, the most glaring of which are recorded in the *Kaliṇgattuparaṇi*. Chōḷa warfare in the north and west spared neither the honour of women nor the innocence of children. But such exceptions only prove the rule that warfare in India was humane, as contrasted with the horrors of war wrought by the foreigners in India:

'For our own part we must confess the conquest of India is repugnant to us, and strikes us with horror on account of the injustice and barbarity of the conquerors, their frauds, extortions and sanguinary feuds.'[1] Mr. Sewell has summed up the evidence as follows: 'Throughout the whole of their dealings with the Portuguese, I find not a single instance in which the Hindu kings broke faith with the intruders, but as much, I fear, cannot be said on the other side.[2] The Europeans seemed to think that they had a divine right to the pillage, robbery and massacre of the natives of India. Not to mince matters, their whole record is one of a series of atrocities.'[3]

[1] Prologue of the Editor of Gaspar Correa's *Lendas da India*.

[2] Cf. Malik Ayaz's letter to Almeyda (De Barros, vol. II, 2-9): 'Once an enemy is conquered, he must be treated as a brother.' But De Barros denies that the Christians had any duties towards the infidels (I. 6. 1): 'There is never a law of God or man runs north of Lat. 53°'.

[3] *Forgotten Empire*, p. 117.

CHAPTER VI

MUGHAL ADMINISTRATION

I

POSITION OF THE EMPEROR

IN Hindustan, as in Central Asia, the Mughals realised the political ideal of Chengiz Khan. They founded a military state where power was centralised in the person of the monarch. A military command conferred by the Mughal carried with it the payment of a lump sum from the Imperial Exchequer. It was the mark of official influence and social respectability. The nature and importance of that command did not conform to any rules. Some won their way to favour at Court by dint of strenuous service done in the field. Others were carpet-knights whose victories in peace had earned for them a military command. Clever courtiers gained it by assiduous attention to the whims and caprices of the emperor.[1] All grants of land or gifts of money were made under his sign manual. There were no written laws to guide the administration of justice.[2] What the emperor willed was law, and what he adjudged was right. He decided questions of peace and war, and conducted negotiations with other powers.

[1] E.g., Birbal (Badauni, Vol. II, p. 260).

[2] Sir T. Roe: Letter dated 29th January, 1616 (Foster: *Embassy of Sir T. Roe*, Edn. of 1926, p. 104). Also De Laet (Trans. by Hoyland and Banerjee, 1928), Part I, Chap. 4.

The despotism was ingeniously maintained by a policy of dividing the nobles and impressing the subjects with imperial grandeur and magnificence. The most powerful nobles were jealously kept at court, and attended the state durbars and royal processions. Others were at the head of armies or in charge of provinces. Prominent subjects vied with each other in the scramble for power and patronage. High on the throne of state in the public Hall of Audience, the emperor received petitions and disposed of them in person.

There too he sat, 'his person loaded with diamonds, rubies, pearls and other vanities, so great, so glorious' to receive envoys and arrange affairs of foreign policy. Such pomp and circumstance was the exclusive privilege of the emperor. Not even the heir-apparent to the throne was permitted to infringe in any particular the royal prerogative. Thus we have in the *Wakiat-i-Jahangiri*[1] and in the letters of Aurangzib special mandates objecting to such small details as the granting of titles to servants, the use of platforms at court, the beating of drums instead of tabors, or the ordering of an elephant-fight. 'Contempt of Court' was used in the widest possible sense, and even absence of intention on the part of the offender was no palliative of the crime. In short, the emperor was the sole director of the state machine, the centre of all aspirations, the object of all reverence.[2]

The despotism was based on the command of a strong army and the possession of a well-filled

[1] E. & D., Vol. VI, p. 325.

[2] *Purchas*: *His Pilgrims* (1905 Edn.), Vol. III, p. 34 ff: IV, p. 436 ff: IX, p. 48 ff.

treasury. To these engines of all despotism, the early Mughal emperors added new ones. They kept their prominent nobles practically as hostages, by insisting on their always remaining at court. An elaborate system of espionage made the emperor acquainted with the deeds and disposition of his local representatives and the feelings and impressions of the common people.[1] Such disaffected chieftains or overgrown subordinates as could not be conveniently overthrown were silently removed by a stealthy dose of poison treacherously administered at a cordial interview. Manucci[2] tells us that a confidential servant kept the poisoned pills and combustible robes of honour, ready for use under Akbar and his successors. This, however, was an extreme measure; and the ordinary expedients were of a more honourable kind. Under Akbar and Shah Jahan the despotism was tempered by a judicious recognition of the rights and prejudices of the subject peoples, and by a sincere desire to rule in conformity with the wishes and feelings of the governed. Both of them employed Hindus as ministers and generals. Their policy was to balance judiciously the conflicting interests of the rival classes in the state. Alike in the army and in the civil administration they employed the men of the mountains, of the coast and the plain; the Sunnis of the empire, and the Shiahs of the north-west; the Mussalmans of Hindustan, and the Rajput natives of

[1] Hawkins, p. 12; Manucci: *Storia do Mogor* (Irvine's trans.), Vol. II, p. 421.

[2] Manucci, Vol. I, pp. 149-50. Regarding the pills, cf. Tod, Vol. I, p. 352; Catrou, p. 134; Herbert: *Travels*, p. 75. Aurangzib tried twice to poison Shah Jahan (Manucci, I, p. 65). Tavernier describes five kinds of *sarapas* or robes of honour.

India. Between the Mughal noble and the Rajput chieftain there was a deep gulf fixed. The Rajput aristocracy was hereditary and feudal; the Mughal held its property at the pleasure of the Padishah.

The admission of Hindus to offices and emoluments was therefore part of a well-considered scheme of policy. Bernier[1] is shrewd enough to observe that the Rajputs acted as a political lever to remove the difficulties of the times. They were eminently faithful to their patrons, had a high sense of feudal loyalty, and were able generals and administrators. They were excellent fighters capable of bringing thousands of soldiers into the field. They were necessary to keep the other native chiefs in check, or to foment dissensions among them with a view to bring them ultimately under the authority of the Mughal. They could be safely used to suppress the rebellions of Mussalman Amīrs or to wage war with Mussalman kings in Persia or in India. It is small wonder, therefore, that special favour was shown to the Rajput chieftains. Some of them were coaxed or bribed, and others coerced by Akbar to attach themselves to the throne by politic inter-marriages. So fruitful was this policy that we find Hindus employed in increasing numbers under his son and grandson. In the *Ain-i-Akbari* list there are 32 Rajputs among the 250 higher *Mansabdars* or Commanders of 500 to 5,000 horse, and 25 Rajputs among the 163 commanders of 200 to 400 horse. We learn from the *Pādishah nāma* that there were 110 Hindus among Shah Jahan's 580 commanders of 500 horse and upwards. But there were only a few Hindustani Mussalmans in the

[1] Bernier (Ed. Constable and Smith), p. 210.

list of *Mansabdars*, perhaps because they represented the race directly supplanted by the Mughal. Manucci says they would not intermarry with the Mughals: so proud a people were the Pathans even after defeat.

II

CHECKS AND LIMITATIONS

The most effective check on Mediæval Mussalman despotism was the Ulema or Doctors of the Faith. They combined the functions of judges and magistrates with those of lawyers and divines. Their rigid formalism and pride of learning stamped their actions with the authority of the Koran, while their worldliness and corruption left no temporal affairs outside the range of their officious interference. Their adherence to the letter of the Prophet's law, and their clever interpretations of dubious points, made them invincible when pitted against the crown. The Mussalman hierarchy, therefore, was a state within the state, and even self-willed monarchs had to bend before its decisions. It regarded holy war with the infidel as a religious duty, and the emperors were subject to its fanatical influence. But in 1579 a document was drawn up [1] by Abul Fazl's father, and signed by the divines and jurists, to the effect that the authority of the just king was higher than that of the Mullahs, and that there was no legal or religious authority above the emperor, save the Koran alone. His was the right to interpret disputed passages, and his interpretation, given 'for the benefit of the nation and as a political expedient,' was binding on the whole

[1] Badaoni, Lowe's trans., p. 279.

nation. Thus the emperor was formally recognised as the supreme head of the state in spiritual matters. There was a partial revival of Islam under Jahangir and Shah Jahan, and Aurangzib entrusted to a committee of Doctors the interpretation of contested points in Muhammadan Law. But the priesthood never regained its old political position. The sanctity of the highest religious office had been added to the strength of despotic regal power.

The military despotism had proved its strength against the Muslim theocracy, but it was not so easily successful against the Mongol aristocracy. We may agree with Abul Fazl[1] that the imperial will could exalt a mere foot-soldier to the rank of Amīr, but it could not, from the necessities of the position, withhold its support from the aristocracy of conquerors. A fair complexion ensured the imperial favour, as it pointed to the probability of a Mongol origin. This was so well known, says Bernier,[2] that those at Court took Kashmiri women to wife in order that their issue might pass for genuine Mongols. An aristocracy based on complexion was nothing new in India. But this aristocracy gave trouble to the emperor. The Mughal governors of provinces were by no means easy to control. Instances of their tyranny and lawlessness abound in the pages of Abdul Khadir Badaoni[3] and Khafi Khan, not to speak of European witnesses. Some were indeed so powerful that the emperors had to wink at their misdeeds. Akbar and Shah Jahan ensured their loyalty and subordination by patronising Rajput Hindus and a few Hindustani Mussalmans.

[1] *Ain-i-Akbari*, Gladwin's trans., Vol. I, p. 228.

[2] Constable's trans., p. 404.

[3] Lowe's trans., p. 288 *et seq.*

Aurangzib would not employ this lever to the requisite extent, and was absolutely helpless. An old woman, unlawfully dispossessed of her land, complained to him for the seventh time that his written order of restitution had not been obeyed by the Viceroy of Bengal. The emperor could only beseech her to lay her complaint before God! This story given by Manucci [1] illustrates Khafi Khan's account of the general laxity of the administration. Under Aurangzib's successors the provincial potentates asserted their independence and the empire fell to pieces.[2]

A third check on Mughal despotism was the hostility of the subject races.[3] The rule of the Pathans had been extinguished, but the ashes had not yet become cold, and the dying embers might be fanned into a flame by the passing news of Mughal reverses, and fed by the uncertain fuel of promised support. The Hindu risings of the period were not political or economic: they were not due to any ambition to have some part in the government or to resistance to the pressure of taxation. They were due to personal slights offered to influential chieftains and to interference with religious worships. Instances in point are the revolt of Jaswant Singh's Rajputs and the insurrection of the Satnamis in the reign of Aurangzib. Even those Hindu chiefs who sought to carve out kingdoms for themselves were adherents of some religious school. If it was not distinctly

[1] Manucci, *op. cit.*; E. and D., VII, pp. 386-7.

[2] *Seir Mutaquerin* (Trans.) I, pp. 44, 49 and 53.

[3] Whose numbers were large: 'The country contains hundreds of gentiles (Hindus) to one Mughal or even to one Muhammadan.' (Bernier, *op. cit.*, p. 209).

religion that fired the nerve of Sivāji, it was certainly religion that united the Sikhs into a brotherhood against the Mussalmans.

Fear of possible invasions from abroad might have acted as a fourth check. It was along the north-western passes that inroads had been made in the past. In Babar's time however, Central Asia was in a state of transition, ending with the settlement of the Uzbegs in Transoxiana and the Kirghi Confederacy in Mughalistan. Babar held Samarkhand for a time as a vassal of Tamasp, the Shah of Persia. The Persian monarch was friendly to Humayun during the period of his enforced wanderings. It was as a mark of friendship that Humayun made him a present of the celebrated *Kohinoor*. But the safety of India was really due to the hostilities between Persia and Turkey, and to the internal troubles in Persia on the death of Shah Tamasp. Kandahar was the bone of contention between Safevi Persia and Mughal India in the succeeding century. The consolidation of Afghanistan dates only from the 18th century, but its founders Nadir and Ahmad were the scourges of India in the declining period of Mughal rule. The eastern frontier also gave some slight trouble in the reign of Aurangzib. The Deccan had remained unconcerned in the politics of Hindustan. But Aurangzib's capture of Bijapur and Golkonda taught the Mahrāthas the way to the north.

The personal character of the emperors was a fifth, and a traditional bid for popularity constituted a sixth safeguard against the abuse of despotic power. The maxims of Akbar and his instructions to his officers have been recorded in the *Ain*. 'It is His

Majesty's constant endeavour to gain and secure the hearts of all men.' Viceroys were instructed to 'constantly keep in view the happiness of the people,' and 'to gain the hearts of all our subjects by a faithful performance of engagements.' The Jesuit Peruschi thought that Akbar conformed to all religions 'in order to obtain popularity.' Jahangir in his 'Institutes' records with exultation the measures taken by him for improving the administration, and the *Intikhab*[1] avers that his whole attention was devoted 'to those things which pleased the hearts of his people.' Shah Jahan went so far in this direction that Tavernier says of him that he ruled not so much as a king over his subjects but as a father over his family. Aurangzib's letters disclose his idea of how kings were to be trained for the throne and how they should conduct themselves after accession. An emperor, says he, ought to stand midway between gentleness and severity: 'Don't be so salty that your subjects would spit you out of their mouths nor so sweet that they may gulp you down.' Secondly, an emperor was never to be fond of ease or inclined to retirement, but should always work in the interests of his subjects. 'So long as a single breath of this mortal life remains, there is no release from labour and work.' 'Sovereignty signifies protection of the people, not self-indulgence and libertinism.'[2]

Lastly must be mentioned the influence of tradition and local customs in a country where the life of the people flowed evenly in set channels and conservative ways. The reverence for custom was retained by the

[1] Pp. 447-9. Cf. *Institutes*, Nos. 6, 12.

[2] Sarkar: *Anecdotes of Aurangzib*, pp. 57 ff.

Mughal emperors, and even those among them who heralded reforms did not make bold to go far in this respect. More than one traveller has mentioned the fact that the non-appearance of a king at the Window would lead to rebellions among the people. Again, there were certain directions in which state aid and encouragement were expected to be given, and certain unwritten ways in which the sovereign was to act. Let us take for illustration the department of Religion, one of the most important, and certainly the most interesting, in this period. Akbar laughed Islam to scorn and violated its tenets; but even he used images on his coins very sparingly indeed. Jahangir introduced the rule of the woman—which is directly condemned by the express injunctions of the Prophet—and there was eventually a revolution. Shah Jahan was popular in spite of all his secret intrigues and affairs of lust, because he let 'sleeping dogs' lie and respected institutions as best he could. Aurangzib imposed a tax on infidels, thereby bringing a hornet's nest about his ears. There was, one may say, a sort of customary contract between the people and their sovereign.[1]

III

CENTRAL GOVERNMENT

The fabric of administration depends for its efficiency on the personal supervision of the monarch. The Mughal emperors were conscious of this fact. Most of them scorned delights and lived laborious days. If there were dullards among them, men who

[1] It is obvious that Smith puts it too strongly when he says that the Mughal emperor was not constrained by any law or custom having the force of law. (*Akbar*, p. 357).

preferred a life of ease and indolence to the uneasiness of wearing the crown, they were weeded out in the process of natural selection by which, as a rule, the succession to the throne was regulated. There was not a single reign which was free from civil war with the other claimants to the throne, or from possible rivals endangering the security of the reigning king. The founder of the empire saw the irresistible tendencies of the situation, and adjured his successor Humayun 'not to slay his brothers but watch them with care.' The weakest period of Mughal rule went with too close an observance of the letter of this advice, for Humayun's brothers were thorns in his side, and their disloyalty accounted for most of his difficulties. Jahangir's brothers had died of drunkenness, but he had a civil war with his sons. He called Shah Jahan 'the wretch', and treated with inhuman severity the disaffected eldest son Khusru. Shah Jahan captured and blinded his younger brother Shahriyar, and ensured the throne for himself by beheading his nephews. If his father had called him a 'wretch', he in his turn called his third son Aurangzib 'a white snake.' As regards the latter, the famous story of the civil war, where he hunted his brothers out and killed them, is immortalized by the hand of the artist, who has painted the scene of the bringing to Aurangzib of the head of the slain Dāra in a silver tray full of crimson blood.[1] Nothing is more painful to the human soul than the history of these kings, their private amours, and their sanguinary feuds with princes of the blood. But these very unedifying wars had an excellent political result. As in the

[1] Havell: *Indian Sculpture and Painting*. Plate

thirteenth century, we have now a succession of able kings on the principle of the survival of the fittest.

Babar's life was full of adventure and daring, and of arduous attempts to found and organise an empire. Humayun divided the days of the week among the avocations which claimed his personal attention. Thursdays and Saturdays were given to religious men and literati, Sundays and Tuesdays to the details of civil and military administration, Fridays to the convocation of assemblies, and Mondays and Wednesdays to music and merry-making. This arrangement, mentioned by Khondamir, was apparently altered by Akbar, who found it necessary to attend every day to every kind of work. Abul Fazl informs us that the emperor ate little and slept less, and that sleep, short as it was, 'looked more like waking.' Details of the daily life of Shah Jahan have been given by Abdul Hamid, and of Aurangzib by Muhammad Kasim. The emperor got out of bed in the small hours of the morning, had definite hours for the different duties of the day, public and private, and retired to bed after 10 o'clock at night. If Shah Jahan had a sleep of six hours, Aurangzib had only three, besides the short nap at noon. The arrangement of time was the same for everybody with a few exceptions. Thursday evenings were given to religious discussions by Akbar, and to prayer and sacred reading by Aurang-zib. Friday was a holiday for the court under the latter, and Wednesday was pre-eminently the day of justice with him and Shah Jahan. It is difficult to believe these details given by the Court historians. What is presented to us is only an ideal, and there must have been frequent departures from the dull routine. But it is clear from all this that the emperors not only reigned but governed hard; they were not do-nothing kings or puppets on the throne.

On three occasions the emperor came directly before the public.[1] Roe writes under date 10th January 1616:—' The king comes every morning to a window called the Jerruco looking into a plain before his gate and shows himself to the common people. At noon he returns thither and sits some hours to see the fight of elephants and wild beasts . . . . from whence he retires to sleep among his women. At afternoon he returns to the darbar. . . . At eight after supper he comes down to the Ghazelkhan . . . . to which are none admitted but of great quality, and few of these without leave.' Business was done only at the last two places, and it was ' publicly propounded.' ' On Tuesday at the Jerruco he sits in judgment.'[2]

These occasions must have been of great importance. They gave the subject direct access to his sovereign. They gave the sovereign first-hand knowledge of the needs and opinions of all sorts and conditions of his subjects. The *Jarokha* freed petitioners from the inevitable expense of making costly presents, or greasing the palm of some insolent underling in order to get a royal interview. To litigants it offered an opportunity of appealing direct to the king without going through the usual judicial procedure which is both costly and tedious. A register was maintained of all public business done at the Durbar

[1] Eliot and Dowson, Vol. IV, pp. 410-413; 550 to 51.
[2] Foster, *op. cit.*, p. 85 f. Cf. Terry (*Voyage*, p. 389).

and the *Diwān-i-am*, and this was open to any one who paid the small fee of one rupee. Sir T. Roe tells us that the king's resolutions were public news every day, and that, if he did not appear in public any day without reason assigned, the result would be a mutiny of the masses. The emperors were fully aware of the importance of these occasions. They had these institutions whether they were in the capital, at Delhi, Lahore or Agra, or camping in the field against a hostile army. Even the austere Aurangzib could not abolish the *Jarokha*, though in his eyes it must have smacked of heathenism.

IV

THE DEPARTMENTS

The work of the central government was divided by Humayun into four departments. First was the military (*Atashi*) department, especially that which related to the artillery and the manufacture of fire-arms. Next came the duties connected with the wardrobe, kitchen, stables, etc., which formed the *Hawai*. Thirdly, there was irrigation (*Abi*), to cut canals and to see to the supply of water. Lastly, there was the *Khāki* which supervised agriculture, resumed *Khālisa* lands, and saw to the erection of public buildings, besides attending to some household affairs. At first each department was placed under a nobleman, but afterwards there was a Prime Minister at the head of all. Under Akbar the office of Prime Minister was a real and onerous one. He was known as *Vakīl* or *Vazīr*, and was the emperor's lieutenant in all matters. He collected the revenue from the crown lands, which he let out on rent, and conferred offices on nobles and subordinates. But his work does not seem to have been clearly defined. It varied, doubtless, with the nature and temperament of his Sovereign, and his own capacity for political affairs. In later times he got control over other departments also,—Army and Foreign affairs, and Correspondence.[1] He was helped by a secretary who had a special staff of clerks. The functions of government were divided in the modern way. The four elements of monarchy, says Abul Fazl, are the *Diwān* (Financier), the *Kāzi* (Chief Justice), the Commander-in-Chief and the Intelligencer. There was a specialisation of offices under these. The work of the emperor's household, with its elaborate organisation for the *harem*, was separated from that of public affairs properly so called. The number of offices was multiplied and their importance reduced, by a minute subdivision of functions and by the privilege of personal interview with the emperor which was granted to the heads of the minor departments as well.[2]

Finance formed the chief department of administration. The *Diwān* received all the revenues of the empire, realised the property of deceased persons, resumed the property of dismissed officials, regulated the *jāgir* and carried out alterations in offices and allowances. Under him were a number of financial

[1] Sarkar: *Mughal Administration*, p. 32.

[2] The chief departments at the close of the period were those of Exchequer and Revenue (*High Diwān*), the Household (*Khān-i-Samān*), Pay and Accounts Officer (*Bakshi*), Law (*Kāzi*), Religious Endowments and Charity (*Sadr*), Censorship (*Muhtasib*), Artillery (*Topkhānah*), Intelligence (*Dāk chowki*). The *Vazīr* had no portfolio. It was an honorific title, but not conferred on any Hindu. As Diwān, he was the head of the Revenue department.

officers and accountants. The *Mir-Mal* was in charge of the emperor's privy purse, the *Mir-Bakshi* was the Adjutant-General, the *Bar-Begi* presented petitioners, and the *Mir Tozak* took charge of the presents they brought with them.

The *Bakshi* was Secretary for War and Paymaster-General. The combination of civil and military rank and functions is illustrated in this office : he recruited the army, assigned posts to commanders in battle, maintained the muster roll of the men, and was sometimes directly in command of a fighting army. As financial officer he maintained a list of the *mansabdars*, arranged their postings at court, in the army or in the provinces, suggested promotions of officers, and countersigned pay-bills. A junior *Bakshi* saw to the promotion and recruitment of the smaller men, verified the documents of the first *Bakshi*, and was responsible for the keeping of the lands confiscated from officers.

The keeper of the seal, and the bearer of the imperial insignia (*kurbegi*), were other important officers. The Accounts department was under a Deputy *Diwān* (*Mustaufi*). There was a special accountant for the army, and one for the imperial workshop. A third had charge of the daily expenditure at Court, and a fourth, of the furniture and stores. Among other officers were the Clerk of the treasury, and the Record-Keeper. There was a special officer to control the supply of grain and to keep the king informed of the daily movements in prices. The king's privy purse was in charge of the *Mir Samān* and the *Diwān-i-Bayutat*, who conducted the expenditure of the royal household.

The *Sadr* was the Chief Justice and Administrator-General, and head of the Ecclesiastical department. He was in charge of lands endowed for pious and learned men, and of the vast sums distributed in charity. He read the *khutba* legalising the accession of a king. The *sadrs* of Akbar's time were notorious for their venality and cruel spirit. So their powers were cut down, and the office abolished in 1582, when the duties of the *sadr* were divided among six provincial *sadrs*.

The *Kāzi* was the chief judge in criminal suits, which were tried according to Muslim Law. He was assisted by two judges. The *Mir Adil* carried out the findings of the *Kāzi*, and tried cases which came under Common Law. All criminal cases in which one of the parties was a Muhammadan had to come before the *Kāzi*. He was expected to be impartial, and to hold trials in the presence of the parties. He was not to accept presents or entertainments. But in practice most *Kāzis* of Mughal times were notorious bribe-takers.

The officers mentioned above were among the 'companions of the king,' others being the palace physician, astronomer, soothsayer and poet. There was a special officer in charge of the Cavalry, another of the Infantry, a third of the Artillery, and a fourth of the Admiralty. Other departments of state were presided over by smaller officers. Thus we have a superintendent of the imperial workshops (*Nazir-Burjutat*) corresponding to our chief engineer for works, another of the Imperial forests (*Mir Barr*), a third of the Imperial kitchen (*Khāna Salār*), and a fourth of the aviaries (*Kushbegi*).

There were four kinds of news-reporters mentioned in *Dastur-ul-aml* of later times: the general reporter (*Waqia-navis*), the special reporter (*Sawanih-nigar*), the criminal intelligence officer (*Khafia-navis*), and the spy who brought oral news (*Harkarah*). The first sent in weekly reports, and the second twice a week. In many cases the *Bakshi* was also a reporter. There was a special reporter only in certain places and at times. The intelligence officers and spies busied themselves with watching the activities of government servants. Capt. Hawkins was surprised to learn that Jahangir had already received a detailed report of his ill-treatment at Surat and that remedial measures had been taken.

Special mention must be made of the emperor's Superintendent of the *Harem*, who had, according to Abul Fazl, the control of the expenditure pertaining to that elaborate establishment. So heavy apparently was the work of this officer that in Aurangzib's reign a great deal of power was delegated to the chief Eunuch. But for a *harem*, perhaps, the influence of the Queen might have been all-important in the administration, like that of Nur Jahan. As it was, the rule of the woman was obviated. The strength of the *harem* was cut down from 5,000 under Akbar to 2,000 under Aurangzib. It was a parliament of races and religions, and its administration was modelled on that of the state. The influence of the *harem* on the government of the empire cannot be over-estimated. The ladies of Akbar's court probably influenced the religious policy of his later years and the adoption by the state of the worship of the Sun and the Fire. Nur Jahan was joint ruler with Jahangir, or rather the *de facto* ruler. Mumtaz Mahal's hatred of the Portuguese resulted in Shah Jahan's capture of Hugli. In the civil war among his sons, his fair daughters were ranged with their brothers on either side, and Aurangzib's final victory was due in no small measure to the support of Roshan Āra. As the emperor attended to a great deal of state work in the *harem*, his women Counsellers[1] there were even more influential with him, and more cognisant of the secret affairs of state than the confidential ministers of the inner council.

The working of the central government was the same whether the emperor was at the capital, in the field or in the provinces. Akbar had his capital at Delhi, Fatehpur, Agra or Lahore. Shah Jahan built a new capital at Delhi, as Agra was too sultry. Under Aurangzib it continued as the chief residence of the emperor, though sometimes the court was at Agra. Even in the same city the emperor frequently changed his residence from fear of plots. The Mughal emperors made frequent progresses of inspection through their dominions, and news came to them from the most distant parts of the empire by the agency of spies and reporters.

The ministers formed a sort of inner Council. It is likely that the chambers in the four corners of the *Diwān-i-khās* were intended for the chief ministers of the state.[2] But it is difficult to determine how far they acted in concert. It is more likely that each minister was responsible to the emperor for the working of his

[1] One of the queens had the royal signet-ring and also the Great Seal of the realm. (Montserrate : *Commentary*, trans. Hoyland and Banerjee, 1922, p. 209.)

[2] E. W. Smith : *Architecture of Fatehpur-Sikri*, Part I, Plates 80 to 84.

own department, and that they never acted as a Cabinet.[1] At the durbar, for instance, the Paymaster-General took orders as to the promotions of military officers from the emperor, and the heads of the military departments introduced the newly-appointed officers to him. Those in charge of the privy purse came next for orders. Then were read the letters from the provinces, after which the *Sadr* recommended men for charities and grants of money. Lastly came the officers in charge of the imperial stables, to display their animals according to rule. So too, at the *Diwān-i-khās* were considered matters relating to crown lands, charities and public works, each subject being introduced to the emperor by the official head of the department.

V

PROVINCIAL GOVERNMENT

The empire was divided into provinces (*Subahs*). A province was not merely an administrative unit of convenient extent, but a historical tract. It contained a number of *Sircars*, every *Sircar* a number of *Mahals* or *Parganas*, and every *Mahal* a number of *Dasturs* or districts. The number of *Subahs* varied at different times. There were 12 in 1580—Allahabad, Agra, Oudh, Ajmir, Ahmadabad, Bihar, Bengal, Delhi, Kabul, Lahore, Multan and Malwa. Later were added Berar, Khandesh, Ahmadnagar (known as Aurangabad after 1695) and Kashmir. The number was still

[1] So Sir T. Roe: 'No counsell. But every officer answers to the king apart his duty.' (Foster, *op. cit.*, p. 105). Montserrate (*op. cit.*, p. 203) says that the emperor asked each counsellor privately for his opinion, and acted on the opinion of the majority.

increased by the separation of Orissa from Bengal, and of Tata from Multan, and the constitution of these into separate provinces. The last additions were in 1720; and consisted of Bijapur, Bidar and Hyderabad. While there was an increase in the number of the *Subahs* occasioned by fresh conquests, there was also a steady increase in the number of *Sircars* and *Mahals* in most *Subahs* as the administrative organisation developed. In the 20 old *Subahs* for instance, the number of *Sircars* rose from 123 in 1594 to 149 in 1695 and 154 in 1720. The total number of *Mahals* in the same was 3,117 in 1594, 3,971 in 1695 and 4,336 in 1720. The extent of each *Subah*, *Sircar* and *Mahal* was varied in accordance with administrative exigencies.

At the head of each province was a *Sepah Śalār*, i.e., Viceroy and Commander of the Forces,[1] known as *Subahdar* after Akbar's reign. He had the command of the local troops, and attended to their equipment and discipline. He had to nominate officers in charge of districts and guards in charge of the highways. He had special instructions to improve agriculture, and to construct and improve reservoirs, wells, water-courses, serais and other pious foundations. He was to adopt a policy of strict neutrality in religious matters, and to set an example to his subjects in religious and orderly life. He was to send two reports to the Court every month. He was advised to subject his conduct to the criticism of a body of experts, and of representatives of public opinion. The *Sepah Śalār* was 'not to subvert ancient families but

[1] *Ain-i-Akbari*, Bk. II, *Ains* 1 and 3; Monserrate in *J.A.S.B.*, 1912, p. 216; Sarkar: *Manual*, pp. 11 and 12.

let an illustrious ancestry redeem unworthy successors.'

The *Subahdar* was assisted by a financial officer (*Diwān*) who was directly appointed by the emperor or by his *Diwān*, and by a Treasurer who disbursed money under instructions from this officer. The Court of Justice consisted of the *Kāzi* and the *Mir Adil*, who administered respectively the Canon and the Common Law. The *Kāzi* conducted the trial and stated the law; the *Adil* carried out the finding of the *Kāzi*. They were appointed by the emperor's *Kāzi*, and acted therefore, to some extent, as checks on the powers of the *Subahdar*.[1] The proceedings were verbal, and no records were kept.

The *Subahdar* checked the accounts of the village officers, sent an abstract of them weekly to the Presence, and submitted a monthly statement of the daily receipts and expenses. 'Every month he shall submit a statement of the condition of the people, of the jāgirdars and neighbouring residents; the submission of the rebellious; the market-places; the current rents or tenements; the state of the destitute poor, and of the artificers; and all contingencies.' It would be an immense gain to social history of the times if we could discover any of the reports of this miscellaneous functionary. He was essentially the man on the spot, and could easily buy up the imperial spies. One sentence in the *Ain* apparently refers to the abuse of power by the district officers. They had to be forbidden to receive presents from subjects, and to 'waive all perquisites—on handicrafts,

[1] There was the inevitable antagonism between the *Subahdar* and the *Diwān*. Instances are cited by Sarkar: *Studies*, pp. 221–24.

market-booths, police, travelling transports, garden-produce, temporary sheds, enclosures, fishing rights, port-dues, butter, oil of sesame, blanketing, leather, wool, and the like malpractices of the avaricious who fear not God.' In the collection of revenue assistance was sometimes received from the *Faujdār*, a military officer in charge of several districts, whose duty it was to bring to reason any rebellious cultivators or collectors of revenue.

European visitors to the Imperial Court and bold Mussalman writers have severely condemned the provincial administration. Badaoni gives detailed instances of misgovernment in Gujarat, Bengal and elsewhere. A Bengal poet of the 16th century, Mukunda Rām, depicts the deplorable condition of the people in consequence. Pinheiro refers to the tyranny of the Punjab governor.[1] According to Roe, the provincial governors of Jahangir 'took life and goods at pleasure.' Hawkins describes the misdeeds of the governor of Gujarat. The *Wakiat-i-Jahangiri* mentions the governor's oppression at Kashmir, and adds that the Amīrs of the frontier posts had assumed almost regal authority. Tavernier complains of the tyranny and extortion of Shah Jahan's viceroy of Sindh. Manucci styles the government of the empire under Aurangzib 'nothing but one vast disorder.' There is something to the same effect in the published letters of that emperor. He tells us that he read the governors of Punjab and Gujarat severe lessons in discipline. The East India Company had to submit to the exaction of the Mughal governor of Hugli and

[1] Letter from Lahore, dated 12th August, 1605 (E. D. Maclagan, J.A.S.B. for 1896).

Balasore. Streynsham Master remarks that the condition of the people was much worse in that province than in Gujarat.

Imperial control over corrupt and cruel governors was either non-existent or ineffectual. The spies and confidential agents sent by the emperor easily colluded with the provincial authorities. The only remedy the emperor could think of was to transfer governors from one place to another.[1] But the governors easily evaded this check by offering a handsome bribe in the name of a present at Court, as the viceroy of Sindh did under Shah Jahan. The frequent changes of governors only added to the sufferings of the subjects, as every new incumbent sought in his province a fresh pasture. Khafi Khan and Manucci agree that Aurangzib could not enforce his orders, and that frequent changes of governors only plunged the Dekhan in chronic misery. The servants of the English East India Company found it impossible to obtain, in the provinces, the concessions promised by the Imperial firman. The remedies applied by the emperors thus proved worse than the disease.

Nor could it be said that there was security for the people against sufferings due to rebellion, robbery or brigandage. Jahangir writes in his *Memoirs* that, notwithstanding frequent massacres, there were almost constant rebellions in Hindustan. There was not a single province in the whole empire in which half a million people had not been slaughtered during his own reign and that of his father. A period of complete repose had never existed. There were organised bands of robbers. The Koolies infested the

[1] Montserrate *Commentary*, *op. cit.*, p. 90.

road from Cambay to Surat, while the sea route was haunted by the Malabar pirates. The 'Raja' of the Grassia freebooters levied blackmail on travellers and caravans. Hamilton refers to the depredations of the Koolies in Gujarat and of brigands in Sindh. If we may believe Manucci, the very villages between Agra and Delhi, the capitals of the empire, contained bands of robbers, which were being gradually dispersed. Such safety as there was in travel was due to the existence of trustworthy guides. In the 18th century the empire could do nothing to stop the inroads of the Mahrāthas, and had to leave to the English the extermination of the Pindaris.

VI

LOCAL GOVERNMENT

Local government differed in different parts of India, as Mughal sovereigns in general respected Indian usages and institutions.[1] There is hardly any evidence of real municipal life; such references as we have seem to indicate that towns were thoroughly under the government officers. It was only in cities, where the corporate life was loose, that there was anything approaching self-governing institutions like those in rural villages. The great bulk of Mughal territory consisted of land-lord villages. But ryotwari holdings persisted in some tracts of India, and continued

[1] Bernier (p. 246) sees in the village system an approach to the modern municipal administration. Cf. Munro (I., p. 280): 'In all Indian villages, there was a regularly constituted municipality, by which its affairs were administered.' So also Malcolm (*Memoirs*, I, chap. 12): 'All just princes founded their chief reputation and claim to popularity on attention to them (village institutions).'

their life unimpeded by influences from outside, as they do to this day in Madras, Bombay and Central India, and as in the Central Provinces in the period of our study.

Every town of any importance had a *Kotwāl* to govern it. This officer had the varied duties of the mediæval English Sheriff and Justice of the Peace. His principal duties related to the preservation of peace and order. He patrolled the city at night,[1] took note of new-comers and aliens, and watched the conduct and morals of the citizens, with the help of an army of spies and detectives. He regulated commercial transactions, supervised weights, measures and coins, appointed guild-masters and brokers, and looked after the welfare of labourers and artisans. He had to discover thieves and stolen property and hand them up to the *Kāzi*. He was responsible for the restitution of the stolen property, whether he was able to detect the criminal or not. In these grave duties the *Kotwāl* was helped by the city army, consisting of a body of infantry and cavalry. He was informed of whatever happened, not only by news-writers and spies stationed in the houses of principal citizens, but by the very sweepers and scavengers of the city, with whom he had secret consultations. But the *Kotwāl* had other functions as well. As a magistrate he was subordinate to the *Kāzi* and took orders from him. His fiscal work consisted in collecting the various dues and cesses from the town and remitting them into the state treasury. He also took charge of the property of deceased or missing persons who

[1] We learn from Thevenot that police officers performed their rounds thrice in the night—9 P.M., midnight, and 3 A.M.

had left no heirs. He set the idle to some handicraft and reduced misdemeanants to righteous living. The nature of city government depended, therefore, on the conduct of the *Kotwāl*.

Villages, whether landlord or ryotwari, had certain common features. The village community was the unit of social, political and industrial life.[1] The *Mukkadam* was to the village what the *Kotwāl* was to the town. He settled with the Government the amount of revenue to be paid by the village, apportioned it among the villagers, and collected it from them. As magistrate he settled petty disputes in the village. He did police work in the way of apprehending criminals and sending them for trial. In the case of land-lord villages, he was appointed by the state for administrative purposes. He then got an allowance from the Government, besides the fees from the villagers and the proceeds of his own share of the village land. Another important officer of the village was the accountant (*Paṭwāri*). He was a servant of the proprietary body in land-lord villages, and a state officer in others. He was paid both by the Government and by the village for keeping the village records and land-registers, the private accounts of the villagers and the public accounts of the village. Among other village officers mentioned in the *Ain* are the Munsiff, the Superintendent, the Land-surveyor and the *Thānadār*. The last was, doubtless, the most important of those functionaries. He had responsible

[1] For Mukunda Rām's description of village life in the 16th century, *see* Das Gupta: Calcutta Readership Lectures, Lecture IV. Still as in the Hindu period villages clustered round cities—210 round Baroda; 2995 round Ahmedabad, according to a Dutch report (De Laet, *op. cit.*, pp. 23, 26).

police duties under the headman or *Mukkadam*. He watched the crops and acted as guide in the precincts of the village. He knew the private character of every villager, and kept watch over all foreigners. He was bound to trace the criminals in the event of theft, robbery or dacoity, or be responsible for the property in dispute, as the *Kotwāl* was in towns. If he was able to trace the criminal to an adjoining village, he shifted the burden of detection and the responsibility for restitution on to the *Thānadār* of that village. The *Mukkadam* presided at meetings of the village assembly, which were held now and then, at which villagers were present either in person or by proxy.

Village officers were controlled by the *Kanungo*, a sort of Revenue Inspector, who maintained a register of transfers of proprietory rights. This officer was subject to the orders of the *Tahsildar*. The district officer had control over these through the *Karkūn* (Registrar of collections) and the *Bikitchi* (Jamābandi Assistant). Where there was no *Kotwāl*, the collector took the duties of that office on himself and supervised the police of the town. In rural tracts the *Faujdār* supervised the roads and paid compensation for day-light robberies if any. There was thus some officer responsible for thefts and robberies,—the *Faujdār* on roads, the *Kotwāl* in the city and the *Thānadār* in the village.

VII

PUBLIC FINANCE

The land-tax taken by Mughal rulers was greater than that levied by other Indian kings, whether before or since, and far greater than that taken by the rulers of foreign countries in the same period. Abul Fazl admits that Hindu kings had taken only a sixth of the produce, as also did the chiefs of the Mongol states in Central Asia in his own day. In Persia the rate was as low as a tenth; in Turkey it was one-fifth. Sher Shah the Afghan had taken a fourth during the period of Humayun's wanderings, and there is evidence that some of the famous Hindu kings had taken the same proportion. Akbar took a third of the produce, and his successors altered the demand as they liked, either by all-round enhancement or by the addition of cesses.

We learn from Babar's *Memoirs* that the land revenue amounted to 2 crores and 60 lakhs. Under Akbar it was 13·21 crores in 1594 and 17·45 in 1605. Jahangir's revenue was about 17½ crores in 1628. Under Shah Jahan it rose to 21·15 crores in 1648. Aurangzib's revenue was nearly 26·35 crores in 1661, 23·31 in 1665 and 20 in 1695. It was 33 crores in 1697, 33·68 in 1700, 29·77 in 1707 and 29·70 in 1720. It is difficult to determine, however, what these figures really represent—whether it is the standard assessment, the demand of some particular year, or the actual collections.

Nothing is more remarkable in Akbar's reign than the assessment and settlement of the revenue from land. In this as in other respects the great emperor was the political heir of Sher Shah the Afghan, who first realised the importance of leaving a clear margin between the gross produce and the state's demand. A thorough-going survey of land was made, the units of measurement being clearly defined by the emperor.

The charge on land was generally a third of the produce, but some concessions were made to those who brought inferior lands into cultivation. This was an indulgence which differed according to circumstances. It is not easy to see, therefore, how the assessors could have carried out Akbar's instructions to the effect that 'Sher Shah's demand was in no case to be exceeded.'

The assessments were to be undisturbed for 19 years. After the 24th year of the reign, the average collection of the previous ten years was made the basis for future settlements. The cultivators were made jointly and severally responsible for the revenue. Needy cultivators, who could not afford the expenses, were given advances which were recovered in easy instalments. This system, promulgated by Todar Mal, went on after his time. It was left unaltered under Jahangir, and was extended to the Dekhan by Shah Jahan in 1654. The total territory surveyed rose from 12·70 crores of *bighas* in 1594 to 31·16 crores in 1720.

In the collection of revenue some consideration was shown for the convenience of the ryot. Arrears were often remitted in the case of small holdings which were not economic, i.e., the cultivation of which would not well pay the husbandmen. Even as regards ordinary collections, a few points may well be noticed. In the first place, the revenue was collected in *dāms*, thereby enabling the cultivator to pay in token coin on the principle of Gresham's Law, and hoarding, or melting for ornament, the gold or silver currency. Secondly, money payments were optional, except in the case of expensive crops like the sugar-cane. Taxes on these could easily be paid in money, as only rich people could afford to grow such crops. When the tax was taken in kind, there were different methods of collection. Sometimes the sown field was divided between the crown and the cultivator, sometimes the crown took its portion counting roughly by heaps, and sometimes there was a precise division of the grain.

The expenses of collection varied at different times, being 8 per cent under Akbar, 10 per cent under Shah Jahan, in whose reign the tax-gatherer (*Crori*) also acted as *Faujdār*, and 4 to 5 per cent under Aurangzib. The *Croris* were allowed a commission at these rates. There were land cesses designed to meet these expenses. The collections were made in four instalments, receipts were given for the amounts collected, and it was the duty of the Collector to see that there were no arrears. With all these regulations, there was a good deal taken out of the pockets of the people which did not find its way to the Imperial exchequer. It was impossible to prevent the frauds and petty pilferings of the tax-collectors, especially when taxes were taken in kind. As regards arrears, it was difficult to obviate the evasion of payment in the troublesome districts. In many cases the land revenue could not be collected without the aid of an armed force.

Though land revenue was the mainstay of Mughal finance, other taxes were collected, and they were of various kinds. There were taxes on men (*jizia*), imposed by Aurangzib in 1677 and abolished in 1722. The poll tax was demanded not only from Hindus but from Christians also. The East India Company evaded it with excuses. Hindu traders had to pay it every year in advance. They got a passport in return, which availed them in practice only in the province in which they lived. There were taxes on pilgrims (*kar*) and on those who were engaged in the various professions. Abul Fazl claims for Akbar the credit of reducing or remitting these taxes: Tolls were abolished and port-dues reduced to 2½ per cent. But Jahangir in his 'Institutes' claims credit for the same action, and Khafi Khan tells us that Aurangzib remitted tolls and house-cesses: the *rahdari* tolls collected on every highway (*guzar*), frontier and ferry, and the *pandari* (ground or house cesses) paid by every trader; the market dues, the collections at fairs and festivals; the taxes on spirits, gambling houses, and brothels; and fines and thanks-offerings. It is probable that these taxes were sometimes remitted, but they were as easily revived when it suited the needs or whims of the monarch. We know that Aurangzib charged a customs-duty, estimated by Manucci at 5 per cent on Hindus and 2½ per cent on Mussalmans. Streynsham Master says that, while the duties came to 2 pagodas on the Mussalmans, Europeans were charged 4 pagodas.

The resources of the Mughals were by no means limited to taxation. The emperor had control of all the savings and estates of his *Mansabdars*. They had to make handsome presents on various occasions. Tavernier tells us that the tyrannical viceroy of Sindh presented Shah Jahan with no less than 50,000 gold *mohur* for a promotion. The emperor expected presents from visitors also. It was well known to European travellers that the importance of a visitor was estimated from the value of the presents he had brought with him. Another source of revenue was the profits of coinage. Under Jahangir the coins were pure and unalloyed. Aurangzib debased the coinage. He got a profit of 11 lakhs from the coins struck at Surat alone. The emperor had the mastery of the hoarded wealth of India. Terry remarks that 'merchants concealed their riches lest they should be made sponges.' But the hoarded riches were brought to the light of day and seized by the emperor from time to time. The estates of a nobleman seized by Jahangir contained 60 maunds of gold, besides silver and jewellery. But the most important heads of imperial receipts were escheat and confiscation. The emperor is 'every man's heir when he dieth, which makes him rich.'[1] The royal title to succeed to the effects of the deceased persons was a constant grievance to the English, whose early treaties stipulate a bar to the exercise of the right.[2]

It is clear that the emperors had a prodigious revenue from all these sources. The effects of Akbar at his death are estimated at £20 millions. This nearly tallies with Ferishta's description[3] of his treasure. Mandelslo was informed that Shah Jahan's treasures amounted to £300 millions. They must have been immense, as one may infer from the costly edifices constructed by him. His throne itself was estimated at 6½ crores of rupees. At the end of the reign he left a reserve of coin and bullion worth 24 crores.

[1] Roe: Letter to Lord Carew, dated 17th January 1616. (Foster, *op. cit.*, p. 89).

[2] E.g., those of 1612 and 1615.

[3] He says that Akbar left 10 maunds of gold, 70 of silver, and 60 of copper bullion; 11 crores of rupees and 1 crore of rupees worth of copper coins.

The main heads of expenditure demand a passing notice. First come the expenses connected with the establishment of the officers of state and of the army. The pay of the *Mansabdar* was given either in land (*jāgir*) or in cash (*naqd*). The former method was begun by Abkar and became usual under Shah Jahan. In most cases the emperor assigned to a chieftain the revenue of a distant province which lay on the verge of imperial control, or that of a newly conquered tract, where the collection not only required the aid of an armed force but constant supervision and control by an officer on the spot. As a rule, old servants retained their jāgirs till their death. The grant of a jāgir was final when the emperor affixed his great seal to it, and also gave an impression of his hand in a red liquid. For smaller purposes there was a privy seal, which was used in sealing letters and despatches. The state-seal of Aurangzib contained his own name and title at the centre, and the names of his ancestors in due order all round, in counter-clockwise direction.

In addition to the permanent pay of the *mansab*, holders of such positions got temporary additions to their rank and emoluments when they were posted to particular offices, such as governorship in provinces. There were no definite rules as regards leave, furlough and pension. It is likely that allowances of this kind could not be claimed as a right, but depended on the will and pleasure of the sovereign. But pensions were given to old officers, sometimes once a year and sometimes in daily doles. If an officer died in active service, the state gave full pay to his heirs ; otherwise, only half the amount was given.

A second main item of public expenditure was the elaborate establishment at the Capital, and the personal expenses of the imperial family. The latter amounted to Rs. 50,000 a day,—Rs. 1,000 in the kitchen alone. The expenditure of the *harem* formed a large part of the expenses of the state. This is estimated at Rs. 30,000 a day by Hawkins, and a crore of rupees yearly by Manucci. Thirdly, the emperor was traditionally bound to patronise artists and men of learning, by permanent assignments or periodical donations. It is related of Bairam Khan that he gave a lakh of *tankas* for a single stanza of Hashim, and another lakh to Rāma Dās, the musician. Akbar gave two lakhs for a stanza of Hussain Maruvi. He patronised in his court a large number of musicians, physicians, philosophers, painters and poets. Jahangir was immensely fond of painting, as Shah Jahan was of music. Some of the permanent results of the state patronage of men of learning remain to this day, in the translation into Persian of the great Epics of India, of the *Atharva-Veda* and *Harivamśa*; of *Leelāvati* and the story of Naḷa.

Another head of Mughal expenditure was that on the public works of the time. Babar tells us that he employed 1,491 stone cutters a day, as many as 680 on his palace at Agra alone, where he built a magnificent *baoli* and other works. Humayun's name is connected with many buildings in Agra and Delhi. Ferishta mentions among them a palace of seven pavilions and a mosque on the Jumna river; but these have not yet been discovered and identified. The magnificent buildings of Akbar at Fatehpur-Sikri and Sikandara have been surveyed and photographed.

The elaborate carving on these structures, and the exquisite finish of the details, imply enormous expenditure from the state treasury. Local tradition has it that building materials were brought from far and near to Fatehpur-Sikri—red sandstone from Bharatpur, coloured marble from Jaipur and Ajmir, and limestone from Jassalmere. Not only building materials but artisans were brought from distant places. Jahangir built lofty mansions for his nobles. Experts in art from foreign countries were largely employed by Shah Jahan, and huge sums placed at their disposal. Thus were erected the Taj Mahal, the Pearl Mosque and the mosque and palace at Delhi. To erect the Taj, 20,000 men worked incessantly for 22 years, says Tavernier. Thus we get some idea of the extent to which the state was an employer of labour. More important for our purpose, however, is the construction of works of utility like tanks, gardens, and the canal from the Chenab, in Shah Jahan's reign, and the embankment on the Ravi put up by Aurangzib after a flood. For these works not only gave employment for labour at the time, but proved to be of lasting benefit for mankind.

There is evidence of a great deal of money and bullion being hoarded by the people. This hoarded wealth was buried underground and was unearthed now and then to become the property of the Crown. At least one traveller has left on record that Indians were under the sway of the mercantilist doctrine which possessed the minds of Europe in the period: 'It is lawful for any nation to bring in silver and fetch commodities, but a crime not less than capital to carry any great sum thence.' But Terry, who makes this remark, does not tell us whether any occasion arose for the export of silver from India. There is no doubt that throughout the period of our study Indian exports exceeded the imports, and the balance had to be paid for by actual imports of specie into this country. Nor do I find any authority in Indian writings for the statement that export of silver was visited with capital punishment. Perhaps the traveller was tacitly assuming in the case of India those conditions and circumstances that prevailed in his own country. Perhaps he assumed, for the natural inflow of bullion into India, the political principles by which the governments in Europe wanted artificially to attract silver into their lands. In any case, it is a relief to turn from the primitive economics of hoarding and mercantilism to traces of true currency policy[1] in the indigenous writings of the time. 'Gold, my son, is fit to be enjoyed. For hoarding, gold is no better than stone.' This was an old Indian saying which expressed the commonsense of the ordinary people, for Badaoni who quotes it was rather a pious Mussalman than a man of the world, much less an economist. If hoarding there was, it was due less to economic ignorance than to the desire for ornament and to the general lack of security ordinarily assumed by the people. This will be clear to those who bear in mind that, in spite of the abundance of gold and silver, and in spite of the facilities for converting them into current coins, the rate of interest remained as high as 15 or 20 per cent.

[1] On Mughal currency and coinage, cf. S. V. Venkateswara in the *Journal of Indian Economics* (Allahabad University), Vol. II, and Moreland: *From Akbar to Aurangzib*, Appendix D.

VIII

ADMINISTRATION OF JUSTICE

Ordinary causes were dealt with by the local authorities in consultation with the law officers. These could be laid also before the governor or the *Kāzi* of the province; and from this latter, appeal lay to the chief *Diwān* or to the chief *Kāzi* of the empire. But the tedious process of a law-suit could be avoided by getting justice at the hands of the emperor in person[1] on Wednesdays. Under Shah Jahan and Aurangzib 'the emperor came direct from the *darśan* window to the *Diwān-i-khās* about 8 a.m. and sat on the throne of justice till midday. This room was filled with the law-officers of the Crown, the judges of Canon Law (*Kāzis*), judges of Common Law (*Adils*), *Muftis*, theologians (*Ulema*), jurists learned in precedents (*Fatawa*), the superintendent of the law court (*Darogha-i-adālat*) and the *Kotwāl* or prefect of the city police. None else among the courtiers was admitted unless his presence was specially necessary. The officers of justice presented the plaintiffs one by one, and reported their grievances. His Majesty very gently ascertained the facts by inquiry, took the law from the *Ulema* and pronounced judgment accordingly. Many persons came from far-off provinces to get justice from the highest power in the land. Their plaints could not be investigated except locally; and so the emperor wrote orders to the governors of those places, urging them to find out the truth and either to

[1] 'Once a week the emperor giveth judgment for crimes capital and civil.' (Roe: *Letter to Lord Carew*, January 17, 1616). Aurangzib had two days a week (Bernier, p. 263).

mete out justice there, or to send the parties back to the capital with their reports.'[1] Jahangir set up bells of justice in his palace and heard complaints from those who rang them.[2] But severe rules had to be enforced against a frivolous use of the bells. Mandelslo tells us that one who rang the bell did so at the hazard of his life. Rarely twenty plaintiffs could be found on Wednesdays in Shah Jahan's reign. 'Few cases came before the emperor except those relating to blood and religion,' says the chronicler, Bihari Mal. Aurangzib had a *Mullah* in each important locality to hear cases connected with religion.

Some reforms in detail were attempted by the Mughal emperors. Akbar prohibited all executions until the sentence had been confirmed by him.[3] Jahangir gave a day's time between the imperial sanction and the actual execution, so as to permit of a reconsideration in the case of hasty orders. But these rules seem to have fallen into desuetude, as they had to be revived under Aurangzib. There was no attempt to reconcile the Hindu and Muslim codes of law,[4] as Sher Shah had made before this period though

[1] '*Studies in Mughal India*' by Sarkar, pp. 14 and 70.

[2] *Memoirs* (Trans. Rogers and Beveridge), Vol. I, p. 7.

[3] The practice continued under his successors: 'When any man deserves death, a courier is despatched (to the emperor) to know his pleasure.' (Thevenot: *Travels*, Part III, p. 19).

[4] Akbar is said to have sanctioned Brāhmanical courts, which followed the *Dharma Śāstras*. We do not know how they worked.

The *Kāzi* alone could put robbers to death. He sat at the western gate in Agra, off the bazaar. Tuesday was the day of execution (*Purchas*, IV, 72—Wm. Finch). The chief *Kāzi* Abdul Wahab Borah amassed 33 lakhs in 16 years.

In 1761 Aurangzib ordered that the Kāzis should attend court every day from 7 to 12 noon, except on Wednesdays when they were to attend on the *Subahdar*. Friday was a holiday.

ineffectually. Aurangzib's penal code was pervaded by the spirit of Islam.[1] But the chief defects of Mughal law were the absence of a proper classification of crimes and the lack of an equitable sense of the relative gravity of offences. Murder was classed among torts, and a composition for homicide was paid to the relatives of the murdered person, like the Teutonic *Wergild.*[2] We read in the *Ain* that among slaves were a class of murderers 'whose guilt had been atoned by payment of money.' These had become slaves to those who had released them. No distinction was made in law between deliberate murder and accidental or justifiable man-slaughter. The gravity of the crime was judged not by the motive which led to it but by the instrument used to accomplish the act. The law was likewise tinged with the peculiar sentiments and prejudices of the age. Drunkenness was a prevalent vice, and we find the use of liquor regarded as a capital offence.

The rules of civil and criminal procedure were the same as in previous times. When a civil claim was proved, the person who gained the suit was put in possession of the property in dispute, and the judge imposed a fine of equal value on the defendant. If the plaintiff lost his cause, he had to pay double the sum that had been sued for. Hindus resorted to the ordeal, whenever the judge could not give a decision

[1] The penal code of Aurangzib is contained in a *farmān* to the Dīwān of Gujarat on June 16, 1672, as well as in *Fatawa-i-Alamgiri.*

[2] If the relatives of the murdered took the 'price of blood' (*diya*), the State did not care. Another punishment was public censure: The face of the culprit was blackened, his hair cut, and he was paraded through the streets (*Ency. of Islam*, I, 132). In Hindu India the head was shaven and the man seated on an ass facing the tail, covered with dust and a garland of old shoes.

even after examining witnesses. Whereas in Europe the ordeal was given up in the 13th century, it was in use in India down to the 18th century. Even as late as 1746 we find the East India Company's factors at Tellicherry applying the oil ordeal in civil cases. Abul Fazl knew eight kinds of ordeal, which were in use among the Hindus. Among them are the usual forms of ordeal by red-hot iron, by boiling ghee or oil, and by poison. Akbar is said to have abolished the ordeal, but the Jesuits of his time declare that he sought at the fire ordeal the proof of the superiority of the Christian religion. In the event of inability to clear off debts, both debtors and sureties were imprisoned or enslaved. It is to be noted that Muhammadan law knows no ordeal. It is strange that Aurangzib did not abolish it among the Hindus.

In murder cases a system of collective responsibility was enforced on villagers and townsmen. The *Ain* observes that 'if the murderer is not discovered, the inhabitants of the town or quarter where the murder was committed shall endeavour to find him; and in default they are subject to whatever fine[1] the judge might think it proper to inflict.' Prevention of crime was secured by the efforts of officers like the *Kotwāl*[2] who were charged explicitly with the duty of inquiring into the occupations of inhabitants and driving away sturdy idlers and vagabonds. A similar duty was performed by the imperial census officers.

[1] Aurangzib, a strict Hanāfi, forbade fines which were against the Koranic law. (1679.)

[2] 'The governor meddles not in criminal affairs; an officer named *Kotwāl* takes cognizance of them.' 'Neither the civil nor the criminal judge can put any one to death. The king reserves the power to himself (Thevenot).

We have a record of the census of 1590 which was a thorough-going survey of the land and its people.

State officers were held responsible for the restitution of lost or stolen property. Abul Fazl says of the *Kotwāl*: 'He shall discover thieves and the goods they have stolen or be responsible for the loss.' There is something to the same effect in the observations of the European travellers. Thevenot says that the *Kotwāl* was answerable for thefts and robberies in the town, and the *Faujdār* in the country round about. Manucci says that the *Kotwāl* had to make good the loss if any one was robbed in the day-light on the public road. But it is difficult to find out how the system worked out in practice. It obtained among the Hindus as well, going back as far as Manu and Yājñavalkya. But Manucci says of the village-guards of the Hindus, who were responsible for preventing thefts at nights, that if any one complained to their superior officers they gave him a sound beating, stripped him of what he had, and threatened to kill him and his people.

Judicial procedure of the Mughal period had its good and bad sides. It was good according to the Persian standard: 'Speedy injustice is preferable to tardy justice.'[1] The summary method of disposing of cases excited the admiration of travellers. Secondly, there was, as Manucci remarks, a remarkable uniformity in the judicial administration, brought about by

[1] 'Trials are quick, and so are executions . . . commonly done in the market place.' (Terry).

'The governor of the town (Surat) judges civil matters, and commonly renders speedy justice.' (Thevenot). But Akbar forbade punishment until he had given orders for the *third* time (Montserrate, p. 209).

the agency of imperial news-writers. On the whole Manucci considered the institutions of the empire as not free from defects indeed, but yet 'little inferior to those of any other nation.' When Bernier assures us that 'a few rupees to the *Kāzi* or his clerks, and a few more expended in buying false witnesses, would have gained the litigant his cause or prolonged it as long as he pleased,' he was making an observation applicable probably to human nature in every clime and country. So also about the employment of torture for judicial and political purposes, some instances of which are on record.[1] A Dutch traveller (1629) swears to two forms of torture having existed among the Muhammadans—whipping, and beating the sole of the foot with a thong. Terry also describes some barbarous methods of inflicting punishment. 'Some malefactors were hanged, some were beheaded, some were impaled, some were killed by elephants, and some were stung to death by snakes.' If crime was rare, it was due not to the terrorism of any savage forms of punishment, but to the peaceful and law-abiding character of the people.

Far the most interesting of the local institutions were the village juries.[2] Differences among villagers were of two classes—social and civil, and there

[1] Montserrate, however, records that 'no one is actually punished with these instruments, which seem to be intended rather to inspire terror than for actual use.' (p. 211).

[2] The vitality of the village judicial administration is proved by the absence of primary courts under the provincial *Kāzis*. It was very seldom that a rich plaintiff carried his case to the *Kāzi* (Sarkar, p. 19). It is a pity that the Persian sources throw no light on the Hindu caste-courts and arbitration boards (records in Mahrāthi inform us to some extent), or about the Brāhmanical courts sanctioned by Akbar. They followed Manu.

were crimes, though rare. All these were dealt with by the panchāyats. The forms of the panchāyat varied in different places, but the principles of their working seem to have been the same in most cases. Civil cases were usually settled by arbitration by the hereditary heads of castes, who were paid fees by their castemen and who held office during good conduct, by the common consent of their constituents. When the cases were referred to government, panchāyats sat upon them. Each of the parties named an equal number of members, and the government appointed the President. Criminal cases of a grave nature were tried by panchāyats called by the head of the district. In emergencies they called in the aid of the panchāyats of the neighbouring villages. In caste-disputes they were aided by panchāyats formed of the heads of castes.

There were no vakils pleading before the panchāyat, and its members got no pay. Their sole reward lay in increase of social influence and personal reputation. The working of the panchāyats was limited and controlled. There were never less than five members, and their decision was expected to be unanimous. If more than one member dissented, the proceedings were invalid. The findings of the panchāyat were transmitted to the governor, and he then delivered judgment. Even after trial by a panchāyat, the accused might appeal for a reversal of the decision or pray for trial by a fresh panchāyat. Boundary disputes were never referred to panchāyats. Nor were petty crimes, which were dealt with by village headmen. Powerful chieftains seldom called panchāyats at all.

IX

THE MILITARY SYSTEM

The most important department of the army was the cavalry. The status of an officer was determined by the number of horses he was expected to maintain for service in the field. A *mansab* of 5,000 horse got its holder a monthly pay of Rs. 28,000 or 30,000, while the horses cost about Rs. 10,000 to maintain. A *mansab* of 1,000 horse entitled its holder to receive Rs. 8,000, one of 100 horse from Rs. 500 to Rs. 900, while the monthly cost of maintenance was estimated at Rs. 3,000 and Rs. 300 respectively. It is clear, therefore, that the higher one went up in the ranks of *Mansabdars* the greater were the profits.[1] The expenses of the *Mansabdars* on other animals and on the infantry they had to maintain, varied with their rank in cavalry. But the real remuneration of the *Mansabdar* did not depend on these figures. The emperor determined the exact number of horses each officer was actually to maintain, as against the number for which he was paid. The difference constituted the profits of the officer, and these were not inconsiderable. Sir T. Roe informs us that the Governor of Patna got pay for 5,000 horse, and maintained only 1,500. Prof. Blochmann reckons the net profits of a *mansab* of 5,000 at £15,000 per annum. The profits, lawfully large, were made unlawfully larger by the dishonesty of most *Mansabdars* who, as Badaoni points out, brought hired horses for the muster, instead

[1] Roe and Terry put it inaccurately when they mention indiscriminately that the payment for each horse was £25 (Roe, p. 89) and £18 (Terry, p. 410).

of maintaining them all through the year. Every *Mansabdar* had to maintain half as many infantry as cavalry; and one-fourth of these were to be matchlock-men, and the rest archers. There were other foot-soldiers under his command, but they received their pay from the state. Besides, the people at large were bound, says Bernier, to follow their ruler in important campaigns.

The total number of *Mansabdars*[1] was 1,388 under Akbar, 2,064 under Jahangir and 8,000 under Shah Jahan. Of the higher *mansabs* of 500 and over, there were 252 under Akbar, 439 under Jahangir and 592 under Shah Jahan. From Akbar's time Hindus were given some of these high posts. But even here the proportion of Hindus employed becomes the smaller as we go higher up the list. There were only two Hindus in the first class of 30 *Mansabdars* of 5,000 horse and over; and 2 out of 9 of 4,000 horse, and 8 out of 17 *mansabs* of 3,000. Hindus held in all 32 out of 252 higher *mansabs* of 500 and over, and 25 out of 163 of *mansabs* from 200 to 400. The number of Hindus employed in higher ranks went on increasing under Jahangir and Shah Jahan. We learn from the *Pādishah-nāmah* that there were 110 Hindus among Shah Jahan's commanders of 500 horse and above. Masters of less than 10 horse were known as *Ahadis*, of whom there were 44,441 in Jahangir's reign.

It is not easy to fix the total number of Mughal cavalry. Ralph Fitch says that Akbar had 30,000 horse

[1] The number of *Mansabdars* in 1690 was about 7,500, paid in cash, and 4,000 jāgirdars. *Br. Mus. Per. Ms.* quoted by Sarkar: *Mughal Administration*, p. 13.

at Fatehpur and Agra, and Abul Fazl that he had never less than twelve thousand in his own stables. If Hawkins may be believed, Jahangir's cavalry was 300,000 strong. The strength of the infantry has been much exaggerated. Abul Fazl says it amounted to 4,400,000, but he apparently includes those who were bound by tenure to give a limited service in certain cases. The strength of the infantry was estimated at 400,000 foot by Careri and Bernier. But the infantry was a despised force. There were a few thousand picked men around the person of the emperor; the rest were a mere rabble of foot-soldiers and camp-followers.

The army arrangements of the empire were not consistent with discipline. Military discipline, applauded by Babar, had become inefficient in the eyes of the Afghan Sher Shah, and relaxed to the point of nothingness through the cpiated ease and idle luxury of the over-kind Humayun. Even under Akbar there was no chain of subordination among the sectional commanders, as each *Mansabdar* had authority over the quota of troops he supplied, and was answerable to the emperor alone. Nor were the soldiers given any training in tactics. The ridiculously small number of officers, as compared with the general levy, explains the disregard of discipline[1] and of instruction in tactics. The vitality of the Tartar had become sapped, too, by the hot climate of India and the easy conditions of settled life.[2] Lucky it was

[1] Though Akbar tried to enforce it strictly (Montserrate, p. 82).

[2] Hence, probably, the remark of Shah Jahan's that one Portuguese could easily beat three Indians, to which Terry adds that one Englishman was better than two Portuguese, and De Laet that a Dutchman was as good as the Englishman (De Laet, *op. cit.*, p. 83).

for the army that there was not much organised resistance. There were a few native chiefs, indeed, who offered a heroic resistance, but they could not present a united front and were easily conquered piecemeal. The futility of the grand army was demonstrated by the first fruits of Sivāji's military organisation.

Was the army efficient in securing the safety of India from foreign invasions? Such security has always depended on the safeguarding of the north-west frontier and the command of the ocean. For in the north-west are the land gates of India, through which invasions have come from pre-historic times onwards, and rolled down into the plains below. By sea the Portuguese had come to India, and the might of the Europeans in warfare was well known to the Mughal emperors. But they never took the lessons of Tamerlane and Albuquerque as seriously as empire-builders ought to have done.

We do not read in the *Ain* of any special measures taken to secure the north-west gates of India from chronic raids from outside or from echoes of the political storms bursting in Central Asia. The only precaution taken was the feeble one of stationing in the frontier provinces a few hundred soldiers more than in the interior provinces. The empire had expanded as far west as Afghanistan, but the Mughal emperors did not understand that the Hindu Kush is the scientific frontier of India, and that it would be difficult to guard effectively any territory to the west of that mountain chain. If the early emperors enjoyed freedom from invasions by the passes, it was due to the conditions then prevailing in Central and Western

Asia. A balance of power existed in those regions as the result of the rivalry of Persia, which was strongly consolidated under the famous Safevi dynasty, with Turkey, which had expanded over Syria under the Osmanli Sultans. The final success of Persia might have affected India, but for the death of Shah Tamasp, which led to internal troubles. After varying fortunes under Jahangir and Shah Jahan, the Mughal strongholds on the border were seized by the Persians and the rebellious Afghans in Aurangzib's reign. Thus Shah Jahan's fatuous war in Balkh had no permanent results, though it cost about four crores of rupees. It was hardly a compensation that the lost territory temporarily yielded a revenue of 22½ lakhs, besides some advantage to India in the matter of Indo-Persian commerce. When the Mughal grasp of the Persian frontier became insecure, the invasions of Nadir Shah and Ahmad Shah were the natural consequences. Nor did the Mughal emperors deal seriously with the question of the thorough subjugation or complete pacification of the unruly Afghan tribes. To Todar Mal belongs the credit of having initiated a Buffer State policy. We learn from the *Khulasāt*[1] that Todar Mal made over part of Multan to the Beluchis so that they might be a 'strong barrier between Hindustan and Khorasan' and thus 'set up a firm rampart on the confines of the two countries.'

There was no better security on the other frontiers, eastern or southern. Under Aurangzib Shaista Khan read the Arakanese severe lessons in discipline, but the Assamese kept Mir Jumla at bay with their guerilla warfare. Southwards lay the Hindu and

[1] Sarkar, *op. cit.*, p. 78.

Mussalman kingdoms of the Dekhan, whose mutual dissensions gave rest to the empire. When Aurangzib overthrew Bijapur and Golkonda, he only broke the barrier against Mahrātha incursions. Bands of Mahrāthas ravaged the plains of Hindustan and levied blackmail wherever they went, while new bands of robbers like the Grassias and the Pindaris added to the sufferings of the people.

Nor can we credit the Mughal emperors with having created a powerful navy for defence on the seas. Akbar's Admiralty department fitted out strong boats, and there were ships built in various parts of the empire. But these were designed for commercial rather than for military purposes. Aurangzib's naval experiment only resulted in the discovery that 'to sail over and fight on the ocean were not things for the people of Hindustan, but only suited to European alertness and boldness.' What had led to this experiment was the capture by pirates of a Muhammadan vessel loaded with cowries, the current money of Bengal. The great distances of the capitals from the coast made effective sea-control impossible, and the empire had to depend on mercenary fleets. The armed flotilla of the Bengal viceroy and fitful subsidies to 'Abyssinian' Siddis on the west coast were the clumsy expedients by which the Mughal government sought to check the pirates of Arakan who swept the Bay of Bengal, the Malabar pirates who rove the western seas, and the Portuguese who harassed pilgrims on their way to Mecca. There was constant trouble especially from the Portuguese, and our records are full of complaints against them. They dominated the route to Mecca and would allow no

Mughal ships to pass, which had not secured a passport from them. The Mughal emperors were content to purchase the passes as demanded (as Akbar was in 1579), but even this did not secure freedom from molestation, as these passports were merely 'letters of Bellerophon.'[1] Of pirates like Henry Avery, the Court writes to 'our General and Council in India' under date 7th August 1696 :—'... Their robberies and villainous practices on the *Gansway* and other ships in the Red Sea belonging to the subjects of the Great Mughal, which we cannot think of without astonishment and detestation.' Khafi Khan says 'when the ships return from Mocha and Jedda bringing gold and silver .... the English spies have found out which ship bears the richest burden and attack it.' 'The Sakanas also, *alias* Bawaril, of Surat are notorious for their piracies.' 'The English pirates not only searched for plunder but stripped the men and dishonoured the women, both old and young.' The Mughal emperors were, in short, helpless in securing the safety of their subjects from these buccaneers. They had conquered Gujarat by land, but left the naval complement of this conquest to the London Company, whose squadrons in the seventeenth century patrolled the pilgrim high-way and acted as a sea-police to the empire. Towards the end of Aurangzib's reign the English were given definite charge of the ships in Bengal, the French of those trading with Persia, and the Dutch of those proceeding to Mecca.

[1] So says Faria-y-Souza (Rolandson : *Tohafat ul Mujahidin*, pp. 90 and 104).

X

INTER-STATE RELATIONS

The relations of Vijayanagar with the Portuguese were guided by economic interests. Through Goa came the horses from Arabia and Persia, which were absolutely necessary to the imperial army. There were legations to Goa in 1547 and 1549. In the former year a treaty was formed, both offensive and defensive, as against all except Ahmadnagar. Cloths from Vijayanagar were not to be sent to the ports of Bijapur, nor iron or saltpetre to be exported there. No Muhammadan ships were to halt at the ports of the Vijayanagar state. In return for these conditions the territories conquered from Bijapur were to belong to Vijayanagar. We do not read, however, of any Jesuits being established at Vijayanagar at any time. The trade relations of Goa and Vijayanagar were so brisk that the roads were lined with shops, and any trader could make profits computed at 25 to 30 per cent. The horse-trade yielded Goa a tax of 120 or 150 ducats on each horse.

Vijayanagar's diplomacy in the Dekhan is a stale oft-told tale. It combined with Ahmadnagar and Golkonda in attacking Bijapur in 1543 and in 1551. In 1551 Rāmarāya had the aid of Golkonda in defeating his two rebel brothers. Later, he assisted Bijapur against a rebellious vassal, and, in 1555, that vassal against the Portuguese. In 1557 the Sultan of Bijapur went to Vijayanagar, but was treated with disrespect. Yet Bijapur and Vijayanagar combined to ravage Ahmadnagar. Soon after, Ahmadnagar and Golkonda combined against Bijapur and Vijayanagar.

Golkonda deserted its ally, and Ahmadnagar was once more ravaged by the Hindus. Rāmarāya sent armies against Golkonda and Bijapur. These passing winds of diplomacy led to the whirlwind of Tālikota in 1565.

Akbar's relations with other states were of a distinctly political character. His spies were at Goa under cover of ambassadors, whenever ships arrived from Portugal, 'in order to estimate how much wealth and how many people have come'. This could easily be believed, as he wrote explicitly in his letter to Abdulla Uzbeg of Turan, dated 23rd August 1586: 'I should undertake the destruction of the Feringhi infidels. . . . They are stumble blocks to the pilgrims and traders. We thought of going in person and cleansing that road of thorns and weeds.'[1] An Armenian Christian is said[2] to have carried a letter from Akbar to Martin de Albuquerque in 1596, but we have no knowledge of the details.

When Akbar was sitting before Asirgarh, he sent an embassy to Vijayanagar. The ambassador, 'a prudent and experienced man,' put up with the Jesuits for a month, and was summoned to see the Emperor after he had waited for 20 days. There was an atmosphere of suspicion as to the motives of the Mughal, and these were well grounded. Xavier wrote that the purpose of this embassy was to conquer Goa and Malabar and the Empire of Vijayanagar. Valentin mentions that Akbar reached Goa and Calicut, perhaps meaning that the Mughal forces or diplomacy went so far. The ambassadors were really spies set upon the enemy

[1] *Akbar-Nāma*, III. 757.

[2] Bartoli: *Missione*, quoted in 'Calcutta Review' No. 163, p. 6.

with a view to ascertain his fighting strength and the condition of his fortresses. No tangible results could therefore follow. Venkaṭa gathered an army which, Coutinho rightly suspected, was for 'driving back the army of Akbar and garrisoning the northern cities and fortresses.'[1] Another Mughal embassy was among those waiting for the Raja's audience in 1604.

Raja Venkaṭa II was by this time seriously contemplating a combination of South Indian forces against the Mughal empire. He sent ambassadors to the new Viceroy of Goa in 1601, and the success of the legation elicited congratulations from Philip III of Spain and Portugal in 1604. There was a return embassy and, after the stormy events at Mylapore, diplomatic relations were resumed in 1608, under instructions from Philip III. The Portuguese Viceroy had already invited Vijayanagar and Bijapur to seek the co-operation of the other Dekhani Sultans. The Bijapur embassy of 1604 came perhaps to invite Vijayanagar to form a defensive alliance against Akbar. The Portuguese were, however, keen on securing the expulsion of the English from Masulipatam. The friendly relations continued till 1610 when the Jesuits were removed from Venkaṭa's court. A memorial against them elicited severe orders from Philip III. It was alleged that they were busy painting indecent pictures to please the Raja.

Jahangir received the embassy of Sir T. Roe from England and Zanbil Beg from Shah Abbas of Persia. Under Shah Jahan no diplomatic relations with the European states were possible as Mumtāz Mahal, the

[1] Heras: *Aravidu Dynasty*, Chs. XVI and XXI. Heras cites Coutinho's letter, dated Chandragiri, August 1600.

lady of the Tāj, hated Christians and especially the Portuguese. Under Aurangzīb there was no attempt at rallying the Muhammadan powers against the Hindus. This is strange, in view of his fanaticism and the warning administered to him by Shah Abbas II:[1] 'Most Zamindars in India are in rebellion as their ruler is weak, incompetent and without resources. Chief of them is the *khafir* Sivaji. . . . You have abandoned the royal practice of doing justice and charity, and are delighting in Satanic magic.' It is doubtful if Aurangzīb could have succeeded in establishing sound and consistent diplomatic relations. That he broke his royal assurance of safe-conduct and security to Śivāji was but too well known to his contemporaries.[2] His anxiety to conquer Bijapur and Golkonda was also very much in evidence.

Perhaps the most significant of the attempts at diplomacy of the time is revealed in Śivāji's letter[3] to Jai Singh in 1666. Śivāji proposes a confederacy of the Hindu powers, including the Rāṇa of Mewar and Jaswant Singh. 'We four will inaugurate a grim war . . . so that nothing may be left of *Aurang* (throne) or *zīb* (lust).' 'This is not the time for fighting among ourselves, as a grave danger faces the Hindus.' 'If two hearts combine they can make a mountain burst.'

[1] Sarkar: *Aurangzīb*, Vol. III, pp. 126–7.

[2] *Surat Factory Records* 1665–7, p. 175. Cf. Thevenot's account: *Indian Antiquary* for 1927.

[3] *Sivaji Souvenir* (1927), pp. 172–8.

CHAPTER VII

HINDU-MUSLIM SYSTEMS OF POLITY

Mahrātha Administration

I

CENTRAL GOVERNMENT

The government of Śivāji was a benevolent despotism. There was no power to check the emperor, and the safety of the empire depended on his benign government. The ministers were merely his servants. Such principles of feudalism as already existed in the Mahrātha country were carefully stamped out. The *Deśpaṇḍes* and *Deśamukhyas* lost their feudal power, were prohibited from building castles, and had to give up their fortresses, which now became outposts for royal garrisons. One is reminded of Norman and Tudor despotism building itself on the overthrow of feudalistic regimes. Śivāji appointed all the *Karkūns* himself, and they alone had authority over the land. Moreover, he was the head of the State in religion. A remarkable instance of the king of the Mahrāthas exercising his powers in this capacity is met with under Sāmbāji, who sanctioned the reconversion of a Hindu who had been put out of caste for having interdined with Mussalmans. The Rāja's despotism may therefore be compared with the Mughal monarchy under Akbar, who became head of the Church about 1581.

The Council of Śivāji consisted of eight *Pradhānas*. They were appointed by the king and held office during his pleasure. Some of them went out on military expeditions, and others were in charge of provinces. They were not entitled to consultation, but the king usually consulted them, and their deputies during their absence.[1] During Śivāji's reign three of the ministers were in charge of provinces, and their representatives resided at court. But these deputies and all the subordinate officers were appointed by Śivāji himself. Those in charge of provinces came to the court with their annual accounts and the revenues due from them. None of these officers was allowed to become hereditary or to be confined to particular families. None of them carried a jāgir. In this respect Mahrātha polity may be contrasted with Mughal polity, where there were tendencies to a disruption in the State through the growth of an aristocratic, political or territorial baronage.

The eight *Pradhānas*[2] were the *Mukhya*, *Senāpati*, *Amātya*, *Sachiva*, *Paṇḍita*, *Nyāyādhīśa*, *Mantrin* and *Sumantra*. The *Mukhya* was the king's vicegerent, and combined civil and military functions. He waged war, and protected the dominions from invasion. He was the chief minister, true to the designation of his office, and he developed into 'Peshwa' in later times. The *Senāpati* had only military functions. He commanded the army, kept army accounts, maintained discipline, and accounted for the spoils taken in war. The *Amātya* was the Chancellor of the Exchequer,

[1] Sarkar cites no authority for styling them a *Cabinet* (*History of Aurangzib*, Vol. V, p. 26.).

[2] *Sabhāsad*, p. 82, 83; Sen: *Śivachhatrapati*, pp. 115-6. The *Pradhānas* took part in the *abhisheka*, and their duties were defined.

and had under him a good staff of clerks to keep accounts and conduct correspondence on financial matters. He also did military work during times of war. The *Sachiva* was the king's Private Secretary. He conducted the royal correspondence and was in charge of the royal seal. His was the duty of consolidating the conquests and restoring peace and order in conquered countries. The *Paṇḍita* was in charge of the department of religion, and of the patronage of learning. He had judicial powers in matters of socio-religious custom and usage.[1] The *Nyāyādhīśa* was the judge in all civil and criminal cases. The *Mantrin* was the minister of diplomacy and head of the Intelligence department. His spies were active in war-time, and he did other war service. The *Sumantra* was in charge of foreign affairs. He received ambassadors, and sent embassies to other States. He was also in military service at times.

A comparison of the Mahrātha council with that of the earlier ages supplies interesting suggestions. We do not find here any of the household officers of the king as in ancient Hindu and in Mughal polity. The queen does not sit in Durbar as she did in Hoysaḷa and even Vijayanagara times. Nor are there any representatives of sections, castes or communities as implied in the ancient *Grāmaṇī*, *Taksha* and *Rathkāra*. The ministry has a distinctly military import, six of the eight *Pradhānas* having military duties. Even the names of some of the offices bear witness to this. In place of the *Pratinidhi* of the *Śukranītisāra* we have the *Senāpati*. The *Sumantra* of that period had financial functions, the

[1] *Āchāra, vyavahāra* and *prāyaśchitta.*

Amātya was the minister for development, and the *Mantrin* the home-minister. It is interesting that while those names are retained, the offices are here given a military character. This is only what may be expected, as Śivāji's state was a military state, and war had not only to feed war but to supply resources for the administration in peace.

The number of ministers was usually eight, which was the norm in Hindu polity. At the coronation of Śivāji we find nine, but this is because the office of *Amātya* was held jointly by two brothers. When the Mahrātha dominions expanded in the South, the office of *Pratinidhi* was created. In Rājā Rām's time the *Pratinidhi* had his seat at Jinji, and he held the first seat in the ministerial council. Every one of these eight ministers had a staff of eight clerks—a secretary, a treasurer, an accountant, an auditor, a record-keeper, a cash-keeper, a correspondence clerk and an emissary.

The most interesting development in the next period is the rise of the Peshwa.[1] The *Mukhya* was at first only one of the ministers, and Bālāji Viśvanāth, the seventh in succession in that office, drew a salary of 13,000 *hūns*, whereas the *Pratinidhi* got 15,000. But the *Mukhya* became the *Peshwa* and a sort of Mayor of the Palace under Bāji Rao I. It was to the interest of the *Pratinidhi* and his settled policy to push forward the expansion of the Mahrātha power in the South. But Bāji Rao got Sāhu's approval for his policy of expansion in the North. He also got himself appointed by the Rāja as the guardian of the minor prince, which meant a virtual supersession of the

[1] Ranade: *Writings*, p. 345; Scott-Waring: *History of the Mahrāthas*, p. 169; Sen: *Mahrātha Administration*, p. 199.

Pratinidhi. Tāra Bāi imprisoned the minor Rājā-Rām at Satara. The Peshwa's power gradually grew, but it excited neither observation nor surprise. Delegation of authority, real or assumed, had been an incident of Mahrātha administration. Sivāji had appointed a council of regency under Jījī Bāi, when he was absent in the North. Kulusha ruled for Sāmbāji; Rājā-Rām's ministers ruled as they liked; and Sāhu's fits of insanity made such rule imperative.

The Peshwa was a colleague of the old nobles and master of the new. Special honours and precedence had to be given to the former, like Āngria and Yādava Rao; but Sindhia and Holkar were the Peshwa's subordinates. All these barons exercised feudal authority which was sovereign within their fiefs (*sarañjams*), but the Peshwa appointed their *Diwāns* and other officers, as was done of old by the Rāja. The feudal nobles rendered military service.

The Secretariat (*Huzūr Daftar*) employed more than 200 *Karkūns.* It kept accounts of the revenues and prepared abstracts (*tarjamas*) of daily registers. At the head of the establishment was the *Huzūr Fadnāvis.* Nāna Fadnāvis introduced many improvements in its working. His Budget (*beheda*) department prepared the abstract of the previous year's accounts (*taleband*) and the estimates (*ajamas*) for the current year. Special accounts were maintained for the military jāgirs. 'Abstracts of all expenditure were arranged alphabetically under the proper heads.' The *Daftar* was neglected under Bāji Rao II, and records removed by interested people.

In the eighteenth century the Rāja of Satara acquiesced in the Mughal supremacy. Sāhu accepted a *mansab* of 10,000 horse from Farrukh Siyar, and in exchange for the *sardeśmukhi* of 10 per cent., bound himself to protect the country, to suppress brigandage and to restore stolen property. He opposed the building of a northern gate to Poona, lest it should be construed as lack of reverence for the *Pādishah.* He sincerely believed in Mughal sovereignty.

The Rāja of Satara appointed the Peshwa and other ministers. The appointment was signalised by a grant of robes of honour by the Rāja.[1] The *Pratinidhi*'s dress of honour in the year 1778 consisted of a 'head-dress and arms.'[2] The formality continued even in later times, when the very household officers of the Rāja were completely under the control of the Peshwa, and the palace accounts subjected to rigorous scrutiny. But pomp and splendour remained as of old, and ceremonial presents (*nazar*) were made to the Rāja. Nāna Fadnavis made two attempts to restore the political power of the Rāja, but in vain. In spite of Nāna, Mahadāji Sindhia got for the Peshwa the title of *Mahārājādhirāja*, and the Rāja of Satara acquiesced in his own impotence.

II

PROVINCIAL AND LOCAL GOVERNMENT

Śivāji's provinces were styled 'Swarājya' of which there were sixteen.[3] Sāhu had thirty-seven. Each province was in charge of an officer, who had the usual staff of eight assistants. The province was called *prānt* and was divided into *mahāls.* The

[1] *Peshwa's Diaries*, IX, 110: cited by Sen: *Mahrātha Administration.*

[2] *Ibid*, IV, 158.

[3] Ranade: *Rise of the Mahrātha Power*, p. 117.

smaller provinces were under *Kāmavisdārs* and the larger under *Māmlatdārs*. These officers were directly under the Central Government. Their pay was usually 4 per cent. of the revenue, besides a lump sum for establishment charges. Some of the local officers were paid only for ten months, though they worked for the whole year. The duties of the *Kāmavisdārs* and *Māmlatdārs* varied, but they included the supervision of agriculture and industries, the appointment of panchāyats for deciding civil and criminal cases, the control of the Police and other officers and the enquiry into the social and religious questions which were referred to them. In the districts of Khandesh, Gujarat and Karnatak there was a *Sarsubahdār* interposed between them and the central government.

The first check on the power of the *Māmlatdār* was the presence of the *Deśmukhs* and *Deśpaṇḍes*. These local officers had been in charge of *pargānas* before Śivāji's time. As they had oppressed the people, Śivāji appointed his own men, and the *Deśmukhs* and *Deśpaṇḍes* henceforth appear as friends and champions of the cause of the ryots, especially against the *Māmlatdārs*. They maintained the accounts and registers of property. They had customary dues from each village in money and in kind, and their interests were therefore bound up with those of the people. Some of them were women.[1]

Another check on the *Māmlatdār* was the provincial staff who were independent of him. They consisted of 12 *Karkūns* and were in charge of

[1] Till 1772: *Peshwa's Diaries*, Vol. VII, p. 113.

various departments of the routine work of administration. From the time of Mādhava Rao I there were also settlement officers. All these *Darakdārs* formed checks on the *Māmlatdār* and also on one another. The Intelligence department was efficient, consisting of numerous spies (*jasuds*) and messengers (*harkaras*).

There were also other checks on the *Māmlatdārs*. They had to pay an advance of revenue, and to conform to the budget (*beheda*) of the central government. They were appointed for short terms only, and frequently transferred from one province to another, under Śivāji. But the tenure was extended under the Peshwas, and the *māmlat* tended to become hereditary. Loose government under Bāji Rao II was marked by frequent changes in the stations of the *Māmlatdārs*.[1]

The capital city was planned by Śivāji on the customary Hindu lines, and on the model of Vijayanagar. According to *Sabhāsad*, Śivāji built in the fortress of Rājgir not only palaces for his queens, separate quarters for the officers, superior nobles and men of note, a council hall and a market, but also stables for elephants, horses and camels, and a storehouse. Rājgir was the capital for sixteen years. The ministers' quarters and the bazaar were situated to the north-east, and the two store-houses, south and south-east. The Mahādeva temple was to the north, with quarters round it for temple servants and dancing girls. Within 200 yards of the *Rang-mahāl* or Palace of Pleasure, stood the citadel to the north and powder magazines to the east. To the north-west of the palace were the elephant stables.

[1] *Bom. Gaz.* (1896), Vol. I, pt. 2, p. 113.

The city was under the *Kotwāl* who had more or less the same functions as in Mughal polity. He decided disputes, fixed the prices of goods, supplied labourers for government work, supervised sales of land, took a census, and kept a record of all men arriving at the city and departing from it. No one in the city could appear in the streets after 10 P.M. without being arrested. 'So strict is the discipline,' records Tone, 'that the Peshwa himself had been kept prisoner a whole night for being out at improper hours.'[1] The villages acted as self-contained political units with democratic institutions, and were recognised by the Peshwas as such. Brāhmans and non-Brāhmans served on the panchāyat, and even the poorest man was heard. There are instances of both village officers and artisans being summoned to the Peshwa's court to give evidence.

The *Patel* had revenue, magisterial, police and judicial functions, and was seldom of the Brāhman caste. His was a hereditary office, whose rights could be sold in whole or in part. Thus the first *Subahdār* of Salsette confirmed as *Patels* those who had been *mhātras* (village headmen) under the Portuguese.[2] He held a high place in society, and was given by the village various perquisites in kind and cash. He controlled the watchmen and enquired into cases of theft and robbery. He had to make good any losses sustained by his co-villagers on account of riots, or of banditti, of thieves, or of robbers. In judicial disputes he had to arrange for arbitration, or to see that a

[1] Tone: *Illustrations of Some Institutions of the Mahrātha People* (1818), p. 55.

[2] Reg. 1 of 1808. *Mhātra* is a corruption of *mahattara*.

panchāyat was constituted. He was responsible to the authorities for the payment of the revenue due from the village, and was liable to be imprisoned for default.

The *Patel's* colleague, the *Kulkarṇi*, was always a Brāhman. Both were surety to the government for the loyalty of the villagers in troublous times. Village records were in the custody of the *Kulkarṇi* and he, like the *Patel*, got emoluments from the villagers in grain and cash. Their assistant was the *Chowgula*.

The communal officers of the village were twelve (*bārā baluti*) assisted in some tracts by another body of twelve (*bārā aluti*). All these were paid by perquisites. Chief of them were the astrologer (*Joshi*), the *Mahar* and the *Potdār*. The Mahar summoned the villagers to the *Patel's* office, acted as the village watchman, looked after the sanitary arrangements, and had his customary share of grain at harvest and perquisite in hides. The *Potdār* or goldsmith was paid by the Central Government,[1] and had his small fee from the village office. Villages had power to borrow for public purposes. The land was owned by the *Mirāsdārs*, and sometimes leased out to tenants. Criminal classes had their dwellings outside the walls of the village. They did police duties, and their *Nāik* or leader was made responsible for thefts and robberies.

III

FINANCE

The revenue system of Śivāji was based on that of Mālik Amber at Aurangabad. Mālik Amber had,

[1] Rs. 4 a month, in 1766.

like Todar Mal in the Mughal empire, surveyed arable land, classified it according to fertility, compiled statistics of the produce, and fixed the assessment payable in money. The great advantage of the system lay in its doing away with intermediaries and making the hereditary *Paṭels* and other revenue officers responsible for the collection of revenue.

Śivāji made the survey more accurate and systematic, fixing the unit of measurement. He used the rod, instead of the rope which could be so used as to swindle the ryot and over-estimate the extent of his land. Secondly, Śivāji classified the land under twelve heads instead of Mālik Āmber's four, and his assessment on each *bigha* ranged, according to its quality, from 5 maunds to 12½. Thirdly, Śivāji's assessment was based on the average of the three previous years, to be paid half in kind and half at a fixed commutation rate.[1] Fourthly, the results of the survey were checked in person by Śivāji's minister, Aṇṇāji Datta, in the Konkan. Aṇṇāji sent a circular letter to the village officers in 1678, and checked their returns in regard to at least one village of each description in each district. His settlement was on fair and equitable principles.[2] In later times the Peshwas attended personally to the work.

Aṇṇāji fixed the land-tax at a third of the gross produce. Śivāji raised it to two-fifths, but abolished the cesses. He retained the customs, and his customs officer at Kalyan is mentioned by Fryer.[3] Settlers

[1] Such, at any rate, was the belief in the Konkan, according to Jervis.

[2] T. B. Jervis: *Memoir of the Konkan*, p. 93.

[3] *New Account of East India and Persia*, (1691), p. 123.

on new land were encouraged by grants of grain, cattle and money, which were recovered in easy instalments.[1]

The chief sources of Śivāji's revenue were the *chauth* and the *sardeśmukhi*, reckoned at a fourth and a tenth of the revenue. Ranade considers the former as the payment for forces to protect the paying country against foreign aggression.[2] When the *chauth* was legalised by the Great Mughal, Sāhu accepted such obligation. In later times the Rāja of Boondi agreed to pay *chauth* to the Peshwas for such protection. One-fourth of this was reserved for the Rāja, and three-fourths spent in maintaining and equipping the troops.

Sabhāsad mentions 32 kinds of gold and 6 of silver coins circulating in Śivāji's dominions. But only two or three of Śivāji's *hūns* have yet been discovered. So most of these must have been foreign coins. Fryer[3] notes that Śivāji allowed foreign coins to circulate freely: he 'would not force his subjects to take those moneys whereby they shall be losers.' We find in his dominions the coins of the Vijayanagar emperors, Devarāya, Rāmachandra and Achyutarāya; and the *hūns* of Gooty, Dharwar, Adoni, Tadpatri and Vellore, among others. Numerous copper coins were issued from Śivāji's mint in 1674. Credit instruments (*huṇḍis*) too were in use and were encouraged.

The rule of the Peshwas witnessed some improvements. The land revenue was made payable in three or four instalments into the village treasury, and receipts were given for payment. *Māmlatdārs* were

[1] *Sabhāsad*, p. 32. [2] *op. cit.*, p. 224. [3] *op. cit.*, p. 80.

instructed not to take from the ryots more than the customary dues; to plant trees such as the cocoanut every year[1] at a progressive rate of 5 per cent; to exempt farm-bullocks and buffaloes from octroi for five years;[2] to give cultivators leases of 5 or 7 years, and to forbid the sale and mortgage of land.[3] Under Mādhava Rao II, there was a grant of subsistence allowance to the *jamābandi* officers, so that they could be thoroughly honest and refrain from levying contributions from the ryots.

Commutation of rent in kind to money was permitted but not encouraged. Cultivation was stimulated in various ways. Where the soil was poor the cultivator benefited by the *batai* system, by which he had to give only a fraction of the normal tax to the State. In rocky parts lands were tax-free (*inām*) or half-free for 20 years. Agricultural loans (*tagai*) were given, either at a low interest or no interest at all,[4] in money or in kind out of the private purse of the *Māmlatdār* or *Kāmaviśdār*. Remission of revenue was made in hard years,[5] in whole or in part, the other part being payable in four annual instalments. Where the camping of officers caused injury to agriculture, compensation was given to the cultivators.[6] The planting of trees was encouraged by making them tax-free,—cocoanut for 20 years, and areca-nut for 15 years. Lastly, dams and canals were paid for by the State either in whole or in moiety, and a grant amounting to a fourth of the expenses was made for roads.

1 In 1747.
2 In 1748.
3 In 1774.
4 as in 1743 and 1750.
5 a half in Pachora, in 1750.
6 In 1768 and 1773.

Such benevolent schemes were in vogue till the days of Bāji Rao II, who introduced the Mughal system of farming out to the highest bidder and brought ruin on the cultivators.

The Peshwas allowed private mints to coin money at a licence fee of Rs. 50 or 100 a year. In 1760 the issue of false coins at Dharwar led to the closure of the mints and the establishment of a State monopoly. At the central mint the charge was only Rs. 7/- per 1,000, of which six went to the government and one to the manager. The excise duty on cotton goods was 2½ per cent. and the customs 5 per cent. reckoned *ad valorem.*[1]

The miscellaneous revenue under the Peshwas compares with the *sair* revenue of the Mughal emperors in regard to presents (*nuzzar*), succession duty, escheats, confiscations from zamindars, mints, customs and excise. There were duties charged on trade, industry and professions, as in the Vijayanagar empire. There were extra dues from land, the triennial tax on *Mirās-dārs*, for instance, and in critical times the *jāsti puṭṭee* of a year's income from all land-holders. The State had the proceeds from house-tax, tax on weights and measures, marriage fees, taxes on sheep and she-buffaloes, pasture fees, forest produce, garden dues, and temple offerings. The profession taxes (*mohatarfa*) were those on palanquin-bearers, shop-keepers, blacksmiths, shoe-makers, oilmen, goldsmiths, potters, basket-makers, boatmen,[2] stone-quarriers and masons. The State had a monopoly in cocoanuts and in ghee. There were dues from towns, like the *kotwāli* and a sixth on the value of houses

[1] *Peshwa's Diaries*, III, p 320.

[2] E.g., in 1742.

sold (*jakat*). In the case of new towns, traders were attracted to them by promise of exemption from taxes,[1] and special privileges were given to founders of new market-towns.

Some of the taxes reflect the social and industrial policy of the government. The State encouraged ship-building, and exempted the builders from taxes. There were Mahrātha merchants trading as far west as Muscat, and as far east as China, and some were doing business with the English. Ships were recovered for merchants from pirates free of charge, no salvage money being demanded. Sometimes the taxes on commodities were remitted partly to augment the supply, as in 1764. There was State regulation of some industries like textiles and lac. The extraction of toddy from cocoanut trees was stopped in 1776. Wine was permitted only to the Portuguese soldiers in service, who were allowed to distil liquor for their own use. They were strictly ordered not to sell or give wine to Brāhmans, Prabhus, Shenois or government servants. The last class enjoyed exemption from ferry-charges and from taxes on personal consumption. But the most interesting point is that the assessment and collection were flexible, and were regulated according to the conditions in each particular district. The condition of the *Mirāsdārs* (proprietors) and *Upris* alike was on the whole satisfactory, as will be seen from Forbes' description of the districts through which he travelled.[2]

[1] For e.g., seven years in 1777.

[2] In 1771. See his *Oriental Memoirs* (1813) I, 204. On *upri* (*upari*) see *supra*, p. 111.

IV

MILITARY SYSTEM

Śivāji's military policy was one of efficiency. The hillsmen formed an excellent infantry, and the hill forts were easily defended strongholds. Of the last, Śivāji had 240, and Sāhu at least one in every taluk. New forts were erected, and each fort was garrisoned by about 500 men. There were three officers of equal authority in each fort, two Mahrāthas and one Brāhman, with a Prabhu as accountant. This organisation was based on the Bijapur system, in which there were three officers in charge of each fort.[1] The Brāhman officers of Śivāji were *Deśasthas*. The Shenois were men with a literary bent and had taken service under the Portuguese. One of the three officers guarded the gates, another kept accounts and conducted correspondence, and the third did commissariat work. In 1761 Śivāji created a reserve fund of one and three-quarter lakhs for the routine repairs of forts in general. From the French at Surat he purchased 80 pieces of cannon and lead for matchlocks.

The infantry were organised in battalions with units of 10 under a *Nāik*, 50 under a *Havaldār*, and so on to a thousand under a *Hazari*, and 7,000 under a *Sarnobat*. Cavalry organisation partly followed the Mughal system. Some cavaliers had equipment from the state. The divisions ranged from 25 troopers under a *Havaldār* to 5,000 under a *Pañcha-hazari*. The main improvement effected by Śivāji was that he had a reserve of one horse for every two troopers, in the interest of speed. The Intelligence department was

[1] Compare the Portuguese system (p. 172 *supra*).

equally efficient: 'He pays his spies regularly, which has greatly helped his conquests by the correct information they give him.'

Śivāji's military discipline was excellent. Pay was punctually and regularly disbursed, in contrast to the Mughal system of keeping soldiers' pay in arrears. There were the usual arrangements according to the principles of Hindu polity, in regard to reward for merit, pensions to widows and orphans, and allowances to the wounded. The widow got half the husband's pay as pension. But no women were allowed in the army. There were strict regulations, enforced by punishments, forbidding the capture of women, children, Brāhmans and cows in the enemy territory.[1] Even Khāfi Khān commends his wisdom in maintaining the honour of women who fell into his hands, and disallowing any dishonour to mosques or to the *Korān*. There were spies, who enabled military discipline to be maintained. In this matter Śivāji got a warning from the defects of the Bijapur system. During campaigns the soldiers were not to give the ryot the least trouble. Funds were furnished for purchasing food for men and fodder for animals in the open market. Everything captured was to be given up to the state. This was an improvement on the system of Mālik Āmber who had anticipated the Mahrātha tactics of harassing the rear of the enemy, plundering the convoy, and cutting off the forage.

Śivāji paid considerable attention to the navy. He took advantage of the ancestral skill and experience of the Malabar mariners. The fleet was 57 sail in 1675, according to Orme's account, but other

[1] Elliot and Dowson, VII, pp. 305, 341.

English reports put the number near 160. According to *Sabhāsad* it was in two squadrons and four hundred strong, and one of the admirals and one of the officers were Muhammadans. Most of the ships formed a mercantile navy, manned by Malabar seamen and plying on the Arabian sea. The President at Surat seems to have remarked[1] that one good English ship could destroy one hundred of them. This remark was probably cynical, and need not be taken seriously.[2] The navy did some fighting with the Siddis and once captured a Portuguese ship near Damaun. Sāmbāji's ships at Rājāhpur (in 1684) are described by Orme[3] as more than a match for the Goa fleet. In any case Śivāji deserves the credit for having understood and maintained the importance of sea-power, while the Mughal rulers were fighting shy of the problem or giving it up in despair.

During the period of Peshwa rule the Mahrātha army was modelled on the Mughal system. Women were allowed in the army, and appear at the battle of Paniput in 1761. The troops of Daulat Rao Sindhia retired in the evening from their barracks to the arrack shop and revelled the whole night in low debauchery.[4] It is clear that the army had become hopelessly demoralised, and that Śivāji's wise restrictions had been helplessly relaxed. The number of non-combatants in the army exceeded that of the combatants. There was luxurious display and the bazaars included wine-stalls,

[1] Sarkar: *Sivaji*, p. 339.

[2] Bishop Heber certifies that 'the ships built by native artists at Bombay are notoriously as good as any which sail from London or Liverpool.' (*Letter*, dated March 1825).

[3] *Military Transactions*, pp. 141, 145.

[4] Broughton, *Letters* of 1809, p. 21.

bullocks, camels and elephants, all in the train, depending for supply on the 'Brinjaris'. Sometimes contributions were taken from feudal chieftains who were subsequently rewarded with fat jāgirs.

Moreover, foreigners were employed in the army. Sivāji had men of all races and religions, including some Portuguese, in his army. Kaṇhoji Āngria employed Europeans long before Sindhia's time. The English officers employed would not face their countrymen and wanted to resign. Jaswant Rao Holkar shot some of them down for such disobedience in the field. One Mr. Lucan, who had left Sindhia's service, was very useful to the British at the battle of Aligarh. But even French officers could not be relied on, as Perron and others made terms with the British government. Mādhava Rao had, in his pay, Evans and fifty others, Europeans of a low type. Baji Rao II had an American, Boyd, who had a pay of Rs. 3,000 per mensem, and eight Portuguese gunners at Rs. 60 each. Boyd's regiment was 1683 strong and cost Rs. 26,000 odd a month. The highest pay of an Indian officer[1] was Rs. 25,000 a year. A large number of Arabs were enrolled after 1742; 'Pindaris' accompanied the army and plundered even Hindu foundations, e.g., Śriṅgeri *Maṭha* in 1791.

Forts were maintained on the revenue of the surrounding villages. Some forts in the Karṇāṭaka were under commanders appointed by the state, but were garrisoned by hereditary servants enjoying rent-free land in payment for service. The artillery was not good. Guns were unwieldy. For good artillery and munitions the Mahrātha relied mainly on the

[1] Karde, in 1762.

English and the Portuguese. The sea was treated as a Mahrātha preserve. The Mahrāthas followed the Portuguese precedent of demanding passes from travellers on the sea. There were an admiral and an *Āmīn* in every ship, the latter being the civil and the former the military head. At first hereditary employees were used as checks on superior officers. But this system was given up later in order to secure undivided command. In the later period naval power was with the Āngrias, but they were independent of the Peshwas.

V

JUSTICE

The machinery of justice devised by Śivāji followed the good old simple Hindu plan. In every village the elders met at a common place, sometimes the *Patel's* office, sometimes the temple, or in the bounteous shade of a spreading tree. The men, though illiterate, were aware of the customary laws of the land. The ordeal was permitted for finding out the truth, but only in cases where the parties were unable to produce documentary or oral evidencc. Criminal cases were first heard by the *Patel.* Appeals lay to the judge (*Nyāyādhīśa*) of the neighbouring town, in both civil and criminal cases. Parties were examined by the *Sabhānāyaka* and cross-examined by the *Mahāpraśnika.*

But the judicial genius of the Mahrāthas sought to avoid resort to the law courts. Arbitration and amicable settlement were encouraged in every way, and often a solatium was offered to the defeated party.

But, if arbitration failed utterly, a panchāyat was instituted, by *Patels* in villages and by *Mahājan* or *Seṭṭ* (leading merchant) in towns. The members of the panchāyat were not allowed to receive payments or presents from the parties. They were chosen by the parties themselves and were bound only by a sense of duty and the fear of public opinion. There were no lawyers, and the members of the panchāyat had to decide questions of law as well as of fact. The winner had to give a fourth of the property in dispute, but this sum was remitted when the party pleaded poverty. The panchāyat's judgment was not binding unless confirmed by the *Māmlatdār*, but he refused to accept it only in cases of proved peculation.

In important cases the panchāyat was recruited from the aristocrats of the locality, the *Deśmukhs* and *Deśpaṇḍes*, from territorial chieftains in the neighbourhood, and from the *Patels* of the adjoining villages. We hear of a case of appeal which was heard by a special council (*majalasi*), consisting of the *Ājusabha* and Brāhmaṇa *sabhā*, whose members were men of substance.

Execution of decrees was helped by social opinion. Debts were usually realised without invoking public aid. *Dharna*[1] was practised against high and low alike. It was by sitting *dharna*—by refusing to take food or water until their dues were paid—that the Muhammadan soldiers of Daulat Rao Sindhia were able to realise their arrears of pay. It was possible, however, for those not responsive to public opinion, to delay matters by obstructive tactics. A suit could be dragged successively through the

[1] Described by Bishop Heber; *Journal* for Sept. 1824.

processes of arbitration, panchāyat, and ordeal, and through the courts of *Māmlatdār*, *Sarsubahdār* and Peshwa.

There was state interference in certain matters of Hindu Law.[1] Adoption required government sanction. The inheritance tax, on succession to the property of a childless brother, was introduced for the first time in Indian polity. Marriage of first cousins was penalised in 1744. In 1789 there was an order forbidding the study of the Vedas by men of the *Prabhu* caste. Bāji Rao II was responsible for a curious piece of legislation. He not only forbade the acceptance of money for giving girls in marriage, but forbade parents keeping their girls unmarried after the ninth year of age.

In murder cases the relatives of the murdered man were compensated. Punishments ranged from fine and confiscation to imprisonment and execution. The amount of fine imposed depended on the means of the party punished, and it was allowed to be paid in instalments. The accused in a criminal case, if there were strong grounds for suspicion, had to pay some fine even if the charge against him could not be legally proved. Sorcery and witchcraft were recognised as offences, and were punishable with fine, imprisonment, excommunication or exile. The punishment for adultery was slavery and penal servitude for men, and hard manual labour in fortresses for the girls. But in prisons the relatives of the prisoners were allowed to see them, and were even provided with rations

[1] But the Mahrāthas allowed full liberty of conscience to their Muhammadan and Christian subjects (Du Perron, I. 384, cited in *Bom. Gaz.*, *op. cit.*, p. 86).

to look after the prisoners. Political prisoners were well treated, and rigour was shown only if they attempted to escape.

Police administration was efficient. The village police officer was the *Mahar* who was under the *Patel*, and the district police were under the *Māmlatdār*. There was the principle of compensation even in the event of non-detection. The robber tribes were made responsible for crimes and criminals, in return for the payment of customary dues. There was an additional police force sent by the *Māmlatdār* to help at fairs and festivals. The city police was under the *Kotwāl*. There were few complaints of insecurity of property. Bāji Rao II introduced a special officer to inspect the police. The Peshwas themselves went on tour every year to receive complaints, and punish offenders. These tours were repeated frequently whenever necessary. Chiefs like Daulat Rao Sindhia similarly went round their estates and were, according to Broughton, always accessible to the people at large. Greater store was set by the prevention than by the punishment of crime.

VI

THE TANJORE MAHRĀTHAS

The political system of the Mahrāthas in South India was to some extent based on the principles described above. The points of distinction that emerge are traceable to the influence of the administrative machinery of Vijayanagar, and were therefore better suited to local conditions. The king was supposed by the ignorant to govern according to his despotic will, says Schwartz, but 'he is in fact more a slave than a king.' He was the head of the State and could carry on the traditions of the government in regard to legislation, taxation, public works and patronage of learning. But the routine work of administration devolved on his ministers and subordinates, and the foreign policy of the king was the sport of political conditions in South India. The situation gave Śivāji slender hopes of support in South India for his life-object of reorganising the shattered forces of Hinduism.[1] He visited the Carnatic in 1676, but to little purpose. The caution of Śivāji to his brother Veṅkāji who founded the Mahrātha state of Tanjore can well be applied to every member of that ruling house: 'Look to the discipline of your army and turn your attention to affairs of moment. This is the time for perfecting great actions. Awake, arise, bestir yourself.' The ease and repose into which the Rājas had fallen had a compensation in the bloom of literature, philosophy and fine arts.

These do-nothing kings inherited political difficulties. They were a foreign dynasty settled in the Tamil country and, like the Nāyaks before them, could not evoke a sentiment of loyalty. Their kinsmen were too far away in the north and west to be counted upon for active help or alliance. Local and dynastic feuds divided Tanjore from the neighbouring kings, and the very fertility of the deltaic region invited invasions from Bijapur, Golkonda and Hyderabad. It was impossible to expect an alliance with Mysore on account of the conflict of interests

[1] Taylor: *Mackenzie MSS.*, Vol. III, p. 369.

over the Kaveri waters. The conditions were such as to baffle the political genius of even the best of kings.

The ministry consisted of the traditional eight (*ashṭapradhānis*), and membership tended to become hereditary. The *Shāhji Vijayam*[1] mentions four as the chief ministers—*Mantrin*, *Senāpati*, *Dharmādhikāri* and *Purohita*. Sometimes the *Senāpati*, also known as *Daḷavāy*, likewise acted as *Mantrin*. The other ministers were the *Pradhāni* or *Diwān*, *Samprati* (Accountant), *Dabīr* (Secretary), and *Rāyasam* (Private Secretary). Judging from the career of individual ministers, it would appear that the *Daḷavāy* or *Senāpati* was the highest in rank, and that below him came in descending order, the *Pradhāni*, *Dabīr*, *Rāyasam* (styled *Sarkele* from the time of Śarabhoji), *Dharmādikāri* and *Samprati*. The *Purohita* stood in a category by himself. Another man in power was the captain of the fort (*Khilledār*) in the capital. The disposition of work among these eight ministers suggests a comparison with Sivāji's ministry, which comprised the *Mantrin*, *Senāpati*, *Nyāyādhīśa*, *Paṇḍit*, *Mukhya*, *Amātya*, *Sumantra* and *Sachiva*. The main point of difference is that the ministers other than the *Daḷavāy* had no military functions, and that there was an irresistible tendency to a combination and hereditary transmission of offices. This accounts for the emergence of trimmers and 'king-makers' like *Rāyasam* Veṅkaṇṇa in 1673 and the Sayyid, the father-in-law of Chanda Sahib, in 1736–40. In the reign of Śarabhoji, the *Daḷavāy* is actually styled Peshwa (1720).

[1] *Trien. Cat. of MSS.*, Madras, II, pt. I.

Provinces were known as *subahs*, which seems to show the influence of Muhammadan rather than of Mahrātha polity. The *Subahdār* had the usual military and civil functions; and was helped in the collection of revenue, where necessary, by a *Havaldār*. The *subah* contained several *sīmai* or *nāḍu*, each of which was divided into *māgāṇams* which again comprised several villages. These are Hindu names, and show that the old Chōḷa nomenclature and arrangements were retained in the local government. The work of the provincial government became considerably lightened by the introduction of the *Puttack* system. The *Puttackdār* was in charge of several villages, not exceeding 128, and was specially instructed to bring backward tracts of land into cultivation. He was responsible for the payment of a fixed revenue. Even apart from this the Tanjore Mahrāthas introduced the system of farming districts to the highest bidder. Thus the work of the *Subahdār* was very much reduced. He had to arrange for arbitration in the case of civil disputes which could not be settled by the parties themselves.

Among the village officers were the Headman, (*Karṇam*, *Kulkarṇi*) and the Watchman (*Kāvalkāran*). They maintained the local accounts and registers (*nāṭṭukkaṇakku*). An abstract of these was submitted to the Central Government through the *Subahdār*. It is interesting to find that among the village servants are included not only smith and carpenter, washerman and barber, but a waterman, whose duty was to supply drinking water to all passers-by. The village assembly was known as *mahājana*. The panchāyats looked after civil and criminal justice in the village. Land in the village was held in one of three forms of tenure. Some was under sole proprietors known as *Mirāsdārs* who owned the land permanently (*ēkabhōgam*); some was held as joint property by the village, the produce being shared by the resident families in a certain proportion fixed for all time (*samudāyam*). Other lands were periodically redistributed among the villagers, and were known as *palabhōgam* because they constantly changed hands. Lands belonging to village officers, and those gifted away to men of learning, were tax-free (*inām*).

Towns under the Tanjore kings were little more than walled villages, where the citadel gave the people shelter in times of stress and disturbance to the public peace. A *Havaldār* with a police force under him was in charge of the town, and the larger forts were under *Killedārs*. The *Killedār* of the capital city had influence with the Central Government. *Havaldārs* helped the *Subahdār* in collecting the revenue and keeping the peace. There was the usual civil army of spies to convey intelligence of the happenings in the rural tracts. The Mahrātha rulers repaired old forts and built new ones, and manned them with soldiers, but their artillery was poor and they had to depend on the European traders for efficient ordnance. The forts could not therefore serve as bulwarks of effective defence, much less of safety from foreign invasion.

Justice was administered by the local officials and panchāyats in cases where voluntary arbitration could not compose civil differences. The king was the highest appellate authority, and appeal lay to his court against the decisions of the local judiciary. The king's court early in the period had only one Civil Judge; but four other judges were added later. The Court heard appeals, original cases from parties who refused to submit their cases to the panchāyat, and high class criminal cases which the panchāyat felt delicate to handle, or where it felt itself powerless to enforce its decision. The court fee was 5 per cent. One exceptional feature of interest in the judicial administration is an institution corresponding to itinerant jurisdiction in England, the royal judges going on circuit and hearing and disposing of cases in the localities concerned. Bartolomeo speaks of this system as prevailing, but there is no reference to it in other sources.

The picture of the civil administration given by Schwartz and Heber[1] suggests a few principles. The land revenue taken varied from 40 to 70 per cent, in accordance with the fertility of the land, the kind and quality of the yield and the economic and political conditions of the time. The normal land-tax was half the net produce. Among the other items the port-dues and customs bulked the largest, European traders being specially encouraged. The excise revenue was farmed out, and included a tax on toddy and liquor. Cesses were levied to pay for the *Kāvalkār* (watchman) and for the local festivals. Among the chief items of expenditure, one notes that on arts and industries, including the local industries of carving and pith-work. The palace library was an institution of which any state may be proud.

[1] See Pearson: *Schwartz* (1834). Heber: Letter to Horton, December 1823. Taylor: *Memoirs of Heber* (1835).

VII

ADMINISTRATION UNDER THE 'NĀYAKS'

The administrative system of the Nāyaks of Madura, Tanjore and Jinji was modelled on the old Vijayanagar polity, modified in such a way as to suit the local conditions. As these were, from the start, primarily military commanders under the Vijayanagar empire, there was a tendency to lay stress on the military aspect of the administration. Being foreign to the country of their charge in tradition, lineage, language and social usages, they had the two-fold duty of protecting their own position in the country of occupation and safeguarding the imperial interests of their suzerain. But they could not overrule the local chieftains who had been in charge of independent principalities in the South. Therefore, the founder of the Nāyak line of Madura felt the necessity for dividing his country into a number of provincial units (*pāḷaiyam*) each under a local chief (*Pāḷaiyakkāṟan*).[1] The original duty of the polegar was to keep men for the protection of the country against thieves. The men had 'the obligation of apprehending thieves or making restitution of goods stolen between sunset and sunrise in the open country, and whether night or day, if among the hills.'[2] Under the Nāyaks, these were allowed to have their own system of government, provided that they rendered their accounts duly to the king, remitted the revenues to the treasury, and provided military contingents in times of necessity.

[1] There were in all 72 such *pāḷaiyams* under the Nāyaks of Madura.

[2] Read's *Letter* to Cornwallis, dated 15th November 1792.

The Central Government under the Nāyak rule was constituted by the king and his council of ministers, based on the old and traditional methods. The *Daḷavāy* ('head of the troops') was the principal officer, and practically the master of the administration. In the case of an able minister like Aryanātha there was the combination of the offices of *Mantrin* and *Pradhāni* also in the same hands. The latter of these officers was the Finance Minister as well as the Judge. The *Rāyasam* (Private Secretary) was the next important officer. There were, besides, the *Kaṇakkan* (Accountant), and *Sthānapati* (Home-Minister) who, as their names imply, were respectively in charge of the royal accounts and provincial affairs. One feature of the administration was that it was dominated by the *Daḷavāy* or Commander, as was naturally to be expected in a military government. Each of these ministers had his own subordinate staff, who were directly appointed by their chief and were responsible to him.

The Nāyak kingdom was divided into a few large provinces, each under a governor and lord of the local polegars. These were directly under the *Daḷavāys* who had 'the chief management of the whole kingdom'[1] and served as the connecting link between the central and the local governments. They wielded enormous powers in their provinces, and a few at least should have become 'more powerful than the Nāyak who then resided at Madura'.[2]

[1] Nieuhoff: *Voyage and Travels into Brazil and East Indies*, ii, p. 297.

[2] Bertrand: *La Mission du Madure*, Letter ii, p. 346 (Mr. R. Satyanātha Aiyer's Tr. in his '*Nāyaks of Madura*').

Village life under the Nāyaks continued as of old, with its revenue and police officials and systems of civil and criminal jurisdiction. The village was self-sufficient and self-governing, and was the smallest unit of administration. A number of villages constituted a *māgāṇa*, which was a sub-division of a *nāḍu*, a number of which in turn went to make a *maṇḍala* or *rāshṭra* (province). One noteworthy feature of the village administration seems to be that the traditional panchāyat system did not find favour under Nāyak rule. We are told that 'each village has two judges, who are much respected by the inhabitants.'[1] Apparently one of these was for civil as the other was for criminal justice.

The Finance department in Nāyak polity was under the control of the *Pradhāni*. Taxes were paid probably in cash, on the model of Vijayanagar finance. The taxes from the villages were collected by the *Maṇiyakkāṟan*, the revenue official, and remitted periodically into the treasury through the polegar and the provincial governor. The main source of revenue was the land-tax which amounted to nearly half the actual produce. Then came the contribution from the polegars (*paishkāsh*) which was equal to a third of what they got from their *pāḷaiyams*. This amount varied with the size of the *pāḷaiyam*, the fertility of the lands and the yield to the agriculturists. The third important source of revenue was fishing, especially for pearls, shipping on the coasts, etc. The Nāyaks of Madura had a fairly long sea-board which was famous from time immemorial for its pearl and *chank* fisheries. Besides these, there were the usual

[1] Nieuhoff: *op. cit.*, p. 297.

taxes and cesses like customs and tolls, export and import dues, taxes on weavers, oil-mongers, etc., and octroi duties. The chief items of expenditure were those on civil, police and military establishments, and on public works and charity. The Nāyaks were builders of religious and secular edifices, and their charities to temples and other pious foundations have been proverbially magnificent.

The military organisation under Nāyak administration calls for few comments. There was the necessity for a strong army, as there were internecine conflicts in South India at the time and threats of invasions by foreign powers. The *pāḷaiyam* system was the creation of such circumstances, and the polegars were expected to maintain an army of soldiers ready to do the fighting at a moment of stress and strain. It may be supposed that the land-forces were well organised and adequate.

But there was one serious defect in the Nāyak military system, as we find in the case of the Tanjore Mahrātha, viz., in regard to the maintenance of a navy and the defence of the coasts. The sea-coast in both cases was of considerable length; but neither the Mahrāthas of Tanjore nor the Nāyaks of Tanjore and Madura who preceded them troubled themselves about it. The rulers of Madura were probably worse sinners in this respect, as they left the defence of the coast to the Portuguese and Dutch merchants who had settled in large numbers there for trade and fishing. The Nāyaks were satisfied if they got the revenues due to them from the ports. The foreign powers were allowed even to develop their own systems of administration. They were only prohibited from erecting any line of fortification in the ports under their occupation.[1] Thus the king allowed the formation of a state within the state.

VIII

MYSORE UNDER THE WOḌEYĀRS

It is interesting to find under the Woḍeyārs the same idea of resuscitation of Hindu polity which appears under Śivāji and the Mahrāthas. The ideal is the preservation of whatever is best in the state, and 'the service of cows and Brāhmans'. 'Devarāya divided his kingdom into four parts, giving the first to the Brāhmans, the second to the gods, the third to charity and the fourth for himself.' Kingship was hereditary, and the dynasty was reinforced by adoption from Ursu families who corresponded to the polegars. Considerable attention was bestowed on the education of princes, and the curricula included military subjects, polity and philosophy, linguistics and religion.

The king was advised by a family council in the early years, and later by experts and hereditary ministers. The powers of administration lay with the *Sarvādhikāri* (chief civil officer), and the *Daḷavāy* (commander of the forces). The two offices came to be united, and the *Daḷavāy* became the *de facto* ruler, who could make land grants independently of the king, and whose approval had to be obtained even for the grants made by the Rāja. The only possible limitation of his power was in the restriction of the duration of his office to a period ranging from 3 to 5 years. His staff consisted of an accountant (*Kāraṇike*) in charge

[1] Nieuhoff: *op. cit.*, p. 294.

of the temple accounts, a treasury officer, one in charge of the stores and of ornaments, a mint-master, an officer in charge of local governments (*hobḷi*) and another in charge of correspondence work.

Districts were originally in charge of polegars, who had control of all local institutions, save that there was an agent (*kārya kartā*) of the Central Government in the newly-conquered tracts and in frontier districts or outposts. Later there were divisions known as *gaḍi*, over each of which was appointed one *Subahdār* assisted by two accountants, clerks and *Tānādārs* and postal messengers (*Añchekāra*). In each was a local militia to maintain peace and order. The organisation has points of comparison with Mughal and Mahrātha institutions, which were also the product of similar conditions.

The work of the Central Government[1] was conducted by eighteen *chāvaḍis* or offices. The *Ekachchāvaḍi* had a general superintendence of all the departments. *Vichāra-chāvaḍis* of which there were two, one for the regions to the south of the river Cauveri and another to the north, were for matters of revenue and justice. *Śuṅkachāvaḍis* regulated and collected duties on merchandise, houses, etc. *Beṇṇe chāvaḍi* was in charge of the *Sarkār* flocks. There were also the *Munkuda-chāvaḍi* for the levy of capitation taxes; *Torya-chāvaḍi* or the Pensions department; *Bhaṇḍār-chāvaḍi* or Exchequer; *Kandāchāra-chāvaḍi* for audit of infantry accounts; *Caravan-chāvaḍis* in charge of cavalry accounts, as well as those of elephants, camels and cattle; *Koṭṭepaṭṭi-chāvaḍi* for keeping forts and other public works in

[1] *Baramahal Records*, Section I, and *Mysore Palace MSS.*

repair; *Bayhin-chāvaḍi* or the Intelligence department; and the *Hul-maidi-chāvaḍi* for collecting a tax on money-rents and for selling the straw that was yielded by the lands leased out.

Corporate life in the villages was fostered by placing on a solid foundation the ancient 'self-governing' *Bārā-baluti* system, consisting of the *Gauḍ* (headman), *Shāṇbōgh* (accountant), *Pañchāṅgam* (astrologer), *Lōhar* (smith), *Dhōbi* (washerman), *Haja* (barber), *Kumbhār* (potter), *Tōṭṭi* (scavenger), *Talāri* (watchman), *Nīrganti* (one who irrigates fields), *Koṭṭe-maṇiyam* (one who repairs mud-forts) and *Pūjāri* (priest). The emoluments of these officials varied according to the nature of their duties, and were usually paid in kind. The *Gauḍa* and the *Shāṇbōgh* were permitted to receive a greater share than the others. Half the pay of the accountant was paid in cash and half in kind. The other village officials and servants had the right of receiving bundles of hay and one measure of corn from the cultivators. These were also given rent-free lands, varying in value from one to six pagodas, according to their status, for their own cultivation. All the village officials were exempt from payment of taxes.

IX

ADMINISTRATION OF MYSORE UNDER HYDER ĀLI AND TIPU SULTĀN

Hyder Āli came to power when Mysore was suffering from repeated incursions of the Mahrāthas. He made few changes in the administrative system of the Woḍeyārs. He abolished the eighteen *chāvaḍis*, which had come down from the time of Chicka Devarāja, and entrusted the affairs to eight *cutcheris* which had fiscal and military functions. His only care was to increase the revenue to the maximum extent, and to maintain a well-disciplined army. He farmed the revenue to the highest bidders. The kingdom naturally fell into sixteen divisions of unequal extent, each of which was placed under a *Subahdār*. The *Subahdār* had his own *Amildār* or Agent and *Sheristadār* or Accountant in each district, whose work was watched by a *Sheristadār* appointed by the Central Government. But a collusion of these officers was not impossible in the circumstances, and the ryot was impoverished by exactions. Hyder was more successful in forming a powerful militia by attracting war-like men from places as far away as Iran and Turan,[1] and by getting them trained and drilled under European officers.

It was left to his son to perfect the system of administration. In this he was assisted by experienced ministers. His passion for novelty led him to change the entire system and to introduce new regulations in every department. The most prominent features of his administration were the expansion of industry and commerce, economy in expenditure, and the personal attention of the Sultān even to the minutest details, which resulted in over-emphasis in military organisation and over-centralisation in polity.

The highest officer of state was the *Diwān* or Prime Minister, which post was occupied by Mīr Sadick, Tipu's evil genius. His department was the

[1] Kirmani: *History of Hyder Naick* (Col. Miles' Trans., p. 309).

Mahalaut (revenue) *cutcheri*, which consisted of himself, his Deputy and eight accountants. The next officer in rank was Pūrṇiah, who presided over the *Toshch-khāna* or Treasury which was in two departments—cash and stores (*Nugdy* and *Jinsy*). The next departments were those of Meer Meerans, which had control of the various divisions of the army; the *zellu cutcheri*, which paid and regulated State servants; the *Sadr cutcheri* (ordnance department) of garrisons and fortifications; and the *Mallik Tujar* or commercial department.

There were similar offices in every province. Tipu Sultān had under him 164 districts, which he grouped under 7 *tukrīs* or divisions in 1784 and 18 in 1791.[1] Over each of these *tukrīs* were placed civil governors (an *Asof*, a Deputy *Asof)*, and from 2 to 4 *Foujdārs*. For every district in their *tukrī* they appointed *Amildārs*, *Sheristadārs* and other officers.

The gross produce of a district was ascertained on an examination of the register of population and produce. The collection of the revenue was entrusted to an *Amildār* from whom a *muchalika* (contract) was taken for the amount. He was to make a circuit through all the villages of his district, and apportion this assessment among the ryots, after a careful measurement of the land by the *derra sultanee.* If the *Amildār* failed to collect the amount required, he was to make good the deficiency, and recoup himself by encouraging farmers to cultivate new lands. In no case was he to resort to undue force and exactions, and, if any ryot absconded, the *Amildār* was to pay a

[1] *Bārāmahāḷ Records*, Section I, p. 151.

fine of 10 to 20 pagodas.[1] He was to collect the tax in four *kists* (instalments), deducting the expenses of collection (10 per cent. of the gross revenue or 18 per cent. of the net revenue), and to remit the balance to the provincial treasury.

The *Amildār* was also the head of the local militia, which was recruited under a system of conscription. At the muster every Friday, each family was to send a representative for undergoing drill and taking military exercise. Absentees were punished with a fine of five *faṇams*. A regular muster-roll was maintained and was submitted to the *Huzūr* along with the account of the fines collected.[2]

The revenue of the State was derived from land-tax, customs duties, anchorage duty, taxes on houses, on grain and other commodities, and the tribute paid by the polegars. A very large portion of the revenue was derived from the department of commerce. A number of products like resin, wax, lac, teakwood, sandalwood, tobacco, pepper and precious metals were state monopolies. For the purpose of selling sandalwood, pepper and cardamums the Sultān established factories *(kōṭis)* in distant places like Muscat and Cutch.[3] He also sent a good deal of the sandalwood to China. There was a Board of Trade of nine commissioners who had jurisdiction over 17 foreign and 30 home factories. Tipu sought to improve

[1] *British India Analysed,* Vol. I, pp. 1-6; 16-20.

[2] *Ibid,* Vol. I, p. 27.

[3] Tipu had a trade Commissioner in Muscat, who sold sandalwood, pepper, cardamums, cinnamon and rice, and got in return copper and sulphur. In one letter Tipu asks him to send saffron seeds and silk worms.

commerce by removing vexatious restrictions such as the duties on the transit of cloth, cotton and thread, and on the export of grain. He encouraged Armenian merchants to bring their silk stuffs, and reduced import duties. He established banking houses *(Mallik Tujar kōṭis)* all over the country. Besides having the entire management of the exchange, they traded in jewels, bullion, spices, perfumes, raw silk, muslins ; also in cloth and grain of every kind.

His passion for novelty is displayed in his military reforms also. For instance, he changed the technical terms of command from French to Persian and Turkish words. He caused to be written a military code *Futtah-ul-Mujāhidin*, 'The Triumph of the Holy Warriors,' which contained details about military exercises, tactics, etc. With the help of French officers, and some deserters and prisoners of war, he got his army trained after the European fashion. The establishment of a military school for some of the *risalas* of infantry was a remarkable step, which might have led to an improvement in the character of the army.[1] The tone of the army was improved by the prohibition of liquor-vending camps.[2] Undue attachment of the men to their officers was obviated by frequent changes in command.

The faith of the Sultān was chiefly in artillery and muskets, and the infantry was the most important branch of the army. The regular infantry was divided into a number of *kushoons*,[3] each of which was placed

[1] Kirkpatrick : *Letter*, No. 364. [2] *Ibid : Letter*, No. 411.

[3] The strength of a *kushoon* was roughly 1,200 men.

under a *Sipāhdār* or *Sipāhsalār*. Four or five *risalas* constituted a *kushoon*; the lowest unit being a *joug*. The *Sipāhdār* was responsible for keeping his men perfect in their exercises. The *Bakshīs* attached to each *kushoon* helped the *Sipāhdār* in mustering the army, and disbursed the pay. Muskets were manufactured in four places in Tipu's kingdom. A manufactory, established at Kankanahaḷḷi, turned out even iron boilers. *Amils* were asked to impress the labour of blacksmiths and artificers.[1]

The regular cavalry was in *mokubs* (regiments), which were subdivided into *teeps* or squadrons and *euz* or troops. A *Bakshi* was placed in charge of every *mokub*. In addition to the regular infantry and cavalry, there were the *silledars* (mounted on their own horse) and the *kuzzaks* or predatory cavalry. The irregular cavalry was by far the most useful: they were inured to fatigue, and more experienced. They were furnished on the contract system, and were mercenary troops. But the most formidable were the *kuzzaks*, who were not paid, but profited by plunder.

The naval experiment is also interesting. At first the navy had been placed under the department of the *Mallik Tujars* or Board of Trade, but in 1796 a separate Admiralty Department was created under a board of eleven (*Meer Yumm*), and about 40 ships were entrusted to their charge. They were also expected to collect together men experienced in naval warfare and to arrange for and supervise the construction of ships. Wilks says there were 100 ships, including

[1] The number of these is given as 80 in Tipu's *letter* dated 13-6-1786.

frigates, in the sea-ports of Calicut, Mangalore and Goa, and that the total cost of the marine[1] absorbed more than a fourth of the state revenue.

Tipu's aversion to the foreigner went as far as the taboo of European medicines, though on one occasion he sent for skilled French physicians and surgeons. He hated Indian Christians, but encouraged the immigration of others into Mysore if they would settle down and be his subjects. He discouraged emigration because the Muslims brought by Hyder from abroad had filled their pockets and quitted the country without leave. He would rather allow export of specie and coin than of commodities to pay for those necessaries of life which were not produced in his own dominions. But he was for discouraging all trade with the Coromandel coast.

The influence of Tipu's religious views on politics has been much exaggerated. He was on good terms with Śriṅgeri and Śivagaṅga *maṭhas* and wrote 40 letters (1791–98). He asked the *Svāmi* to pray for the prosperity of the country. He presented vessels to the Melkōṭe temple.[2] His new calendar was based on the 60-year-old cycle of the Hindus, and adopted the solar year and the thirteenth intercalary month. He appointed Brāhmans in the departments of revenue and intelligence. His fanaticism showed itself in outside wars in Malabar and Coorg and in putting down rebellions. He put up the mosque at Seringapatam on the site of an old Hindu temple; but Kirmāni says that he acquired the site by paying the Hindu owners for it.

[1] 28 lakhs out of 95 lakhs of rupees.

[2] *Mys. Arch. Sur. Rep.* for 1908, para 79.

X

THE POLITY OF THE SIKHS

A theocratic state was formed in the Punjab by the organizing ability of the Sikh Gurus.[1] Its roots were watered by Akbar's toleration and eclecticism. Its central place was Amritsar, where Akbar gave Guru Rāmadās a jāgir, and the beautiful tank was excavated in 1577. Its bible was the *Grandh Sāhib* which was compiled by Guru Arjun and elicited the admiration of Akbar as 'a volume worthy of reverence.' Its finances were organized, the frequent presents and occasional contributions being collected systematically by local agents and remitted to the Guru annually at the Assembly. The Guru encouraged a lucrative trade in horses with Turkestan, and his followers became the finest horsemen of the time.

Guru Har Govind gave a military and political stamp to this organization. He sanctioned hunting as a pastime and meat-eating to his men. He insisted that all presents to the Guru should take the form of horses, arms and military equipment. He maintained 300 horse and 60 artillery, and his stables could hold 800 horses. The paraphernalia of royalty were added —the crest, the umbrella and the sword. The congregation came to be styled Durbar, and the temple was the Durbar Hall. The Durbar was the court of the Guru, who had jurisdiction in all civil and criminal cases. A theocratic community of monks and mendicants was thus gradually transformed into a flourishing military state of which the Guru was the veritable head (*Saccha Pādshah*).

[1] Dabistan, Vol. II, pp. 217-82.

Guru Govind laid the foundations of the Khālsa in 1695. He enjoined on his followers the worship of *śakti* and the wearing of steel weapons, in place of a divided allegiance to the plough, the loom and the pen. The initiation into the Khālsa (*pāhul*) was by drinking water stirred by a dagger (*kṛpaṇa*). He bestowed on his followers a distinct political existence, and inspired them with the desire of being socially free and nationally independent.

Under Banda the Khālsa soldier became an adept in the use of arms, and trained in guerilla warfare. In the 18th century the military community took advantage of the confusions in the Punjab due to the invasions of Nādir Shah and Ahmad Shah Abdali. The Khālsa became transformed into a compact and united kingdom, and assumed regal powers as the Abdali had foreseen. Jassa Singh occupied the Punjab and coined money in the name of the Khālsa. Later coins bear the legend of Grace, Power and Victory.

Cunningham[1] terms their organization a theocratic, confederate feudalism. The Sikh people met once at least every year at Amritsar. It was on the occasion of the Rāma festival, when the cessation of the periodical rains rendered military operations practicable. Their assembly was termed *Gurumata*, for they sought wisdom and unanimity of counsel from their teacher and the book of his word. The leaders who thus met owned no subjection to one another, 'but the notion of a chain of dependence was acknowledged as the law, and the federate chiefs partitioned their joint conquests equally among themselves, and divided their

[1] Cunningham : *History of the Sikhs*, p. 104.

respective shares in the same manner among their own leaders of bands, while these again subdivided their portions among their dependents agreeably to the general custom of subinfeudation.' The subdivisions were sometimes so minute that two or three or ten Sikhs became co-partners in the rental of one village or of one street in a town. Corresponding to the Mahrātha *chauth*, the Sikhs levied the *rākhi* from the territories conquered but not occupied. The levy varied in amount from a fifth to a half of the government share of the produce.

The Sikhs were in confederacies known as *misals* of which a dozen were important, each being independent in its local concerns. The strength of the confederacy varied from two to twenty thousand. The total force was estimated at 300,000 in 1783 and 248,000 in 1803. All the Sikhs were horsemen. The soldiers were experts in the use of the matchlock, but they had forty pieces of field artillery also in 1800. The order of the *akālis*, with their blue dress and bracelets of steel, owned no subjection to earthly governors, and the more warlike among them acted from time to time as the armed guardians of Amritsar. Their passions had full play till Ranjit Singh's time.

The last Sikh *Gurumata* was held in 1805. The *misals* had served their ends, being democratic bodies under a military leader. It was now felt that the rude system of mixed independence and confederacy was unsuited to an extended dominion. The mass of the people remained satisfied with their village freedom, to which taxation and inquisition were unknown. A single authority was virtually admitted in the person of Ranjit Singh, who laboured to give unity and coherence to the scattered elements and to mould the Sikh nation into a Commonwealth.[1]

Ranjit Singh's main achievement was the political unification of the Punjab. He, like Hyder Āli, was unlettered, but showed genius as general and statesman. He had a talent for the selection of subordinates, and was generous to those who did him service. He had a freedom from bigotry and an intelligent curiosity in all matters of moment. He chose the best men, irrespective of caste, colour or creed. He trained his army on the European model and employed some European officers. As head of a military state, he showed energy and vigour, but evinced a commendable moderation in the exercise of power. He honoured men of reputed sanctity, and attributed every success, whatever his own share in it, to the favour of God bestowed on the Commonwealth or Khālsa. He is represented to have outraged decency by appearing in public inebriated and surrounded with courtesans. This picture has perhaps been overdrawn. In any case his rule was popular, founded as it was on the feelings of the people and the fashions then in vogue. When his genius was no more and a limit had been set to Sikh militarism and dominion, the vital spirit of the race began to consume itself in domestic contentions.

The machinery of administration[2] consisted of the standing army, the revenue farmers, the *Kārdārs*, Jāgirdars and certain governors of large provinces. There were several Jāgirs formed by grants of land,

[1] Cunningham : *History of the Sikhs*, Ch. IV.

[2] Report of Captain Murray, cited by Tupper : *Our Indian Protectorate*, pp. 260–63.

whether to the conquered chieftains themselves or to court officers or favourites. The *Ijāradār* was the farmer of the government share of the produce. Both Jāgirdārs and *Ijāradārs* collected their dues through *Kārdārs*. The *Kārdār* had the duties of protecting his charge, increasing the cultivation, punishing theft, and causing restitution to be made to the complainant. If thieves or cattle were traced to any village, custom rendered it equitable to demand the restitution from the village as a whole.

The prosecutor in a case of theft had to deposit a fourth of the value of the lost property. If successful, the suitor in a civil case paid *shukarāṇa*, a present of gratitude; if unsuccessful, a fine. Civil and matrimonial cases were referred to panchāyats consisting of men chosen by the parties themselves. Resort was sometimes had to ordeals by water, by boiling oil or by bearing a heated plough-share. Bloodshed might be atoned by the price of blood (*khūnbaha*) or by a matrimonial alliance (*nāta*).

XI

CIVIC CONDITIONS IN THE MALABAR COAST

The country west of the Western Ghats exhibits a picture of Hindu communities developing their peculiar political and socio-religious institutions unhindered by influences from outside. The king was never despotic. His power had been limited in the earliest ages by the rights of the sixty-four original villages, which constituted a primitive democracy. When the introduction of monarchy was found necessary in the interests of an integration and consolidation of these communities, the power of the king was still limited to 12 years in duration, and his ministry were checked by the Nairs.[1] These limitations continued, down to the 18th century.

Of political importance is the festival known as *Mahāmakhạm* described in a Malayāḷam manuscript diary[2] of the Zamorin, dated 1683, and in the ballad known as *Māmāṅkappāṭṭu.* The festival was held every twelfth year at the capital city of Tirunāvāyi. At this festival the Zamorin was seated in his tent on an open plain, and any chieftain who could break through the ranks of his guards and slay him, could gain the crown for himself.[3] To this end a jubilee was proclaimed throughout the land on the completion of the twelve years, and the Zamorin was allowed to retain the throne only if he could protect himself against all comers. If he was not able to hold his own, he was either beheaded or had to retire into a temple. The last evidence of this festival being held is in 1743.

The military and social prestige enjoyed by the Nairs was an effective check on the Zamorin's despotism. We read in 1746[4] that 'the Nairs, being heads of the Calicut people, resemble the Parliament, and do not obey the king's dictates in all things, but chastise his ministers when they do unwarrantable acts.' Another check on the Zamorin's power had been the sanctity attached to the Brāhman hierarchy and priesthood. To these may be added the influence of a hereditary

[1] Day: *Land of the Perumals*, p. 42.
[2] Quoted by S. V. Venkateswara: *History of the Zamorins*, p. 25.
[3] Hamilton: *New Account of the East Indies*, Vol. I, p. 310.
[4] Diary of the Tellicherry Factory, 2nd May, 1746.

ministry and the political influence wielded by the Moplah merchant-princes.

The country was divided into *nāḍs*, and each *nāḍ* into *deśams*. These were military divisions.[1] The ruler of the *deśam* was the *Deśavāḻi*. His general powers included control over public properties and collection of the revenue. He was entitled to certain customary payments, the chief of which was the marriage fee. In judicial affairs he was assisted by two or three local men known as *Pramāṇis*. These formed a kind of jury, and cases were decided by them in the presence of the *Deśavāḻi*. Judges were paid for their service. The *Deśavāḻi* got a rupee on every case tried, and the *Pramāṇis* half a rupee each, in cases involving more than Rs. 15. In criminal cases the verdict of old men was taken into consideration.[2]

The *Nāḍuvāḻi* was the ruler of the district, and the superior of the *Deśavāḻi*. He was responsible for the collection of taxes, and commanded the forces. He administered justice in person, when influential persons were concerned. His power was so great that, even if the Zamorin found him disobedient or traitorous, he could not confiscate his property, though he could dismiss him.

The chief of the *Nāḍuvāḻis* was the minister of the State. To him, in the absence of the king, appeals went on the decrees of the other *Nāḍuvāḻis*. After the 15th century the ministership became hereditary in the family of the Māṅgāṭ Acchan at Calicut, as of the Pāliyat Acchan at Cochin. The power of the minister was so great that as soon as a Zamorin died,

[1] Warden's Report of 12th September, 1815, paras. 63, 64.

[2] Philipp: *Account of the Malabarians*, p. 83.

and before his obsequies were over, the authority complete as of right devolved on the Māṅgāṭ Acchan, who except in name was the Zamorin for the time.[1]

The system was feudalistic in several ways. The *Nāḍs* and *Deśams* were designated by the allotted quota of Nairs each was required to bring into the field. The manuscript diaries of the Zamorins are full of instances of 'sword and cloth' being given to the Nair chiefs. These are simply symbols of the investiture of feudal authority. 'The lands of the vassals could be confiscated on their dying without heirs; their heirs had to pay *reliefs* on coming in possession of their ancestral holdings; and they were obliged to have the Zamorin's permission to adopt children.'[2]

The administration of justice was efficient. The ordeal was used both in civil and in criminal cases. The diary of the Tellicherry Factory[3] records the Zamorin's permission to the East India Company to employ the ordeal in civil cases, in 1728. Hamilton[4] notes in 1707 that in criminal cases 'the trial by truth is by ordeal by boiling oil.' The system was so far effective that large cargoes of merchandise brought by foreign merchants could be disembarked and deposited in the open streets and market places.

There are evidences of a trial by combat substituted for that by ordeal at the option of the parties. The *aṅkam* was 'the money which the Rāja received as umpire between two combatants under a system of

[1] Visscher: *Letters from Malabar, V.*; Ikkuṇḍa Paṇikkar's letter to the second Malabar Commission, 29th March, 1793.

[2] Græme's Report of 1822, p. 5.

[3] Diary of the Tellicherry Factory, 6th May, 1728.

[4] *New Account*, Vol. I, p. 315.

battle by wager. These quarrels were meant to wipe off stains cast on the individual's honour.' A shade of chivalry and knight-errantry is discernible in this combat, for a later development of the system showed the combatants 'not necessarily the principals in a quarrel, but generally their champions.' The Nairs entered the field in a purely Spartan spirit: to them loss of life weighed as a feather in the balance as against loss of honour. Thus in the fighting 'it was indispensable that one should fall.'[1]

[1] Græme's Report, p. 26.

CHAPTER VIII

OUR HERITAGE

I

THE family was the foundation of social and political life. The sex-instinct was not brushed aside as unholy, even by philosophers who became forest-dwellers in the evening of life. They were jealous of the sex-complex, and sought to conquer it, not by repression but by purification in the life of the home and the family. They sought to ensure 'the perennial breed of noble bloods' which was necessary to carry on the traditions of the community. This was out of the question where the best men were condemned in cloistered seclusion to lead a life of single-blessedness and sterility. Indian society, while it aimed at the obviation of diffused sexuality, made the production of man-power the debt (*ṛṇa*) of each generation to its predecessors and its duty to its successors. The eternal theme in Indian art is the woman as Mother in the happiness of the home, with suckling babies at her breast or grown up children at her feet. We do not find the girl in her teens, the beauty in the bud, in which the lewd and wanton might revel.

The sex-instinct was sublimated in the family. Exogamy and endogamy were worked into a scheme whereby physical degeneracy and predisposition to disease were checked, without sacrificing homogeneity in cultural life. A judicious use of hypergamy enabled communities in lower cultural grades to get increasing strains of better blood and a rise in the social scale.

From a regulated family life flowed ideas of chivalry and gentleness, compassion for the weak and the distressed, a conception of beauty and grace pervading the acts of daily life, and a self-denying affection and readiness to make sacrifices. The consequent losses to individualism and enterprise are a matter of opinion, when we consider the attendant evils. Some early communities evolved from status to contract, discarding or outgrowing the significance of the family as a political unit. But India aimed at the sublimation of the institution, with a deliberately conceived social and political purpose.

Political life reflects the trend of social thought in this direction. There is an anxiety, even in the earliest texts, to preserve intact the laws and custom of the family (*kula*) as well as of the community. Sometimes the family had expanded into a self-governing clan, and political law-givers bear witness to its strength and invincibility. The codifiers of sacred laws show even greater anxiety to preserve the laws of the clan (*kuladharma*), side by side with those framed for the groups bound by increasing ties of local contiguity. The idea was Indian rather than Aryan, and appears even in a more intensive form in the south. In the village life of the Tamil country, as evidenced by mediæval inscriptions, the political sins of the father, or even of a distant kinsman, are visited on all the scions of the family, who are disqualified from wielding political power and holding public offices.

II

The conception of design and order in Nature suggested a plan and purpose in society. The uniformities of Nature help to maintain her forces and move towards the end of creation. Life cannot exist unless the rhythm and sequence in Nature's phenomena could be calculated and acted upon. The iron laws of *ṛta* and *satya* suggest similar laws in society holding the entire fabric together, allowing each part freedom to develop along its particular lines. *Dharma* means that which holds the limbs of society in equilibrium. It is eternal (*sanātana*), and has its parallel in the ageless order and design in Nature. As every limb of Nature is at liberty to move, subject to her laws, so in social life are individuals allowed to develop their own powers consciously within the limits devised for the up-keep of society. Here is *sva-dharma*. It is laid down that progress could be achieved in the best way if every one acted according to his bent, his inborn tastes and natural aptitudes, taken in connection with the circumstances of his breeding and training. A reconciliation between unrestricted individualism and selfless subordination to social purpose, was provided in the grouping of peoples in communities and grades according to their outlook on culture and on life. Such a social division of labour was intended to develop the best in each member, so as to contribute that best to the common life of the whole.

The link between *sanātana-dharma* and *sva-dharma* was thus found in *varṇāśrama-dharma*. The beginnings of the system go back to the earliest Vedic age. It was not, and could not be, devised by any brain, Aryan or Dravidian, as has been so often suggested. Vedic Aryas were in communities, which differed in social habits and cultural outlook as well as in territorial habitat. They were in contact with non-Aryan communities, who likewise differed even to a greater extent among themselves. From this heterogeneity, a scheme of solidarity emerged as the result of time and experience. There is no evidence of its appearing full-fledged, as Athena from the head of Zeus. The *ganas*, *vrātas*. *gṛtsas* and *śardhas* of Vedic times, some high, some low (*mahat* and *kshullaka*), some bent on military achievements and some on the arts of peace (*kshattṛ* and *saṅgṛhītr*), are evidence of this heterogeneity. Pronounced, likewise, were the cultural differences among the non-Aryan peoples, Rākshasa, Piśācha, Nāga, etc. A system which could weld these diversities into a unity could compel the allegiance of the constituents only by its sweet reasonableness and its pragmatic value. In fact, the communities were divided into social groups more or less, as persons and schools vastly varying in political thought find their equilibrium in political parties :—the group that was inclined to philosophise, and revelled more in culture of the spirit than in that of the flesh; the group actuated by ambition, love of power and domination over others; the group whose watchword was material prosperity and economic affluence. Outside these there were the masses of those drifting aimlessly, who attached themselves to one or other of the above groups. The cultural conditions here considered crystallised in a social organisation of people in accordance with the dominating purpose in life,—*dharma*, *kāma* and *artha* being pre-eminently the pursuits of the Brāhmaṇa, Rājanya and Vaiśya respectively.

It would be difficult to show that any one of these groups was superior to the others, or was regarded as such. The difference was functional rather than racial. The word *varṇa*, like the word *rūpam* in the early Vedic texts, cannot be proved to refer to complexion or to physical structure, as it came to do in later times. The groups have their analogues in the *Avesta*, and the Iranian denominations do not at all suggest the idea of colour or complexion. Different rules had to be laid down for Brāhmaṇas, Rājanyas and Vaiśyas in accordance with the objective of each. The Brāhmaṇa had to conserve his energy for intellectual, religious and philosophical purposes. Therefore, immunity from disturbance even in times of war, a certain cloistered seclusion, the rigidity of discipline implied in *satyam*, *ahimsā*; *brahmacharyam* and *aparigraham*—truthfulness, harmlessness, continence and poverty—were prescribed for him as helpful in his line of evolution. The *Rājanya* had to develop power, and the discipline for him consisted in physical exercises and military training. *Rājadharma* allows hunting and even gambling, albeit breaches of *satyam* and *ahimsā*, on account of their social and military virtues. The Vaiśya had to seek popularity rather than power, the gentle influence over his fellowmen, on which his success in industry and commerce and his social standing so largely depended. Truth was considered out of the question in trade, as it was occasionally in statecraft and diplomacy. But the Vaiśya was allowed to accumulate riches by untiring patience and industry, while the social uses of anger and indignation were permitted to the ruling classes, who had to punish the wicked and develop the military spirit. Rights and duties were prescribed for each class in such a way as to develop the virtues needed to attain its objective.

At the same time this division of labour, based on the preference of men in regard to their goal in life, was subordinated to the general scheme for the common good. Co-operation of all the classes was needed in the daily administration, and is provided for in the political institutions that were devised and worked. A passage in the *Mahābhārata* provides for the presence in the king's Council of representatives of the three classes, and even of the outer masses of the population. Hindu polity maintained this co-operation even as late as Mahrātha times. It is proof of the vitality of the scheme that such co-operation could be taken for granted. A sort of balance of power, which would ensure it for all time, was provided, the most advanced intellectuals stripping themselves of active power in the administration and of control over the economic conditions of the country. The force of intellect could outstrip even a combination of wealth and power, if the intellectual resources were organised and concentrated in the interests of self-assertion and monopoly. In the earlier stages, the foremost thinkers of India were scattered in Vedic schools, evolving differing social systems and textual recensions. A good instance is furnished by the schools of *Yajur-Veda* in five different parts of the Jumna-Ganges region and the surrounding tracts—the *Kāṭhaka* of the Doab, the *Kapisṭhala* of the Punjab, the *Maitrāyaṇi* of the Rajputana region, the

Vājasaneyi to the East and the *Taittirīya* to the South. In later times sectarian differences succeeded the local—*Vaishṇava*, *Smārta*, *Śaiva*, etc.

In course of time the *varṇas* crystallised into rigid castes. This was due in part to the efficiency of each type of system and training in attaining its objective, still more to the influence of local communities, and lastly to the great value that Indians, like the Greeks, attached to heredity and environment. It was economically necessary, and perhaps socially justifiable, that the Vaiśya communities of a locality (*varga*) should preserve as their exclusive possession the industrial skill developed in each group (*śreṇi*) on account of its particular economic resources and environment. In fact, skill in technique and trade secrets could be monopolised and handed down only by exclusiveness. Their native instincts (*jāti-dharma*) and the indigenous institutions preserving their peculiarities (*deśa-dharma*) were respected and retained in the schemes of Indian polity. But they were made to feel the commonness of their interests with other communities having a similar outlook in life, and a cultural homogeneity was thus evolved. It was held that the primary duty of the state was to preserve this social scheme of life and to protect each section of the people in the legitimate exercise of its duties and rights.

III

Indian polity effloresced from Indian socio-sophy. It is a declared duty of the head of the State and of the Government to preserve and protect *dharma*. This appears in all texts, religious, secular and political. Vedic texts regard the king as the embodiment of *dharma*. The Sūtras have special sections on *Rājadharma*, and these are illustrated by episodes in the Epics. Kāḷidāsa considers it as coming down from time immemorial that it was the duty of the king to protect the *varṇas* and the *āśramas* in the lawful exercise of their rights and duties. Kauṭilya warns the king that he would bring ruin on himself and his kingdom, if he departed from the *dharma* pertaining to castes and allowed the social scheme to drift into chaos. Some of the provisions of the *Arthaśāstra* are based on this view, and would in these days be regarded as *prima facie* negations of individual liberty. No man had a right to give up home life, for instance, unless he had provided for the upkeep of his family before entering upon asceticism. Heretical orders were not allowed to concentrate in towns, but were to be kept under observation or distributed among rural tracts. Men pursuing new occupations were to be jealously watched. At the same time, Kauṭilya is anxious to perpetuate local and communal self-governing institutions in their common life, special laws, immunities and customs. The local regulations were binding in so far as they were consistent with the laws of the *dharma* of the particular castes and social orders concerned.

The rules of *dharma* were deduced by the most advanced and unselfish men, as in best accord with Vedic practices. These came into existence in different places and at different times, developed into local customs and usages, and were codified in the post-Vedic period. It is not easy to account for the binding authority of particular codes, like those of Manu and

Yājñavalkya, even in matters of civil law, on the assumption that they were devised by single men and were accepted by their compeers under the awe of religion. Some of these rules breathe differences undoubtedly based on local customs and practices. Baudhāyana and Āpastamba, for instance, sanction cousin-marriage in the south; and different though similar concessions are made to Aryan communities in other parts of India. It is important to remember that none of these codes depended for its sanction on any act of State or Legislature. So far as they can be dated, they were formed after the religious differences in India had begun to assert themselves in every Indian State. Many of the basic principles are found alike in various Hindu codes and in those of the Buddhists and the Jains, in spite of the variations necessitated by altered religious conditions and social circumstances.

If the fundamental aim of the State was to preserve the Indian outlook on life and those institutions which were held necessary to perpetuate it, the question arose as to what was the binding authority, in cases of differences in opinion, as to the interpretation or the relative importance of the injunctions. It is characteristic of Indian polity that the will of the majority was not considered as always settling the issue, even where men of quality and learning alone were consulted. It is significant that agreement among the learned and good (*dharmajña samayah*) is recognised as of binding force, but not the will of the majority. No meeting was valid unless men of quality were present, and the opinion of the men of quality was acceptable only when they were bold enough to speak out their mind. One condition of such boldness was the freedom from allegiance to political power, whenever a lack of governance or positive misgovernment sought to threaten the very foundations of society. We have evidence of the creation of such referees or classes of referees even in Vedic times. At the coronation of the king all classes swore allegiance. The Brāhman did homage with the remarkable qualification that he owed a higher loyalty to truth and justice: 'Oh men, here is your king. Soma is the king of us Brāhmans. Our loyalty abides to him, as well as *now* to this king,' —that is to say, so long as they lived within his dominions and were protected by him. There are references to the emigration of such votaries of truth and justice from states where misgovernment prevailed. Here was a power potent to check injustice when political powers had lost their moorings. But there was no danger of a State within the State or of a theological class holding the head of the State in awe. For the members of this class were scattered in different rural tracts, and the rule of their life was poverty and contentment. They expressed their ideas on politics and the burning questions of the day, only when consulted, whether individually or collectively. Any fear of concerted action among them was made impossible by circumstances.

The very monarch of a State was so protected and fortified with pomp and splendour that he had no need to identify himself with any party in the State, which might have the majority for the moment, in order to preserve his crown, but could take a detached and impartial view in all matters. Once the king was chosen, his person became sacrosanct, and he could stand above contending parties and their conflicting interests. By his ability to reconcile these was his efficiency judged, both at the time of selection and afterwards. To this end, the system of primogeniture was somewhat relaxed. When the throne became vacant the choice was made, from among the members of the royal family, of that prince who had the best qualities, as determined by a general consensus of opinion among secular leaders and men of learning and character. It is clear in the early texts, as well as in inscriptions of mediæval times, that an agreement was arrived at without cleaving the State into parties. The welfare of the State was thus in the hands of men who could put the interest of the whole State before that of any party or section thereof.

If the will of the majority was not applied in matters of high politics and general policy, it had its place in the discussion of administrative details. The impartial king was to consult his ministers individually for their opinions, discuss these in general council, and abide by the view of the majority in matters of detail. This Executive Council was to consist of men who were experts in the departments of administration, men of tested character and integrity, irrespective of considerations of caste or creed.

Communal representation, while thus denied in the Central Government, was accepted for certain purposes. The principle of consulting representative opinion was recognised in the formation of a larger Council for important administrative purposes and exigencies, in which the Vaiśyas or men of wealth were most largely represented and could make their voice effectively felt, while the men in power were there also in good number, and the Brāhman and the Śūdra had only a few representatives—just enough to enable them to present their view-points for consideration. In local government various communities had organisations of their own. In the larger council and in town corporations, the predominant communities had the preponderant voice. A sort of balance and harmony was thus secured between the general principle of efficiency, most necessary in the Central Government, and the need for respecting the feelings and opinions of the various groups and communities in the State.

It cannot be said that the will of the majority was the deciding principle, even in local institutions. We have some knowledge of the details of government at Vaiśāli, the city of the Licchavis, which furnished a model of organisation to the Buddhist monastery. The President of a meeting was carefully selected as the man above parties. If any matter came in for heated discussion and cleft the assembly into parties, whatever the disparity in numbers between them, the vote of the Assembly was not binding. The Chairman declared his opinion that it had become a party question, and a Committee was immediately appointed to bring about a reconciliation. If the Committee agreed, settlement could be along their lines; if they differed among themselves, the matter was brought for discussion again before the general body, and the process was gone through until some sort of compromise was arrived at. Members of adjacent localities were sometimes consulted, and put on the Committee of Arbitration. No stone was left unturned in the matter of securing peace and conciliation. The formation of permanent parties was thereby effectively prevented. In certain matters, indeed, unanimity was insisted on, as by the Buddha in the case of admission of a new Bhikshu into the order, or of a local panchāyat deciding civil or criminal causes. We may discover the analogue in education where, the same mentality is in evidence. Profundity was the aim, and perfection was looked for, rather than a percentage of success in the performance. The scholar who could answer all the questions got a hall-mark, and he who made one or more mistakes had to appear again.

It will be clear from the foregoing that deliberate purposes and aims run through the ages as the end of the State in ancient India. Their preservation was helped by the principle of toleration accepted even by the various conquerors. The Indian genius lies in inclusiveness, the consolidation of various principles and their reduction to a state of stable equilibrium, where cultural ends are placed foremost, and the whole is never lost sight of in the elaboration of the parts. The party system is foreign to the genius of India. Nor could it be conceived of among a people whose cultural outlook ripened into a sense of kinship with all men and of the sanctity of all life. Herein lies India's cultural distinctiveness in public life and political organisation. Political differences were not pressed to a breaking-point, but were healed and set at rest by the genius for conciliation characterising the common sense of the people. The function of arbitration is conceived as higher than the iron rule of efficiency. The monarch or the president of a corporate body is regarded as justifying his existence by his virtue of impartiality, of detachment from passing political interests. A whole class of intelligentsia, divorced from power and wealth, existed and secured the same end. They enjoyed social prestige in spite of, or rather because of poverty. The State was thus enabled to secure a free and fearless expression of opinion on matters of administration.

IV

The main cultural outlook of India is also evidenced in the machinery of administration. India is cut up by geographical barriers and by ethnic and linguistic differences into a number of fairly large states. The political horizon of her philosophers was confined to the country, even when her cultural influences permeated other parts of Asia. Megasthenes and other travellers have averred that Indians never attempted any conquests abroad. This aversion to political domination over other peoples had its reflex in the internal polity of India. The states into which the country was naturally divided were taken as political units, and forms of government so devised as to make for their political stability and inter-relationship. 'Imperialism was unknown in ancient India.' In the Maurya empire the independence of the local and provincial parts was recognised and respected, subject to a formal acceptance of the titular suzerainty of the emperor and the reception of the imperial viceroy. In the Gupta empire there was similar independence on the basis of hegemony, and the conquered kingdoms retained their institutions as of old, and their captured princes were liberated and reinstated. Harsha's power has been exaggerated. Even by the testimony of his friends, his contemporaries Pulakeśin, Śaśāṅka and Narasiṁhavarman were no less great than he, and he had little political influence beyond the open expanse of the Gangetic region. The Chōḷa empire meant supremacy in South India, but not extinction or interference, generally speaking, as its policy towards the other ancient kingdoms of the south.

The solitary exception to this principle is perhaps to be found in the expansion of Vijayanagar. By the 15th century India had been drawn into the vortex of the world's politics, and a larger and more powerful political organisation than that of the prevailing local states was found to be essential for self-preservation. The genius of India, in adapting her political organisation to altered forces, is clear in the building of this empire and of the later Indo-Islamic structure known as the Mughal empire. The centre of gravity had now shifted from the local states to the imperial government. Forms of government were freshly forged so as to ensure safety and efficiency at the centre. The older institutions of the localities, surviving in their varieties from the Vedic age onwards, still retained their political individuality in the various parts of the empire, and were appreciated and adopted as the basis of the new provincial organisation. But the form of government in the empire was strong, unitary and centralised, so that India could hold her own against the other nations of the world.

The empire of Vijayanagar and the Mughal empire were stable forms of organisation, as they were based on the political experience of India. Till the tenth century the congeries of small states could continue in relations of war and peace without endangering their existence, on account of general community in cultural ideas and a certain political tolerance. The Hindukush had been the geographical or natural frontier on the north-west. Tribes rolled down into the Punjab for plunder, and some of them made settlements on Indian soil as political units. But these conquerors were gradually conquered by the culture of India, and gave up ideas of rampant militarism or political domination. The ethics of warfare in mediæval India rendered her unable to cope with invaders like the Mussalmans by land and the Portuguese by sea. Portuguese accounts of India make it clear that Hindu ethical principles meant a handicap against enemies who were not hampered by humane considerations in their assertion of might and strength. Instances abound of Hindu delicacy of feeling, chivalry, faithfulness and honesty, as against the treachery, cruelty, terrorism and conquest at any cost, characterising the conduct of the enemy nations. If Hindu *dharma* was to be maintained, there ought to be greater power and concentration of forces.

The first idea that dawned upon the Hindus was that of a confederacy. The Rajputs formed one against the Turks, and the South Indian powers against the Taghlaks. These were formed for the temporary purpose of resisting the advancing waves of Islam. They could not develop into federations, as the local, communal and linguistic differences and jealousies asserted themselves, even in the presence of external dangers. The differences were so profound, as in the case of ancient Greece, that no really binding influence could overcome them if the provinces were to be autonomous. Even in Mahrātha polity the centrifugal forces proved incessant sources of strife, as soon as the cementing force of Sivāji's personality was removed by death. Not even the developed machinery of the Mughal empire could help the provinces suffering disruption and dismemberment in the eighteenth century. It was not only that they were divided from one another, but each was divided in itself by local jealousies, party factions, communal feuds and sectarian differences. The lesson of history is that no abiding economic interests, nor even waves of religious enthusiasm, could unite all India in the absence of strong political organisation at the centre. The geographical and cultural unity of India and her political history alike point to the need for a strong central government and the dangers of instability for any feeble form of federalism.

V

There is no evidence that the Central Government at any time was autocratic, that is, based on the will of one man. The ancient Rāja was rather an impartial arbitrator than master of the state. He was selected by the ministers and the leaders of the people who were the king-makers (*rāja-kartr*). If he ruled badly and set selfish or class interests above the common weal, good men left the state, and this was the signal for his expulsion or deposition. This primitive expedient did not suffice as the state grew larger, and we have the gradual evolution of ministerial responsibility. Evidence of ministerial opposition to the declared wishes of the Rāja is found in the inscriptions of Aśoka and Rudradāman; in Purāṇic texts relating to the Śuṅgas and Kaṇwas;

in Jaina tradition about Vasubandhu, the Gupta minister; and in other places. By the Gupta period it had become an accepted political doctrine that the ministers were there to see that even a bad king ruled in accordance with the wishes of the people. They were, it is true, selected by the king and not elected by the people; but they were selected for those very qualities of detachment and impartiality which were considered the qualification of those in charge of the government. It was therefore that Aśoka had to bend to their will, and Rudradāman to restore from his privy purse the expenditure, though for public purposes, incurred by him against their views. It was therefore that the threat of Vasubandhu to resign had its effect.

Kauṭilya lays down that the ministers were to be consulted individually as well as in Council, and that their opinion should be binding on the king. Ministers on other duty or away from the capital were to be consulted by correspondence. Later works like the *Śukranītisāra* demand that these transactions should be in writing and that the decisions of the ministry should be signed and sealed, so that the king could not alter them or evade their import. The prominence of the ministry is in evidence under Muhammadan rule also, whether we think of Makbul Khān, Abul Fazl, Āli Mardan Khān, Asof Khān or Jaswant Singh. The ministry became so prominent under the Mahrāthas that its chief developed into a Mayor of the Palace, overshadowing the throne. Such a consummation could be reached only where the ministers looked forward less to royal favour than to the interests of the people.

The organisation of the ministry discloses some peculiar features. There was a king's Council of three or four or more ministers in early times, and the number became fixed as eight in mediæval times. There was an outer Council of eighteen *Tirthas*, which developed and replaced the body of fifty-four described in the *Mahābhārata*. They represented the heads of departments in the State. Here we have a line of departure from what is familiar to us as the distinction between the 'Curia Regis' and the 'Magnum Concilium' of mediæval England. The reason is that, the heads of revenue being settled in India, there was no need to consult the non-official nobility with a view to exploiting fresh resources. Indian polity attached more importance to effectual checks on expenditure. The budget of a Hindu State may be described as the adjustment of expenditure to income, rather than the discovery of resources for meeting increasing expenditure.

The departments required expert knowledge. But, in the Indian view, there was even more need for protection against the tyranny of the expert. So the departments were not rigidly exclusive. Whether in Hindu or in Mughal polity the ministry was a hierarchy, where the members were of unequal power and influence. All of them came into contact with the Sovereign, but some had the power to check or veto the proposals of others. No proposal could be carried out unless it had gone through more than one minister. To the same end, we have a provision in the Hindu codes that no minister should be in charge of the same portfolio for more than three years. The proposal of the expert for the time was thus subjected to the scrutiny of those who had been experts in the same department some years earlier. In Hindu polity the expert's proposal was checked also by other ministers from various points of view, the highest check being by men who were attached to the king by excellence of character as well as by expert knowledge.

Local variations determined the foundation of the smaller states or provinces. In the earlier period the local states got their distinctiveness on account of geographical, racial or linguistic features. This distinctiveness they retained even under expanding empires, like those of Aśoka and the Guptas. In Mussalman times the culture of Bengal was peculiar to it, as was that of the Punjab, and these two provinces were political units, not much inferior in status to the kingdom of Delhi. In Mughal, Mahrātha and Vijayanagar polity there was a provincial organisation on similar lines.

Under the Mughal and Vijayanagar emperors we have a landmark in the history of the provincial system. Each province served as a cultural unit, whether we consider Agra, Oudh or Allahabad; Āndhra, Koṅkaṇa or Chōḷa. Its type of culture and its characteristic language and traditions were retained and allowed to develop. At the same time provincial and local jealousies were kept in check by tight control from the centre. Provinces were subdivided, or new provinces created out of existing ones, when altered political conditions required a revision of the system in the interests of the efficient handling of provincial affairs by the Central Government. But in any such revision the cultural and historic as well as the linguistic and geographical unity of the province was a primary consideration. The growth of national feeling in a province showed itself in the development of its vernacular literature, in economic life and institutions, and in particular systems of social life and civil law.

Yet the inherent defects of the polity showed themselves. Whether under the Vijayanagara, the Mughal or the Mahrātha scheme, the Central Government may be described as having looked inwards into the provinces, breathing life into their polity, unifying them and contributing to a common life, attending to matters which were of general importance, and having a broad, as distinguished from a compartmental, outlook in internal administration. But the empire as a unity concerned itself much less with states outside India and the relations with them. Imperial defences were not properly provided for, even by the Mughal empire. In the army the aim was to unite the provincial resources into a national army, but not to distribute this army so as to keep the weak spots of India on the north-west frontier safe from foreign invasion. Vijayanagar fleets scoured the seas and did some good work in establishing commercial relations with other powers, but neglected their function as bulwarks of defence against foreign fleets on the open seas. This fact is all the more remarkable as the Portuguese roved the seas, and their piracy was a constant worry to the Mughal empire. Vijayanagar appreciated the horses that came from the trade with the Portuguese, but could not look ahead or scent any political danger. Śivāji's polity was a growth from local fortresses and cultural types, which he succeeded in unifying into a living political system. He formed a fleet, and was not unmindful of the part it might play in the destiny of India. But his successors; even those who were champions of a strong and centralised polity, could not look outwards as he did. They neglected the fleet and failed to foresee the ultimate outcome in politics of their relations with the European powers.

In the case of none of these empires—Mahrātha, Mughal, Vijayanagar—could it be said that they could take an all-Indian view, and appreciate that an Indian government had duties in the frontier provinces which were not the concern of any of the provinces. It can therefore be said that none of these governments was really a central one; and no government could be stable in India unless it had powers at the centre, independent of the parts or provinces. An evident danger of Indian polity has been the centrifugal tendencies in politics. This danger asserted itself even when provincial autonomy had been broken by the Mughals and by the Mahrāthas, by strict supervision from the centre, and by the subdivision of ultimate power in the province: the political, economic and judicial heads being independent of one another, and responsible only to the Central Government.

In local institutions the main principle was the freedom of each locality to act according to its own ideas, to enact its own laws, and to insist on the observance of local custom and traditions. This was a feature in both Aryan and non-Aryan villages and townships, in quarters in towns and corporations in cities. This was recognised in civil law, and in the administrative courts of the corporations concerned, whether they were based on communal, caste, professional, racial, or local grouping. In Pre-Mussalman India there was insistence on attention to rural life. The importance of a town or a city was gauged by the number of villages with which it came into effective social and economic contact. Thus we have towns which served ten villages, a hundred villages or hundreds of villages. They seem to have served as places for the concentration (*saṅgrahaṇa*) and joint purchase or sale of agricultural produce and requirements. The villages and parts of towns governed themselves on a co-operative basis. Details of such self-governing corporations are familiar to us in the Buddhist books and in South Indian inscriptions. The point to note is that local polity was based on the effective independence of the rural tracts in the matter of self-government in social, economic, political, religious, educational and other concerns. The Central Government did not interfere with local autonomy, except on the invitation of the local bodies when they were helpless against over-powerful chieftains, or in the way of audit and supervision of public funds, as in the Chōḷa empire. The stress on village life is of great importance, as India has a predominantly agricultural population. The integrity and independence of village life was maintained by Muhammadan rulers in spite of their partiality for city life, and local panchāyats continued to function effectively far into the nineteenth century. The care of the Central Government for the common villager is evidenced by the details of social and economic life recorded in the village surveys undertaken from time to time. These are mentioned in Kauṭilya's *Arthaśāstra*, the South Indian inscriptions, the *Ain-i-Akbari* and other records.

VII

Consistently with the general outlook on polity, there was attention to the various aspects of administration. In early times justice was regarded as the most important. The king was the supreme arbitrator and his court the seat of justice, both in Aryan and in South Indian polity. The finding in regard to fact was left to panels of judges, and the award lay with the king. In republics there was an officer who had a Book of Precedents or Record of Case Law, which was consulted so that punishments might be uniform. The local juries and panchāyats settled civil disputes, and their decision was binding, provision being made for challenging the fairness of the judges, if they were inclined to partiality or corruption. One interesting provision peculiar to India is the responsibility of the state for the detection of the criminal in cases of theft and robbery. The fact of the crime being proved, the local police officers must detect the criminal or be responsible for the restitution of the lost property. This institution existed both in cities and in villages, and throughout the ages, according to the testimony of travellers. In regard to criminal law the main principle was that one suspected of crime should be let off if there was at any stage reasonable presumption of his innocence. To this end the criminal's case was referred successively to various officers, any one of whom could liberate him, but all of whom had to agree if he was to be found guilty. It is important to remember that the accepted aim in judicature was to secure gratuitous justice during the preliminary trials by respectable fellow-men. There were no lawyers, and all opportunities were given to decide matters by voluntary arbitration. During Mughal rule the Persian principle was applied, that even 'speedy injustice was preferable to tardy justice,' and the law's delays were dreaded.

In regard to taxation, we see certain principles always in operation. Agricultural produce contributed most to the State revenue. A sixth of the yield was the standard tax in Hindu polity, and taxes on moveables varied from two to ten per cent. In mediæval times when India was in the regular stream of the world's commerce, the revenue from other sources became equal to that from land. There was, as a rule, no gain to the State from coinage, the intrinsic value of the coin agreeing with its face value. This principle was in prevalence in Hindu administration, when the coin was looked upon as merely a nugget of gold (*nishka*) or a piece of silver (*veḷḷi*). Roe and Terry have remarked that the Mughal currency was the purest in the world, superior even to the Spanish. Śivāji allowed all coins to circulate in his kingdom at their intrinsic values. Debasement of the coinage appears as the last resort of kings in financial embarrassment, and is followed by the downfall of the government. It must be added that when political exigencies led to a temporary sophistication of the currency, the purity of the coinage was restored as soon as normal conditions were resumed.

Some channels of expenditure were prescribed by custom and tradition. The most important of these come under the class of public works. In Hindu polity attention was chiefly bestowed on irrigation works, the cutting of new canals and the construction of tanks, wells, and reservoirs. Hindu religious sentiment set a premium on this kind of work, and directed individual charities towards the sinking of wells. The soul in heaven was fed by the feeding of thirsty crops on earth. The Mughal emperors also paid prominent attention to this department, as the Afghans had done before them for economic gain. Attention to roadways and to foreign trade and its development was a matter of secondary importance, as India was practically self-sufficing. The stores of grain at the capital and in the imperial cities came to the rescue in famine times, rather than speedy transport of goods from other localities. There was not much expenditure on education or medicine, as the teacher and the doctor could be easily found in every unit, teaching being regarded as the duty of particular classes in the State, and being gratuitous or inexpensive, like such forms of medical relief as were then available. Services and salaries were no doubt an important item, and this was perhaps swelled by an elaborate system of pensions, not only for servants who survived but for their families, in the event of death before their time. But there was a saving, as honorary work was utilised and encouraged. The fact that there was no continuity of employment when political conditions altered had perhaps this advantage, that among the non-officials there were men capable of active service and with some experience of state affairs. These became the leaders of public opinion and contributed weight and responsibility to public agitation.

Another head of expenditure was the patronage of high erudition, and of experts in the fine arts. The indigenous arts of India could not be left to private encouragement, and it was the business of the State to see that they did not languish. The arts were not merely for pleasure, but were so directed by æsthetic tradition as to contribute to the highest cultural aims of India. The industrial arts were sufficiently advanced not to require bolstering up by protective duties or bounties. Such attention as was given them was with a view to directing labour into those channels which were for the greatest good of the state, and diverting it from occupations which were not for the common good, by preferential rates of taxation and by avenues of public employment.

VIII

The principle of polity was not *laissez-faire*. It was the duty of the State, with due regard to individual and communal liberty, to help the many-sided development of the individual, as well as of those social ideas and institutions which would make this development permanent and universal. The State had thus the duty of educating all, and of preventing the emergence of anti-social impulses in individuals and in society. The ideal of a good State in its relation to its subjects is thus laid down in one of our earliest texts: there was in it 'no thief, no villain, no drunkard; none who neglected religious rites, none uncultured, no man incontinent, and gay as libertine, no woman who was unchaste.' An idyllic picture, indeed, but one which shows that the criterion of political progress (like that of military progress laid down by Julius Cæsar) was the extent to which the worst man had improved in social ethics. It was the self-imposed task of India not only to educate her own peoples and her conquerors and visitors, but to convert to her cultural altitude the states of Serindia and the regions lying beyond the seas. It redounds to the credit of her conquerors that the fundamental ideas of Indian polity and society were preserved through time, adapted to altered conditions. May the same genius for integration and adaptation, without losing sight of the destiny of the soul, animate her political progress in the vaster times yet to come!

INDEX